CELESTIAL NAVIGAT
(UPON OCEANS ENDORSEMENT)
VOLUME VI

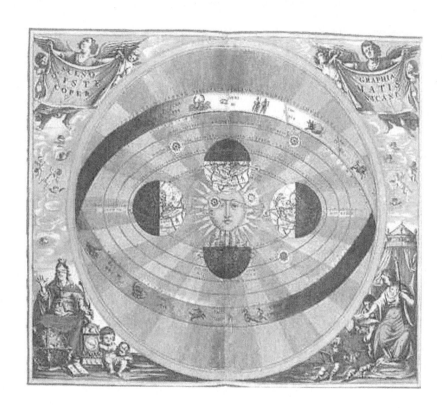

By

Alexander F. Hickethier MBA

i

Revised October 18, 2020. We have reviewed the publication and corrected errors, typos and added questions to reflect changes in the USCG data base.

Every effort has been made to assure that this book is accurate, current, and complete as of date of publication. However, as in the case of all human endeavors, there can be no guarantee that this work does not contain errors or omissions. Therefore, the prudent mariner will not rely only on this or any other single source when guiding his vessel.

Please report any errors or omissions to the publisher.

Printed in the United States
First Edition
ISBN 978-1480163737

Published by:
Alexander F. Hickethier MBA
20555 Bee Valley Road;
Jamul, CA 91935
www.mmts.com

Forward

I have developed this series of textbooks to assist the merchant mariner in mastering the theory and calculations required to passing the U.S. Coast Guard Licensing Examination for the Master 500 GT to 2nd Mate Unlimited Upon Oceans Endorsement.

The textbooks are modular in design and incorporate theory, practical exercises and actual U.S. Coast Guard examination questions. As the Mariner progresses from one license level to the next the appropriate information is provided. For example an individual preparing for an Inland or Near Coastal license through Master 1600 GT would use the first four volumes (Shiphandling and Deck Seamanship, Marine Safety, basic Terrestrial navigation). Whereas a Master NC needing the Upon Oceans Endorsement would use Volume VI, Celestial Navigation (Upon Ocean Endorsement) and a Mariner studying for 3rd/2nd Mate Unlimited Upon Oceans would use all six volumes.

A description of each manual follows:

Volume I - Shiphandling and Deck Seamanship

This manual provides an in-depth understanding of Basic Shiphandling and Deck Seamanship, including Shiphandling, Marlinspike, Cargo Rigs and Rigging, Towing and Anchoring.

Volume II - Marine Safety

In the second manual, I provide a concise treatment of Fire and Firefighting, First Aid, Damage Control, and Pollution Control, pollution, basic stability, the use of The Code of Federal Regulations and The Chemical Data Guide.

Volume III - Practical Navigation for Master NC

In this volume, I combine theory and practical application in all aspects of Terrestrial Navigation to a level to meet the needs of a Master, of 100 GT through 2nd Mate. Subjects covered are Chart and Publications, Range of Lights, Gyro Compass, Aids to navigation, Piloting, Dead Reckoning and Current Sailing, Electronic Navigation, Weather, Tides and Currents.

Volume IV – Basic Terrestrial Navigation (Plotting)

The textbook is an integrates theory using actual U.S. Coast Guard Long Island plotting questions and specifically designed practical navigation exercises and problems to teach the skills required to successfully complete a U.S. Coast Guard plotting examination.

Volume V – Advanced Terrestrial Navigation (Problems)

The workbook is an integrated text using actual U.S. Coast Guard questions and specifically designed practical navigation exercises and problems to teach the skills required to successfully complete a U.S. Coast Guard Master 500 GT through 2nd Mate Navigation problems

Examination. It incorporates Special Bearing problems, Geographic and Luminous Range problems, and Compass Correction problems determining compass error by terrestrial observation, RPM and fuel calculations.

Volume VI - Celestial Navigation (Upon Oceans Endorsement)

This volume is a comprehensive work on Celestial Navigation, it's theory and practice and is designed for Master through 2nd Mate Unlimited. It uses actual USCG exam questions as it teaches the celestial calculations in easy to understand steps; with additional USCG questions at the end of each chapter, when appropriate. Subject matter areas covered includes: all Celestial Navigation subjects, The Sailing's, compass adjustment theory and problems; and other upon oceans examination requirements.

Volume VII- Advanced Subjects for Master Unlimited Upon Oceans

The last Training Manual in the Deck License Series is designed to be used with the other five training manuals for mariner preparing for licenses above 2nd mate unlimited. It includes all subject matters areas required for Master/Mate Unlimited, Deck and Rigging calculations, and Celestial Navigation calculations for the Moon, ex-meridian, unidentified Stars not using the star finder, Moonrise and Moonset and Latitude by moon and planets.

Recommended Supplemental Manuals:

Deck Officers:

Volume I: Deck Calculations worked-out for Master 500 GT through 2nd Mate Unlimited Upon Oceans.

Volume I provides an in-depth understanding of Basic Deck and Stability Calculation found US coast Guard Merchant Mariner Examinations through 2nd Mate Unlimited,

> **Chapter 1,** including Stowage Calculations, Lumber and Dunnage Stowage, Stowage Factors, Size of lines and Block and Tackle, lifting stress, Anchoring calculations, Humidity and Dew Point Calculations and Rules for bearings.

> **Chapter 2,** includes Stability Terminology, Calculating Period of Roll and Estimating GM, Freesurface, Floodable Length Curves, Loll, Final Draft, TPI, Trim, LCG, Final KG, Freeboard Draft, LCG and Double Bottom Tankage.

Volume II: Terrestrial Navigation Calculations worked-out for Master 500 GT through 2nd Mate Unlimited Upon Oceans.

Volume II provides an in-depth understanding of Terrestrial Calculation found US Coast Guard Merchant Mariner Examinations through 2nd Mate Unlimited.

Chapter 1, Tides and Currents.

Chapter 2, Speed by RPM, SOA, Slip and Fuel Consumption Calculations

Chapter 3, Compass Deviation Table Construction, Deviation by Celestial Observation (Amplitude and Azimuth), and Deviation by Terrestrial Observation.

Chapter 4, Time Zone Calculations, (Sunrise and Sunset, Time tick, and Estimated Time of Arrival).

Volume III: Celestial Navigation Calculations worked-out for Master 500 GT through 2nd Mate Unlimited Upon Oceans Endorsement.

Volume III provides an in-depth understanding of Terrestrial and Celestial Calculation found on the US Coast Guard Merchant Mariner Upon Oceans Examinations through 2nd Mate Unlimited.

Chapter 1, Nautical Publications and Equipment

Chapter 2 The Sailings, Parallel, Mid-Latitude, Mercator and Great Circle.

Chapter 3, Magnetic and Gyro Compass Error Calculations (Amplitude, Azimuth and Polaris)

Chapter 4, Time and Time Zone Calculations (Sunrise and Sunset, Time Tick, Time of Meridian Transit and Estimated Time of Arrival)

Chapter 5, Determining latitude (Local Apparent Noon and Latitude by Polaris)

Chapter 6, Determining Position by Sight (Any Body)

Chapter 7, Star Identification, and Star and Planet Selection.

ACKNOWLEDGMENTS

There are numerous people who made this book possible. In particular I profusely thank my, dear friend Master mariner and educator Dr. Hu Jia-Shen for his support and encouragement while completing the works for both Deck officers and Engineers.

ALEXANDER F. HICKETHIER MBA

ABOUT THE AUTHOR

 **Alexander F. Hickethier** is the Vice-President Maritime Institute Inc. for Curriculum Development and International and Academic Affairs. He is a visiting navigation department professor at Shanghai Marine University, Shanghai, China and National Kaohsiung Marine University, Kaohsiung, Taiwan. He is an approved instructor of 23 Marine/STCW US Coast Guard (USCG) approved courses. He has designed and implemented 25 USCG approved Maritime courses of which 7 are approved e-Learning courses, Authored or co-authored 7 maritime textbooks, 3 navigation workbooks and 3 Engineering workbooks. He holds a BBS and MBA from National University.

TABLE OF CONTENTS

NAUTICAL PUBLICATIONS
and
EQUIPMENT

Chapter 1

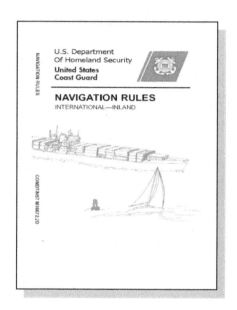

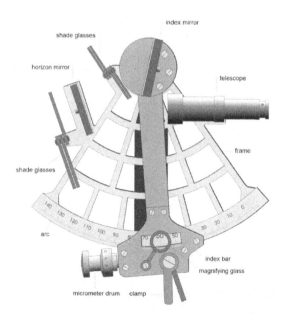

NAUTICAL PUBLICATIONS

Every vessel should carry the charts and publications required for its safe operation. These include the Navigation Rules and Regulations Handbook, all charts applicable for the vessel's navigational area of operation, and appropriate publications pertinent to navigation.

Included here is a listing of the some of the more commonly used publications, and the agencies responsible for publishing them. Naturally, not all of them will be applicable to all vessels.

Navigation Rules and Regulations Handbook

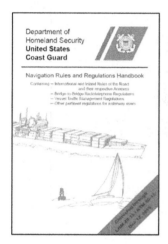

The U.S. Coast Guard publishes the Navigation Rules and Regulations Handbook. This publication, officially known as Commandant Instruction M16672.2d, contains the Inland Navigation Rules enacted in December 1980 and effective on all inland waters of the United States including the Great Lakes, as well as the International Regulations for the Prevention of Collisions at Sea, enacted in 1972 (1972 COLREGS). Mariners should ensure that they have the updated issue.

Sailing Directions (Enroute and Planning Guides)

National Imagery and Mapping Agency *Sailing Directions* consist of **37 Enroutes** and **5 Planning Guides**. *Planning Guides* describe general features of ocean basins; *Enroutes* describe features of coastlines, ports, and harbors.

Sailing Directions are updated when new data requires extensive revision of an existing volume. This data is obtained from several sources, including pilots and foreign Sailing Directions.

One book comprises the *Planning Guide* and *Enroute* for Antarctica. This consolidation allows for a more effective presentation of material on this unique area.

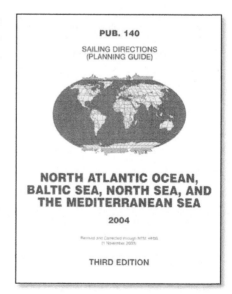

The *Planning Guides* are relatively permanent; by contrast, *Sailing Directions (Enroute)* are frequently updated. Between updates, both are corrected by the **Notice to Mariners.**

Sailing Directions (Planning Guide)

Planning Guides assist the navigator in planning an extensive oceanic voyage. Each of the Guides provides useful information about all the countries adjacent to a particular ocean basin.

The limits of the *Sailing Directions* in relation to the major ocean basins are shown in the below:

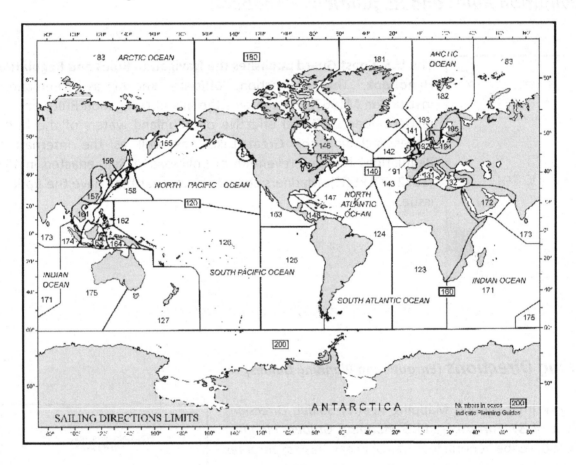

Planning Guides are structured in the alphabetical order of countries contained within the region. Information pertaining to each country includes Buoyage Systems, Currency, Government, Industries, Holidays, Languages, Regulations, Firing Danger Areas, Mined Areas, Pilotage, Search and Rescue, Reporting Systems, Submarine Operating Areas, Time Zone, and the location of the U.S. Embassy.

Sailing Directions (Enroute)

Each volume of the *Sailing Directions (Enroute)* contains numbered sections along a coast or through a strait. Figure on page 1-4 illustrates this division. Each sector is sub-divided into paragraphs and discussed in turn. A preface with information about authorities, references, and conventions used in each book precedes the sector discussions. Each book also provides conversions between feet, fathoms, and meters, and an Information and Suggestion Sheet.

A foreign terms glossary and a comprehensive Index- Gazetteer follow the sector discussions. The Index-Gazetteer is an alphabetical listing of described and charted features. The Index lists each feature by geographic coordinates and sector paragraph number.

U.S. military vessels have access to special files of data reported via official messages known as Port Visit After Action Reports. These reports, written in text form according to a standardized reporting format, give complete details of recent visits by U.S. military vessels to all foreign ports visited. Virtually every detail regarding navigation, services, supplies, official and unofficial contacts, and other matters is discussed in detail, making these reports an extremely useful adjunct to the *Sailing Directions*. These files are available to ".mil" users only, and may be accessed on the Web at: http://cnsl.spear.navy.mil, under the "Force Navigator" link. They are also available via DoD's classified Web.

Coast Pilots

The **National Ocean Service** publishes nine *United States Coast Pilots* to supplement nautical charts of U.S. waters. Information comes from field inspections, survey vessels, and various harbor authorities. Maritime officials and pilotage associations provide additional information.

Coast Pilots provide more detailed information than *Sailing Directions* because *Sailing Directions* are intended exclusively for the oceangoing mariner. **The *Notice to Mariners* updates *Coast Pilots*.**

Each volume contains comprehensive sections on local operational considerations and navigation regulations.

Following chapters contain detailed discussions of coastal navigation. An appendix provides information on obtaining additional weather information, communications services, and other data. An index and additional tables complete the volume.

Light Lists

The **United States publishes two** different light lists. The U.S. **Coast Guard publishes** the *Light List* for lights in U.S. territorial waters; **NIMA publishes** the *List of Lights* for **lights in foreign waters**.

Light lists furnish detailed information about navigation lights and other navigation aids, supplementing the charts, *Coast Pilots*, and *Sailing Directions*. Consult the chart for the location and light characteristics of all navigation aids; consult the light lists to determine their detailed description.

The *Notice to Mariners* corrects both lists. Corrections which have accumulated since the print date are included in the *Notice to Mariners* as a *Summary of Corrections*. All of these summary corrections, and any corrections published subsequently, should be noted in the "Record of Corrections."

A navigator needs to know both the identity of a light and when he can expect to see it; he often plans the ship's track to pass within a light's range. If lights are not sighted when predicted, the vessel may be significantly off course and standing into danger.

A circle with a radius equal to the visible range of the light usually defines the area in which a light can be seen.

On some bearings, however, obstructions may reduce the range. In this case, the obstructed arc might differ with height of eye and distance. Also, lights of different colors may be seen at different distances. Consider these facts both when identifying a light and predicting the range at which it can be seen.

Atmospheric conditions have a major effect on a light's range. Fog, haze, dust, smoke, or precipitation can obscure a light. Additionally, a light can be extinguished.

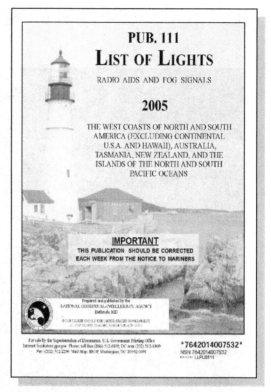

Always report an extinguished light so maritime authorities can issue a warning and make repairs.

On a dark, clear night, the visual range is limited by either: (1) luminous intensity, or (2) curvature of the Earth.

Regardless of the height of eye, one cannot see a weak light beyond a certain luminous range. Assuming light travels linearly, an observer located below the light's visible horizon cannot see it. The Distance to the Horizon table gives the distance to the horizon for various heights of eye.

The light lists contain a condensed version of this table.

Abnormal refraction patterns might change this range; therefore, one cannot exactly predict the range at which a light will be seen.

The American Practical Navigator (Pub 9)

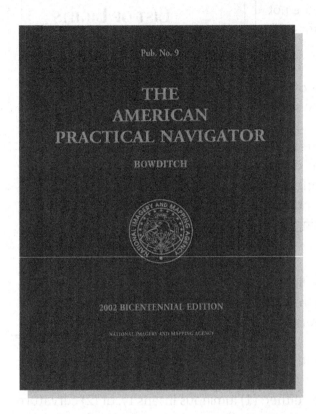
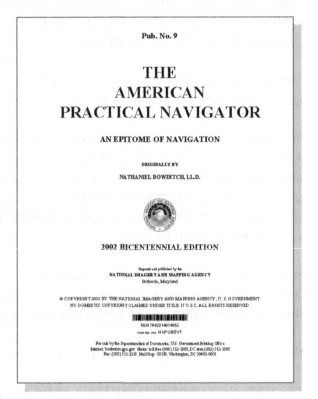

The American Practical Navigator (Pub 9) is a publication, which describes the modern principles of marine navigation and includes the formulas, tables, data and instructions required by navigators to perform the computations associated with dead reckoning, piloting, and celestial navigation. The publication also contains sections addressing the Practice of Navigation, Navigational Safety, Oceanography, Weather, and Electronic Navigation.

Notice to Mariners

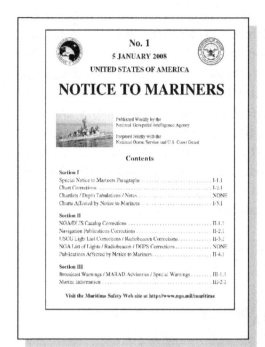

The **Notice to Mariners** is **published weekly** by the **National Imagery and Mapping Agency (NIMA)**, prepared jointly with the National Ocean Service (NOS) and the U.S. Coast Guard. It advises mariners of important matters affecting navigational safety, including new hydrographic information, changes in channels and aids to navigation, and other important data. The information in the *Notice to Mariners* is formatted to simplify the correction of paper charts, sailing directions, light lists, and other publications produced by NIMA, NOS, and the U.S. Coast Guard.

It is the responsibility of users to decide which of their charts and publications require correction.

Suitable records of *Notice to Mariners* should be maintained to facilitate the updating of charts and publications prior to use.

Notice to Mariners No. 1 of each year contains important information on a variety of subjects which supplements information not usually found on charts and in navigational publications. This information is published as **Special Notice to Mariners Paragraphs**. Additional items considered of interest to the mariner are also included in this *Notice*.

Summary of Corrections

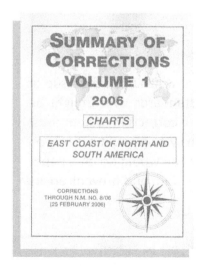

A close companion to the *Notice to Mariners* is the **Summary of Corrections**. The *Summary* is published in five volumes. Each volume covers a major portion of the Earth including several chart regions and their sub-regions. Volume 5 also includes special charts and publications corrected by the *Notice to Mariners*. Since the *Summaries* contain cumulative corrections, any chart, regardless of its print date, can be corrected with the proper volume of the *Summary* and all subsequent *Notice to Mariners*.

Local Notice to Mariners

The *Local Notice to Mariners* is issued by **each U.S. Coast Guard District** to disseminate **important information affecting navigational safety within that District.** This Notice reports changes and deficiencies in aids to navigation maintained by the Coast Guard. Other marine information such as new charts, channel depths, naval operations, and regattas is included. Since temporary information of short duration is not included in the NIMA *Notice to Mariners*, the *Local Notice to Mariners* may be the only source for it. Since correcting information for U.S. charts in the NIMA *Notice* is obtained from the Coast Guard local notices, there is a lag of 1 or 2 weeks for NIMA *Notice* to publish a correction from this source. The *Local Notice to Mariners* may be obtained free of charge by contacting the appropriate Coast Guard District Commander. Vessels operating in ports and waterways in several districts must obtain the *Local Notice to Mariners* from each district. See below for a complete list of U.S. Coast Guard Districts.

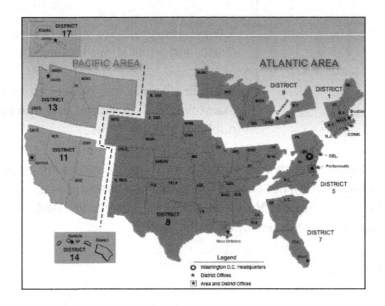

Electronic Notice to Mariners

One major impediment to full implementation of electronic chart systems has been the issue of how to keep them up to date. The IMO, after reviewing the range standards which might be employed in the provision of updates to ECDIS charts, decided that the correction system must be "hands off" from the mariner's point of view. That is, the correction system could not rely on the ability of the mariner to enter individual correction data himself, as he would do on a paper chart. The process must be automated to maintain the integrity of the data and prevent errors in data entry by navigators.

Chart No. 1 Chart Symbols and Abbreviations

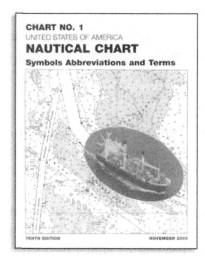

Chart No. 1 is not actually a chart but a book containing a key to chart symbols. Most countries which produce charts also produce such a list. The U.S. *Chart No. 1* contains a listing of chart symbols in four categories:

1. Chart symbols used by the National Ocean Service
2. Chart symbols used by NIMA
3. Chart symbols recommended by the International Hydrographic Organization
4. Chart symbols used on foreign charts reproduced by NIMA

Subjects covered include general features of charts, topography, hydrography, and aids to navigation. There is also a complete index of abbreviations and an explanation of the IALA buoyage system.

NIMA *International Code of Signals (Pub. 102)*

This book lists the signals to be employed by vessels at sea to communicate a variety of information relating to safety, distress, medical, and operational information. This publication became effective in 1969.

According to this code, each signal has a unique and complete meaning. The signals can be transmitted via Morse code light and sound, flag, radio telegraph and telephone, and semaphore. Since these methods of signaling are internationally recognized, differences in language between sender and receiver are immaterial; the message will be understood when decoded in the language of the receiver, regardless of the language of the sender.

The *Notice to Mariners* corrects *Pub. 102*.

Sight Reduction Tables Pub. 229

Without a calculator or computer programmed for sight reduction, the navigator needs *sight reduction tables* to solve the celestial triangle. Two different sets of tables are commonly used at sea.

NIMA *Pub. 229, Sight Reduction Tables for Marine Navigation*, consists of six volumes of tables designed for use with the ***Nautical Almanac*** for solution of the celestial triangle by the **Marcq Saint Hilaire** or **intercept** method. The tabular data are the solutions of the navigational triangle of which two sides and the included angle are known and it is necessary to find the third side and adjacent angle.

Each volume of *Pub. 229* includes two 8 degree zones, comprising 15 degree bands from 0 to 90 degrees, with a 1 degree overlap between volumes. *Pub. 229* is a joint publication produced by the National Imagery and Mapping Agency, the U.S. Naval Observatory, and the Royal Greenwich Observatory.

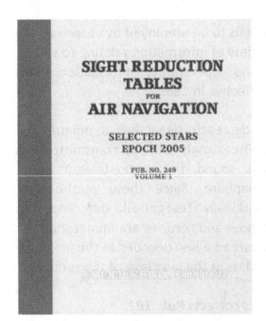

Sight Reduction Tables for Air Navigation, Pub. 249, is also a joint production of the three organizations above. It is issued in three volumes. Volume 1 contains the values of the altitude and true azimuth of seven selected stars chosen to provide, for any given position and time, the best celestial observations. A new edition is issued every 5 years for the upcoming astronomical epoch. Volumes 2 (0 to 40) and 3 (39 to 89) provide for sights of the Sun, Moon, and planets.

Radio Navigational Aids PUB. 117

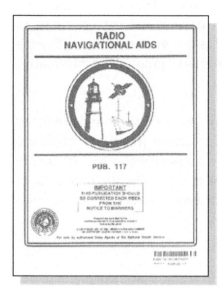

The Radio Navigational Aids (Pub 117) publication contains a detailed list of selected worldwide radio stations that provide services to the mariner. The publication is divided into chapters according to the nature of the service provided by the radio stations. The services include RDF and Radar Stations; stations broadcasting navigational warnings, time signals or medical advice; communication traffic for distress, emergency and safety including GMDSS; and long range navigational aids. It also contains chapters describing procedures of the **AMVER System**, and the interim emergency procedures and communication instructions to be followed by U.S merchant vessels in times of crisis

The Nautical Almanac

For celestial sight reduction, the navigator needs an **almanac** for ephemeris data. **The *Nautical Almanac*,** produced jointly by H.M. Nautical Almanac Office and the U.S. Naval Observatory, is the most common almanac used for celestial navigation. It also contains information on sunrise, sunset, moonrise, and moonset, as well as compact sight reduction tables. The *Nautical Almanac* is published annually.

Current Tables

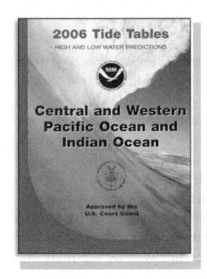

The Tidal Current Tables informs the reader on the expected behaviors of the oceans along the eastern and western coasts of North and South America, as well as the western coasts of Europe and Africa, and its waves through charts, graphs, and informative writing.

Topics include daily predicted times of slack water and predicted times and velocities of maximum current (flood and ebb), the speed of a current at times between slack water and maximum current, and the duration of weak current near the time of slack water. This book is published as one part in a set of four volumes listed below:

Tidal Current Tables: Atlantic Coast of North America
Tidal Current Tables: Pacific Coast of North America
Tide & Tidal Current Tables: New York Harbor to Chesapeake Bay
Tide Tables: Central & Western Pacific Ocean

Tide Tables

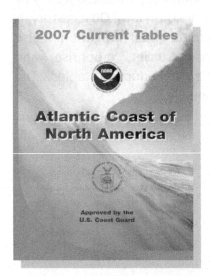

As an example the Central and Western Pacific and Indian Ocean Tide Tables contains full daily predictions for 76 reference ports and differences and other constants for about 2,600 stations in North America, South America, and Greenland.

It also contains a table for obtaining the approximate height of the tide at any time, a table of local mean time of sunrise and sunset for every 5th day of the year for different latitudes, a table for the reduction of local mean time to standard time, a table of moonrise and moonset for 8 places, a table of the Greenwich mean time of the Moons phases, apogee, perigee, greatest north and south and zero declination, and the time of the solar equinoxes and solstices, and a glossary of terms.

This book is published as one part in a set of four volumes as listed below

Tide Tables: East Coast of North and South America
Tide Tables: Europe and West Coasts of Africa
Tide Tables: West Coast of North and South America

Chemical Data Guide for Bulk Shipment by Water

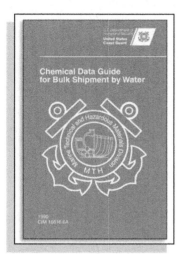

Chemical Data Guide for Bulk Shipment by Water: Marine Technical and Hazardous Materials Division.

The data in this guide was compiled from a number of sources in the interest of safe water movement of bulk chemicals. Hopefully, by providing key chemical information in an easy to use form, this guide can help prevent or at least minimize the harmful effects of chemical accidents on the waterways.

CELESTIAL NAVIGATION EQUIPMENT

Chapter 1

TELESCOPIC ALIDADE

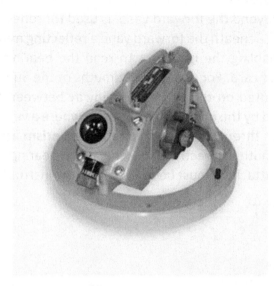

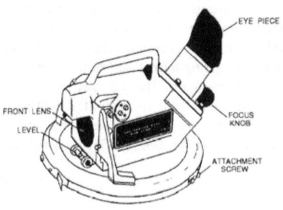

A **telescopic alidade** is a telescope equipped with crosshair, level vial, polarizing light filter, and internal focusing. The telescope is mounted on a ring that fits on a gyro repeater or magnetic compass. The optical system simultaneously projects an image of approximately 25 degrees of the compass card, together with a view of the level vial onto the optical axis of the telescope. By this means, both the object and its bearing can be viewed at the same time through the alidade eyepiece. Older models of the telescopic alidade have a straight-through eyepiece telescope, whereas the model shown in the figure has the eyepiece inclined at an angle for ease in viewing.

AZIMUTH CIRCLE

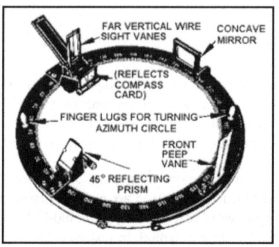

To take an azimuth of a celestial body, you must use the **azimuth circle.** An azimuth circle is a nonmagnetic metal ring sized to fit upon a 7 1/2 inch compass bowl or upon a gyro repeater. The inner lip is graduated in degrees from 0° to 360° in a counterclockwise direction for taking relative bearings. Two sighting vanes (the forward or far vane containing a vertical wire and the after or near vane containing a **peep sight**) facilitate the observation of bearings and azimuths. **Two finger lugs** are used to position the instruments exactly while the vanes are being aligned. A hinged **reflector vane**, mounted at the base and beyond the forward vane, is used for reflecting stars and planets when you are observing azimuths. Beneath the forward vane a **reflecting mirror** and the extended **vertical wire** are mounted, enabling the navigator to read the bearing, or azimuth, from the reflected portion of the compass card. For observing azimuths of the Sun, an additional **reflecting mirror and housing** are mounted on the ring, each midway between the forward and after vanes. The Sun's rays are reflected by the mirror to the housing where a vertical slit admits a line of light. This admitted light passes through a **45 degree reflecting prism** and is projected on the compass card from which its azimuth is directly read. When both bearing and azimuths are observed, two spirit levels, which are attached, must be used to level the instrument.

SEXTANT

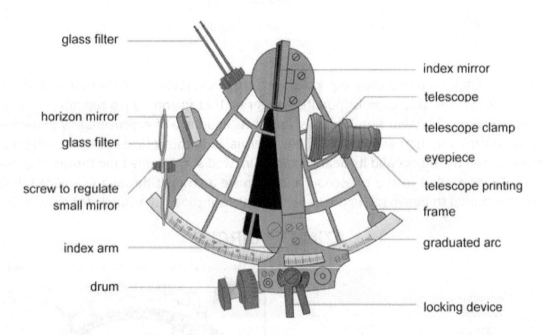

One of the better known navigational instruments is the **sextant.** It is used to measure angles that ultimately result in determining the ship's position at sea. The sextant is capable only of measuring the angle between two objects. Its principal function in navigation is measuring the angle between a heavenly body and the visible horizon.

The figure above shows the parts of a marine sextant. The **frame** is on which the other parts are mounted. The **graduated arc or limb**, graduated in degrees. (The word sextant is derived from the Latin word sex; meaning six. In old-fashioned sextants the limb was one-sixth of the arc of a circle. The **limb** on a modern sextant however contains more than one-sixth of the arc of a circle.) The **index arm,** pivots about the exact center of curvature of the limb. The lower end of the arm is provided with an index mark (to indicate the reading) and with a **micrometer drum.** The **index mirror** is mounted perpendicular to the plane of the **limb** at the upper end of the **index arm.** Half of the horizon glass is silvered over like a mirror; the other half is clear. At zero reading, the **horizon glass** is supposed to be exactly parallel to the index mirror. The **telescope** is supported in a collar attached to the **frame.** It directs the observer's line of sight to the **horizon glass**, a line parallel to the plane of the **frame,** and also magnifies the horizon. **Glass Filters** reduce the glare of light reaching the eye.

MICROMETER

The figure below shows the micrometer arrangement on a sextant. The limb on this sextant has teeth that mesh with teeth on the **micrometer drum. One complete rotation of the drum moves the index arm 1 degree along the limb.** The limb and micrometer drum can be separated by disengaging the tangent screw. This process is accomplished by squeezing the two small **levers** that project below the arm.

Looking at the figure to the right, see if, you can figure out how to read the altitude. On this type of sextant, altitude can be read to the nearest tenth of a minute. It's easy to see that the altitude is somewhere between **57 degrees and 58 degrees** - the indicator on the arm shows you that on the main scale. Inboard of the tangent screw is the micrometer drum, graduated from **0 to 60**. Each graduation represents **1 minute (1')**. A smaller cylinder, inboard of

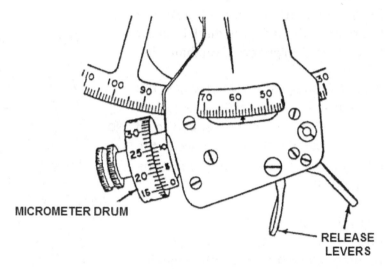

MICROMETER DRUM

RELEASE LEVERS

the drum, is graduated from 0 to 10. It is the vernier of this type of sextant. Each graduation on it represents one-tenth of a minute (0.1'). The index mark for the drum is the 0 on the vernier, **which is between 16 and 17**. Thus, the altitude is a little more than 58 degrees 16 minutes. To find, to the nearest tenth of a minute, how much more the altitude is, start along the vernier scale from 0 and locate the **first graduation that lines up with a graduation on the drum.** Here, it is readily apparent that the first graduation that so lines up is 3. Therefore, the sextant shows an altitude of **58 degrees 16.3 minutes**.

Index Correction

Practically every sextant has a small error, called the **index error,** which is allowed for by applying the **index correction (IC)** to every sextant reading. To find the IC, place the index mark at 0 degrees on the limb scale, and level the sextant toward the horizon. If there is no IC, setting for zero altitude will bring the direct and reflected images of the horizon exactly into line. If the two images are not exactly in line when the instrument is set at zero, the IC is the amount shown to the right or left of zero after they are brought into line. A few graduations have been inserted to the right of the 0 degree mark to allow for an IC that might occur on that side.

After the images are lined up, if the index lies to the **right** of 0 degrees, then the IC is plus and must be **added** to all sextant readings. If the index lies to the **left**, the IC is minus and must be **subtracted**.

This little jingle will help you remember how to apply the IC to the sextant reading: **When it's on, it's off, when it's off, it's on.** In other words when the reading is on the drum scale, the correction is subtractive; when the reading is off the drum scale, the correction is additive.

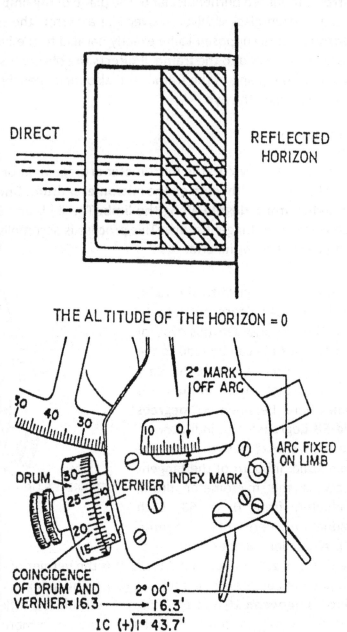

DIRECT

REFLECTED HORIZON

THE ALTITUDE OF THE HORIZON = 0

2° MARK OFF ARC

ARC FIXED ON LIMB

DRUM

VERNIER   INDEX MARK

COINCIDENCE OF DRUM AND VERNIER = 16.3

2° 00'
16.3'

IC (+)1° 43.7'

Care of Sextant

Accuracy of the sextant depends on exact adjustment and alignment of its various parts. A slight shock, for instance, can disturb the adjustment and alignment enough to produce a material error. **In handling the sextant**, **exercise great care** to avoid striking it accidentally against any object. Accidental dropping will, of course, either temporarily or permanently destroy its value as a navigational instrument. **Protect it** against exposure to **salt spray** while you are waiting to get a sight. If no shelter is available, use a towel to protect the sextant.

Alexander F. Hickethier MBA (c) 1988-2019

Moisture must not be permitted to accumulate on the mirror or glass surfaces. These surfaces should be dried with a good grade of lens paper or a piece of clean, soft linen. Silk or chamois may scratch the mirrors, and cotton cloth or waste may leave particles of lint adhering to the glass. **Alcohol** is an **excellent glass cleaner** and is safe to use on a sextant.

Never use brass polish on the arc or vernier because it eventually abrades the graduations on the scale. When **cleaning** becomes necessary, use **ammonia**. Subsequent rubbing with thin oil and lampblack will restore the distinctness of faded markings. A drop or two of light oil should be applied occasionally to the **sextant's working parts**.

Adjusting screws on the sextant should never be manipulated unless absolutely necessary and then only by authorized persons who must exercise the greatest possible caution. Minor adjustments are described below. All other adjustments should be made by trained personnel or at an authorized optical shop.

Sextant adjustment

The navigator should measure and remove the following adjustable sextant errors in the order listed:

1. **Perpendicularity Error:** Adjust first for perpendicularity of the index mirror to the frame of the sextant. **To test for perpendicularity**, place the index arm at **about 35°** on the arc and hold the sextant on its side with the index mirror up and toward the eye. Observe the direct and reflected views of the sextant arc, **as illustrated below**. If the two views are not joined in a straight line, the index mirror is not perpendicular. If the **reflected image is above** the direct view, the mirror is inclined forward. If the **reflected image is below** the direct view, the mirror is **inclined backward**. Make the adjustment using two screws behind the index mirror.

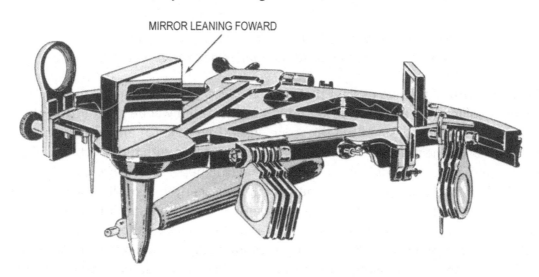

MIRROR LEANING FOWARD

Testing the perpendicularity of the index mirror: Here the mirror is not perpendicular

2. Side Error: An error resulting from the horizon glass not being perpendicular is called **side error**. To test for side error, set the index arm at zero and direct the line of sight at a star. Then rotate the tangent screw back and forth so that the reflected image passes alternately above and below the direct view. If, in changing from one position to the other, the reflected image passes directly over the un-reflected image, no side error exists. If it passes to one side, side error exists. **In the illustration below**, observations without side error (left) and with side error (right). Whether the sextant reads zero when the true and reflected images are in coincidence is immaterial for this test. An alternative method is to observe a vertical line, such as one edge of the mast of another vessel (or the sextant can be held on its side and the horizon used). If the direct and reflected portions do not form a continuous line, the horizon glass is not perpendicular to the frame of the sextant. A third method involves holding the sextant vertically, as in observing the altitude of a celestial body. Bring the reflected image of the horizon into coincidence with the direct view until it appears as a continuous line across the horizon glass. Then tilt the sextant right or left. If the horizon still appears continuous, the horizon glass is perpendicular to the frame, but if the reflected portion appears above or below the part seen directly, the glass is not perpendicular. **Make the appropriate adjustment using two screws behind the horizon glass.**

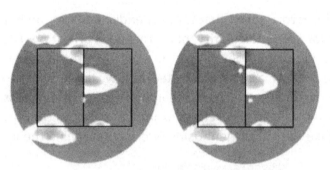

Testing the perpendicularity of the horizon glass. On the left,
side error does not exist. At the right, side error does exist.

3. **Collimation Error:** If the line of sight through the telescope is not parallel to the plane of the instrument, a **collimation error** will result. Altitudes measured will be greater than their actual values. To check for parallelism of the telescope, insert it in its collar and observe two stars 90° or more apart. Bring the reflected image of one into coincidence with the direct view of the other near either the right or left edge of the field of view (the upper or lower edge if the sextant is horizontal). Then tilt the sextant so that the stars appear near the opposite edge. If they remain in coincidence, the telescope is parallel to the frame; if they separate, it is not. An alternative method involves placing the telescope in its collar and then laying the sextant on a flat table. Sight along the frame of the sextant and have an assistant place a mark on the opposite bulkhead, in line with the frame. Place another mark above the first, at a distance equal to the distance from the center of the telescope to the frame. This second line should be in the center of the field of view of the telescope if the telescope is parallel to the frame. Adjust the collar to correct for non-parallelism.

4. **Index Error: Index error is the error remaining after the navigator has removed perpendicularity error, side error, and collimation error.** The index mirror and horizon glass not being parallel when the index arm is set exactly at zero is the major cause of index error. To test for parallelism of the mirrors, set the instrument at zero and direct the line of sight at the horizon. Adjust the sextant reading as necessary to cause both images of the horizon to come into line. The sextant's reading when the horizon comes into line is the index error. If the index error is positive, subtract it from each sextant reading. If the index error is negative, add it to each sextant reading.

End-of-chapter questions

1. What is the principal function of a sextant in navigation?

    a. Measuring ranges to other ships
    b. Measuring the angle between a heavenly body and the visible horizon
    c. Determining the courses of the ships
    d. Determining the true bearings of navigational aids

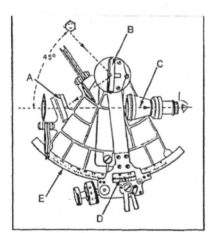

Diagram for Questions 2 through 4

2. The index arm of the sextant pivots about the exact center of curvature of the part of sextant marked:

    a. B
    b. E
    c. A
    d. C

3. What part of the sextant is the horizon glass:

    a. C
    b. E
    c. A
    d. C

4. What part of the sextant is parallel to the horizon glass when the index mark is at zero and there is no index correction?

    a. B
    b. C
    c. D
    d. E

5. How many degrees is the sextant index arm moved by one complete rotation of the micrometer drum?

    a. 10 degrees
    b. 5 degrees
    c. 2 degrees
    d. 1 degree

6. The micrometer drum of the sextant is graduated in:

    a. half seconds from 0 to 180
    b. half seconds from 0 to 20
    c. seconds from 0 to 60
    d. minutes from 0 to 60

7. You have sighted on the horizon to determine the index correction of a sextant. The index mark falls on the arc just to the left of the 0 degree line. If the drum and vernier read 9.4', what is the index correction?

    a. + 50.6'
    b. + 9.4'
    c. - 50.6'
    d. - 9.4'

8. Which of the following cleaning agents is used to clean the mirror or glass surface of a sextant?

    a. Saltwater
    b. Alcohol
    c. Ammonia
    d. Soapy water

9. Which of the following cleaning agents is used to clean the limb and the vernier of the sextant?

    a. Brass polish
    b. Alcohol
    c. Ammonia
    d. Soapy water

ANSWERS
    1. b
    2. a
    3. c
    4. a
    5. d
    6. d
    7. d
    8. b
    9. c

Alexander F. Hickethier MBA (c) 1988-2019

The Magnetic Compass Adjustment and Correction

Chapter 2

The Magnetic Compass

The principle of the present day magnetic compass is in no way different from that of the compass used by the ancients. It consists of a magnetized needle, or array of needles, pivoted so that it will rotate in a horizontal plane. The superiority of the present-day compass results from a better knowledge of the laws of magnetism which governs the behavior of the compass, and from greater precision of construction.

Magnetism

Any piece of metal on becoming magnetized, that is acquiring the property of attracting small particles of iron or steel, will assume regions of concentrated magnetism, called **poles**. Any such magnet will have at least **two poles**, of unlike polarity. **Magnetic lines of force (flux)** connect one pole of such a magnet with the other pole as indicated in the figure.

The number of such lines per unit area represents the intensity of the so-called magnetic field in that area.

If two such magnetized bars or magnets are placed side by side, the like poles will repel each other, and the unlike poles will attract each other.

Magnetism is in general of two types, permanent and induced. A bar having permanent magnetism will retain its magnetism when it is removed from the magnetizing field. A bar having induced magnetism will lose its magnetism when removed from the magnetizing field. Whether or not a bar will retain its magnetism on removal from the magnetizing field will depend on the strength of that field, the degree of hardness of the iron (retentively), and upon the amount of physical stress applied to the bar while in the magnetizing field. The harder the iron the more permanent will be the magnetism acquired.

Terrestrial Magnetism

The accepted theory of **terrestrial magnetism** considers the **earth as a huge magnet** surrounded by lines of magnetic force which connect its two magnetic poles. **These magnetic poles are near, but not coincidental, with the geographic poles of the earth**. Since the **north seeking end** of a compass needle is conventionally called **a red pole, north pole, or positive pole,** it must therefore be attracted to a pole of opposite polarity, or to a **blue pole, South Pole, or negative pole**. The magnetic pole near the north geographic pole is therefore a blue pole, South Pole, or negative pole; and the magnetic pole near the south geographic pole is a red pole, North Pole or positive pole.

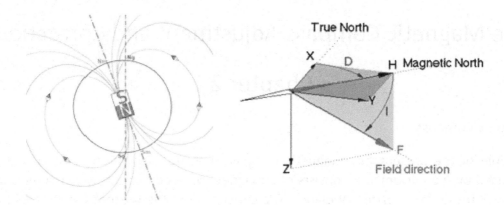

Figure 1   Terrestrial Magnetism

The figures above illustrate the earth and its surrounding magnetic field. The flux lines enter the surface of the earth at different angles to the horizontal, at different magnetic latitudes. This angle is called the angle of magnetic dip, 0, and increases from zero, at the magnetic equator, to 90 degrees at the magnetic poles. The total magnetic field is generally considered as having two components, namely **H**, the horizontal component, and **Z**, the vertical component. These components will change when the angle **D** changes such that it is maximum at the magnetic equator and decreases in the direction of either pole, and **Z** is zero at the magnetic equator and increases in the direction of either pole. The **X** coordinate is the **North** axes and **Y** is the **East** axis.

Since the magnetic poles of the earth are not coincidental with the geographic poles, it is evident that a compass needle in line with the earth's magnetic field will not indicate true north, but **magnetic north**. The angular difference between the true meridian (great circle connecting the geographic poles) and the magnetic meridian (direction at the lines of magnetic flux) is called variation. This variation has different values at different locations on the earth. These **variation** values may be found on the **compass rose** of navigational charts. See figure 2 to the right. The variation for most given areas undergoes an annual change, the amount of which is also noted on all charts.

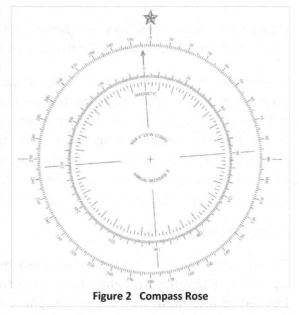

Figure 2   Compass Rose

Ships Magnetism

A ship while in the process of being constructed will acquire magnetism of a permanent nature under the extensive hammering it receives in the earth's magnetic field. After launching, the ship will lose some of this original magnetism because of vibration, pounding, etc., in varying magnetic fields, and will eventually reach a more or less stable magnetic condition. This magnetism which remains is the so-called permanent magnetism of the ship.

The fact that a ship has permanent magnetism does not, of course, mean that it cannot also acquire induced magnetism when placed in a magnetic field such as the earth's field. The amount of magnetism induced in any given piece of soft iron is dependent upon the field intensity, the alignment of the soft iron in that field, and the physical properties and dimensions of the iron. This **induced magnetism may add to or subtract from the permanent magnetism** already present in the ship, depending on how the ship is aligned in the magnetic field. The softer the iron the more readily it will be induced by the earth's magnetic field, and the more readily it will give up its magnetism when removed from that field.

The magnetism in the various structures of the ship which tends to change because of cruising, vibration, or aging, but does not alter immediately so as to be properly termed induced magnetism, is called subpermanent magnetism. This magnetism at any instant is recognized as part of the ship's permanent magnetism, and consequently must be corrected as such by means of permanent magnet correctors. This subpermanent magnetism is the principal cause of deviation changes on a magnetic compass. Subsequent reference to permanent magnetism in this chapter will refer to the apparent permanent magnetism which includes the existing permanent and subpermanent magnetism at any given instant.

A ship, then, has a combination of permanent, subpermanent, and induced magnetism, since its metal structures are of varying degrees of hardness. Thus, the apparent permanent magnetic condition of the ship is subject to change from departing, excessive shocks, welding, vibration, etc.; and the induced magnetism of the ship will vary with the strength of the earth's magnetic field at different magnetic latitudes, and with the alignment of the ship in that field.

Resultant induced magnetism from earth's magnetic field

The above discussion of induced magnetism and terrestrial magnetism leads to the following facts. **(Figure 1, page 2-2)** A long thin rod of soft iron in a plane parallel to the **earth's horizontal magnetic field, H**, will have a **red (north) pole** induced in the end toward the north geographic pole and a **blue (south) pole** induced in the end toward the south geographic pole. This same rod in a horizontal plane but at right angles to the horizontal earth's field would have no magnetism induced in it, because its alignment in the magnetic field is such that there will be no tendency toward linear magnetization and the rod is of negligible cross section. Should the rod be aligned in some horizontal direction between those headings which create maximum and zero induction, it would be induced by an amount which is a function of the angle of alignment. If a similar rod is placed in a vertical position in northern latitudes so as to be aligned with the **vertical earth's field, Z**, it will have a blue (south) pole induced at the upper end and a red (north) pole induced at the lower end. These polarities of vertical induced magnetization will be reversed in southern latitudes.

The amount of horizontal or vertical induction in such rods, or in ships whose construction is equivalent to combinations of such rods, will vary with the intensity of H and Z, heading, and heel of the ship.

Ship's Heading

Ship's heading is the angle, expressed in degrees clockwise from north, of the ship's fore-and-aft line with respect to the true meridian or the magnetic meridian. When this angle is referred to the true meridian, it is called a true heading. When this angle is referred to the magnetic meridian, it is called a magnetic heading. Heading, as indicated on a particular compass, is termed the ship's compass heading by that compass. It is always essential to specify heading as true heading, magnetic heading, or compass heading. To obtain the heading of a ship, it is essential that the line through the pivot and the forward lubber's line of the compass be parallel to the fore and aft line of the ship. This applies also to the pelorus and gyro repeaters, which are used for observational purposes.

Variation

Variation is the angle between the magnetic meridian and the true meridian, measured from true north. If this angle is to the right of the true meridian, the variation is easterly, and if the angle is to the left of the true meridian, the variation is westerly. The local variation and its small annual change are noted on the compass rose of all navigational charts. Thus, the true and magnetic headings of a ship differ by the local variation.

Deviation

As previously explained, a ship's magnetic influence will generally cause the compass needle to deflect from the magnetic meridian. This angle of deflection is called **deviation**. If the north-end of the needle points east of the magnetic meridian, the deviation is **easterly**; if it points west of the magnetic meridian; the deviation is **westerly**.

Heading relationships

A summary of heading relationships follows:

(1) **Deviation** is the difference between the compass heading and the magnetic heading.

(2) **Variation** is the difference between the magnetic heading and the true heading.

(3) **Algebraic sum of deviation and variation** is the **compass error.**

The following simple rules will assist in naming errors and in converting from one heading expression to another:

(1) **Compass least (less than magnetic heading), deviation east.**
Compass Best (greater than magnetic heading) deviation west.

(2) In correcting (going from compass to magnetic to true), apply the sign algebraically **(+East, -West).** In uncorrecting (going from true to magnetic to compass), reverse the sign **(-East, +West)**

Use of compass heading and magnetic heading for adjustment

The primary object of **adjusting compasses** is to **reduce deviations** (to make the magnetic heading and the compass heading identical, or as nearly so as possible). "The two methods of accomplishing this are as follows:

(1) Place the ship on the desired magnetic heading and correct the compass so that it reads the same as this magnetic heading. This is the preferred method.

(2) Place the ship on the desired compass heading and determine the corresponding magnetic heading of the ship, and correct the compass so that it reads the same as this known magnetic heading. This method is used whenever it is impractical to place the ship on a steady magnetic heading for direct correction.

In using the magnetic heading method, the deviations of the compass are easily observed as the difference between the compass reading and the known magnetic heading of the ship. The difficulty in using this method lies in placing the ship on the desired magnetic heading and holding the ship steady on that heading while adjustments are being made.

When using the compass heading method, the ship can easily be brought to any desired compass heading, but the difficulty is in the determination of deviations. Further difficulty arises from the fact that the steersman is steering by an uncorrected compass whose deviations are changing as the necessary adjustments are being made. Therefore, as each adjustment is being made, the steersman should attempt to hold the ship steady on that heading by some means other than the compass being corrected.

Adjustments by this method are made as a series of approximations for example:

Place the ship on any desired compass course, and correct the compass to read the corresponding magnetic heading. This will probably leave the ship on a course other than the desirable cardinal and intercardinal headings for compass adjustment. For accurate results, the above procedure should be repeated.

If the compass has no appreciable deviations, the deviations taken on compass headings will closely approximate those taken on magnetic headings. However, as the magnitude of errors increases, there will be a marked difference between the deviations taken on compass headings and those taken on magnetic headings. The Napier's Diagram affords a method of converting compass course to magnetic course, or vice versa, regardless of whether the deviations were taken on magnetic headings or compass headings.

Methods of placing ship on magnetic headings

A ship may be brought on a magnetic heading by reference to a gyrocompass. The magnetic variation is applied to true heading to determine the gyro course which must be steered in order to place the ship on the desired magnetic heading. If the gyro compass has any error, it must be taken into consideration. It is well to calculate all such problems through true headings, since short cuts on this procedure frequently lead to errors.

The difference between gyro heading and magnetic heading will be constant on all headings as long as the gyrocompass error is constant, and the variation does not change. This gyrocompass error may be determined by a comparison of the calculated true azimuth of the sun and the azimuth as observed on a synchronized repeater.

It is to be remembered that gyrocompass have certain errors resulting from latitude and speed changes as well as turning errors, and that these errors are not always constant on all headings. For these reasons, the gyro error must be checked constantly, especially if the gyro is being used to obtain data for determining residual deviation curves of the magnetic compass.

A ship may be placed on a magnetic heading by aligning the vanes of an azimuth circle with the sun over the topside compass. The sun is a distant object whose azimuth (angle from the north) may be computed for any given time. Methods of calculating azimuth by Polaris and sun are discussed in **Chapters 19, 20 and 21** By setting the line of sight of the vanes at an angle to the right (or left) of the fore-and-aft line of the ship equal to the difference between the computed magnetic azimuth and the desired magnetic heading of the ship, and then swinging the ship until the sun is aligned with the vanes, the ship will be on the desired magnetic heading. The azimuth circle must always be kept level while making observations, particularly of celestial bodies.

A distant object (ten or more miles away) may be used in conjunction with the. Azimuth circle or placing the ship on magnetic headings provided the ship stays within a small area. This procedure is similar to that used with the sun except that the magnetic bearing of the object is constant. With an object 11.4 nautical mile distant; a change in position of 400 yards at right angles to the line of sight introduces error of one degree.

A. PROCEDURES FOR MAGNETIC COMPASS ADJUSTMENT (CHECK OFF LIST) A. DOCKSIDE TESTS AND ADJUSTMENTS

1. Physical checks on the compass and binnacle.

   (a) Remove any bubbles in compass bowl

   (b) Test for movement and sensibility of compass needles

   (c) Remove any slack in gimbal arrangement

   (d) Magnetization check of spheres and Flinders bar

   (e) Alignment of compass with fore-and-aft line of ship

   (f) Alignment of magnet trays in binnacle.

   (g) Alignment of heeling magnet tube under pivot point of compass

   (h) See that corrector magnets are available

2. Physical checks of gyro, azimuth circle, and peloruses.

    (a) Alignment of all gyro repeater pelorus or dial pelorus with fore-and-aft line of ship.

    (b) Synchronize gyro repeaters with master gyro.

    (c) Make sure azimuth circle and peloruses are in good operating condition.

3. Necessary data

    (a) Past history or log data which might establish length of Flinders bar.

    (b) Local apparent time and watch setting.

    (c) Azimuths for given date and latitude

    (d) Ranges or distant objects in vicinity (local charts). (e) Correct variation (local charts).

4. Precautions

    (a) Determine transient deviations of compass from gyro repeaters, doors, guns, etc.

    (b) Secure all effective magnetic gear in normal sea-going position before beginning adjustments.

    (c) Whenever possible, correctors should be placed symmetrically with respect to the compass.

5. Adjustments.

    (a) Place the Flinders bar according to best available information.

    (b) Set spheres at mid-position, or as indicated by last deviation table.

    (c) Adjust heeling magnet, using balanced dip needle.

    (d) Adjust degaussing compass compensating coil currents.

B. ADJUSTMENTS AT SEA

These adjustments are made with the ship on an even keel and after steadying on each heading. When using the gyro, swing from heading to heading slowly and check gyro error by sun's azimuth or ranges on each heading. Be sure the gyro is set for the mean speed and latitude of the vessel. Note all precautions in section A-4 above. (**"Oscar Quebec"** international code signal should be flown to indicate such work is in progress.)

    1. Come to a cardinal magnetic heading, e.g. east (090 degrees) Insert fore-and-aft B magnets, or move the existing B magnets in such manner as to remove all deviation.

2. Come to a south (180 degree) magnetic heading. Insert athwartships C magnets, or move the existing C magnets, in such manner as to remove all deviation.

3. Come to a west (270 degrees) magnetic heading. Correct half of any observed deviation by moving the B magnets.

4. Come to a north (000 degree) magnetic heading. Correct half of any observed deviation by moving the C magnets.

(The cardinal heading adjustments should now be complete).

5. Come to any inter-cardinal magnetic heading e.g. northeast (45 degrees). Correct any observed deviation by moving the spheres in or out.

6. Come to the next inter-cardinal magnetic heading, e.g., southeast (135 degrees). Correct half of any observed deviation by moving the spheres.

The inter-cardinal heading adjustments should now be complete, although more accurate results might be obtained by correcting the D error determined from the deviations on all four inter-cardinal headings.

7. Readjust the heeling magnet to remove oscillations of compass card, with ship under rolling conditions on a north and south heading.

8. Secure all correctors before swinging for residual deviations.

9. Swing for residual un-degaussed deviations on as many headings as desired, although the eight cardinal and inter-cardinal headings should be sufficient.

10. Should there still be any large deviations, the procedure under **"Adjustments' at Sea"** will have to be repeated. If the resulting deviation curve is still unsatisfactory, analyze it to determine the necessary corrections.

11. ·Record deviations and the details of corrector positions on standard form and in the Compass Record Book.

12. Reline degaussing compass compensating coil adjustments.

13. Swing for residual degaussed deviations with the degaussing circuits properly energized.

14. Record deviations for degaussed conditions.

The above check-off list describes a simplified method of adjusting compasses, designed to serve as a simple workable outline for the novice who chooses to follow a step-by-step procedure. The **"Dockside Tests and Adjustments"** are essential as a foundation for the **"Adjustments at Sea"** and if neglected may lead to spurious results or needless repetition of the procedures at sea. Hence, it is strongly recommended that careful consideration be given these dockside checks prior to making the final adjustment to allow time to repair or replace faulty compasses, anneal or replace magnetized spheres or Flinders bar, realign binnacle, move gyro repeater if it is affecting the compass, or to make any other necessary preliminary repairs. It is further stressed that expeditious compass adjustment is dependent upon the application of the various correctors in a logical sequence so as to achieve the final adjustment with a minimum number of steps. This sequence is incorporated in the above check-off list and better results will be obtained if it is adhered to closely

COMPASS ERROR BY TERRESTRIAL OBSERVATION

1. 03751 When proceeding up a channel on course 010° per gyro compass, you notice a pair of range lights Lin alignment with the masts of your vessel when viewed forward. A check of the chart shows the range to be 009° T and the variation to be 15° W. If the ship's course is 026° psc, what is the deviation for the present heading?

    A. 2° W
    B. 2° E
    C. 1° W
    D. 1° W

2. 03752 While your vessel is proceeding down a channel you notice a range of lights in line with your vessel's mast. If your vessel is on course 001° per gyro compass and the charted value of the range of lights is 359° T, what is the gyro compass error?

    A. 2° W
    B. 2° E
    C. 1° E
    D. 1° W

3. 03753 Your vessel is proceeding up a channel, and you see a pair of range lights that are in line ahead. The chart indicates that the direction of this pair of lights is 343° T, and the variation is 5° west. If the heading of your vessel at the time of the sighting is 344° per standard compass, what is the correct deviation?

    A. 11 E
    B. 1° W
    C. 4° E
    D. 4° W

4. 03754 Your vessel is proceeding up a channel, and you see a pair of range lights that are in line ahead. The chart indicates that the direction of this pair of lights is 014° T, and the variation is 11° E. If the heading of your vessel at the time of the sighting is 009° per standard compass, what is the correct deviation?

    A. 5° E
    B. 5° W
    C. 6° E
    D. 6° W

5. 03755 Your vessel is proceeding up a channel, and you see a pair of range lights that are in line ahead. The chart indicates that the direction of this pair of lights is 186° T, and the variation is 11° W. If the heading of your vessel at the time of the sighting is 193° per standard compass, what is the correct deviation?

    A. 4° E
    B. 4° W
    C. 7° E
    D. 7° W

ANSWERS

1. 03751 A

T	009°
V	15° W
M	024°
D	**2° W**
C	026°

2. 03752 A

T	359°
E	**2° W**
G	001°

3. 03753 C

T	343°
V	5° W
M	348°
D	**4° E**
C	344°

4. 03754 D

T	014°
V	11° E
M	003°
D	**6° W**
C	009°

5. 03755 A

T	186°
V	11° W
M	197°
D	**4° E**
C	193°

Deviation Table Construction

1. 4000 You are swinging ship to determine the residual deviation by comparing the magnetic compass against the gyro compass. The gyro error is 2° E. The variation is 8° W. After completing the swinging you have the following readings:

HEADING	HEADING	HEADING
PSC - PGC	PSC - PGC	PSC - PGC
358.5° - 350°	122.5° - 110°	239.5° - 230°
030.5° - 020°	152.0° - 140°	269.0° - 260°
061.5° - 050°	181.0° - 170°	298.0° - 290°
092.0° - 080°	210.0° - 200°	327.5° - 320°

What is the deviation on a magnetic compass heading of 057°?

A. 1.0° E
B. 1.5° E
C. 1.0° W
D. 0.5° W

2. 4001. You are swinging ship to determine the residual deviation by comparing the magnetic compass against the gyro compass. The gyro error is 2° E. The variation is 8° W. After completing the swinging you have the following readings:

HEADING	HEADING	HEADING
PSC - PGC	PSC - PGC	PSC - PGC
358.5° - 350°	122.5° - 110°	239.5° - 230°
030.5° - 020°	152.0° - 140°	269.0° - 260°
061.5° - 050°	181.0° - 170°	298.0° - 290°
092.0° - 080°	210.0° - 200°	327.5° - 320°

What is the deviation on a magnetic heading of 143°?

A. 2.0° W
B. 1.5° W
C. 0.5° W
D. .0°

Alexander F. Hickethier MBA © 1988-2019

3. 4002. You are swinging ship to determine the residual deviation by comparing the magnetic compass against the gyro compass. The gyro error is 2° E. The variation is 8° W. After completing the swinging you have the following readings:

HEADING	HEADING	HEADING
PSC - PGC	PSC - PGC	PSC - PGC
358.5° - 350°	122.5° - 110°	239.5° - 230°
030.5° - 020°	152.0° - 140°	269.0° - 260°
061.5° - 050°	181.0° - 170°	298.0° - 290°
092.0° - 080°	210.0° - 200°	327.5° - 320°

What is the deviation on a true heading of 258°?

A. 0.5° W
B. 0°
C. 0.5° E
D. 1.0° E

4. 4003. You are swinging ship to determine the residual deviation by comparing the magnetic compass against the gyro compass. The gyro error is 2° W. The variation is 8° W. After completing the swinging you have the following readings:

HEADING	HEADING	HEADING
PSC - PGC	PSC - PGC	PSC - PGC
358.5° - 354°	122.5° - 114°	239.5° - 234°
030.5° - 024°	152.0° - 144°	269.0° - 264°
061.5° - 054°	181.0° - 174°	298.0° - 294°
092.0° - 084°	210.0° - 204°	327.5° - 324°

What is the deviation on a gyro heading of 058°?

A. 1.5° W
B. 1.0° W
C. 1.0° E
D. 0.5° W

5. 4004. You are swinging ship to determine the residual deviation by comparing the magnetic compass against the gyro compass. The gyro error is 2° W. The variation is 8° W. After completing the swinging you have the following readings:

HEADING	HEADING	HEADING
PSC - PGC	PSC - PGC	PSC - PGC
358.5° - 354°	122.5° - 114°	239.5° - 234°
030.5° - 024°	152.0° - 144°	269.0° - 264°
061.5° - 054°	181.0° - 174°	298.0° - 294°
092.0° - 084°	210.0° - 204°	327.5° - 324°

What is the deviation on a magnetic compass heading of 166°?

A. 2.0° W
B. 1.5° W
C. 1.0° W
D. 0.5° W

Deviation Table Construction

Problem 1. 4000

T 022	T 022	+w	T 052	T 052
E 2E	V 8W	-E	E 2E	V 8W
G 020	M 030	↓	G 050	M 060
	D .5W	↑		D 1.5W
	C 030.5	+E		C 061.5
		-W		

M	D		M	-		
030	0.5W		**057**	=	1.5W	**ANS: C**
060	1.5W			-		

Problem 2. 4001

T 112	T 112	+w	T 142	T 142
E 2E	V 8W	-E	E 2E	V 8W
G 110	M 120	↓	G140	M 150
	D 2.5W	↑		D 2.0W
	C 122.5	+E		C 152.0
		-W		

M	D		M	-		
120	2.5W		**143**	=	2.0W	**ANS: A**
150	2.0W			-		

Problem 3. 4002

T 232	T 232	+w	T 262	T 262
E 2E	V 8W	-E	E 2E	V 8W
G 230	M 240	↓	G260	M 270
	D 0.5E	↑		D 1.0E
	C 239.5	+E		C 269
		-W		

T	M	D	T	-		
232	240	0.5E	**258**	=	1.0E	**ANS: D**
262	270	1.0E		-		

Problem 4.   4003

T 052		T 052		+w		T 082		T 082
E 2W		V 8W		-E		E 2W		V 8W
G 054		M 060		↓		G 084		M 090
		D 1.5W		↑				D 2.0W
		C 061.5		+E				C 092
				-W				

G	M	D	G	-			
054	060	1.5W	**058**	=	1.5W	ANS: A	
084	090	2.0W		-			

Problem 5.   4004

T 142		T 142		+w		T 172		T 172
E 2W		V 8W		-E		E 2W		V 8W
G 144		M 150		↓		G 174		M 180
		D 2W		↑				D 1W
		C 152		+E				C 181
				-W				

M	D	M	-			
150	2.0W	**166**	=	1.5W	ANS: B	
180	1.0W		-			

Additional USCG problems worked-out for this chapter can be found in **Celestial Navigation Calculations (Upon Oceans Endorsement) Worked-Out for Master 500 GT through 2nd Mate Unlimited, Volume 3, part 1, Chapter3 Deviation Table Construction.**

THE SAILINGS
BY CALCULATION
Chapter 3

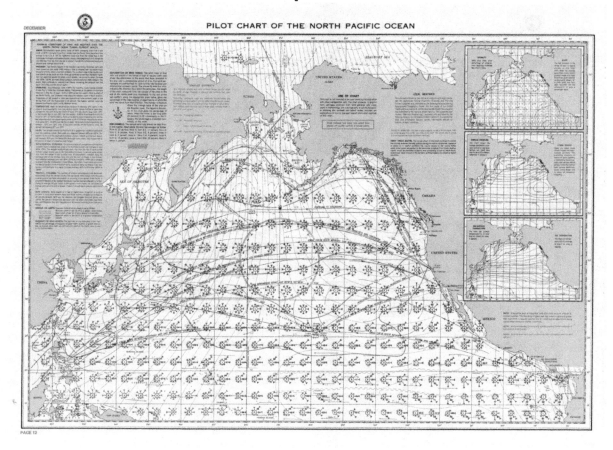

USCG SAILINGS WORKED-OUT
WITH EXCERPTS
AMERICAN PRACTICAL NAVIGATOR
CHAPTER 24

by
ALEXANDER F. HICKETHIER MBA

THE SAILINGS

INTRODUCTION

Introduction

Dead reckoning involves the determination of one's present or future position by projecting the ship's course and distance run from a known position. A closely related problem is that of finding the course and distance from one known point to another known point. For short distances, these problems are easily solved directly on charts, but for long distances, a purely mathematical solution is often a better method. Collectively, these methods are called **The Sailings**.

Navigational computer programs and calculators commonly contain algorithms for computing all of the problems of the sailings.

Rhumb Lines And Great Circles

The principal advantage of a rhumb line is that it maintains constant true direction. A ship following the rhumb line between two places does not change true course. A rhumb line makes the same angle with all meridians it crosses and appears as **a straight line on a Mercator chart**. For any other case, the difference between the rhumb line and the great circle connecting two points increases (1) as the latitude increases, (2) as the difference of latitude between the two points decreases, and (3) as the difference of longitude increases. A great circle is the intersection of the surface of a sphere and a plane passing through the center of the sphere. It is the largest circle that can be drawn on the surface of the sphere, and is the shortest distance along the surface between any two points. Any two points are connected by only one great circle unless the points are **antipodal** (180° apart on the earth), and then an infinite number of great circles passes through them. Every great circle bisects every other great circle. Thus, except for the equator, every great circle lies exactly half in the Northern Hemisphere and half in the Southern Hemisphere. Any two points 180° apart on a great circle have the same latitude numerically, but contrary names, and are 180° apart in longitude. The point of greatest latitude is called the **vertex**. For each great circle, there is a vertex in each hemisphere, 180° apart in longitude.

At these points the great circle is tangent to a parallel of latitude, and its direction is due east-west. On each side of these vertices the direction changes progressively until the intersection with the equator is reached, 90° in longitude away, where the great circle crosses the equator at an angle equal to the latitude of the vertex. On a Mercator chart a great circle appears as a sine curve extending equal distances each side of the equator. The rhumb line connecting any two points of the great circle on the same side of the equator is a chord of the curve. Along any intersecting meridian the great circle crosses at a higher latitude than the rhumb line. If the two points are on opposite sides of the equator, the direction of curvature of the great circle relative to the rhumb line changes at the equator. The rhumb line and great circle may intersect each other, and if the points are equal distances on each side of the equator, the intersection takes place at the equator.

Great circle sailing takes advantage of the shorter distance along the great circle between two points, rather than the longer rhumb line. The arc of the great circle between the points is called the **great circle track**. If it could be followed exactly, the destination would be dead ahead throughout the voyage (assuming course and heading were the same). The rhumb line appears the more direct route on a Mercator chart because of chart distortion. The great circle crosses meridians at higher latitudes, where the distance between them is less. This is why the great circle route is shorter than the rhumb line.

The decision as to whether or not to use great-circle sailing depends upon the conditions. The saving in distance should be worth the additional effort, and of course the great circle route cannot cross land, nor should it carry the vessel into dangerous waters. **Composite sailing** may save time and distance over the rhumb line track without leading the vessel into danger. Since great circles other than a meridian or the equator are curved lines whose true direction changes continually, the navigator does not attempt to follow it exactly. Rather, he selects a number of points along the great circle, constructs rhumb lines between the points, and follows these rhumb lines from point to point.

Kinds Of Sailings

There are seven types of sailings:

1. **Plane sailing** solves problems involving a single course and distance, difference of latitude, and departure, in which the earth is regarded as a plane surface. This method, therefore, provides solution for latitude of the point of arrival, but not for longitude. To calculate the longitude, the spherical sailings are necessary. Do not use this method for distances of more than a few hundred miles.

2. **Traverse sailing** combines the plane sailing solutions when there are two or more courses and determines the equivalent course and distance made good by a vessel steaming along a series of rhumb lines.

3. **Parallel sailing** is the interconversion of departure and difference of longitude when a vessel is proceeding due east or due west.

4. **Middle- (or mid-) latitude sailing** uses the mean latitude for converting departure to difference of longitude when the course is not due east or due west.

5. **Mercator sailing** provides a mathematical solution of the plot as made on a Mercator chart. It is similar to plane sailing, but uses Meridional difference and difference of longitude in place of difference of latitude and departure.

6. **Great circle sailing** involves the solution of courses, distances, and points along a great circle between two points.

7. **Composite sailing** is a modification of great-circle sailing to limit the maximum latitude, generally to avoid ice or severe weather near the poles.

2403. Terms And Definitions

In solutions of the sailings, the following quantities are used:

1. **Latitude (L)**. The latitude of the point of departure is designated L_I; that of the destination, L_2; middle (mid) or mean latitude, L_m; latitude of the vertex of a great circle, L_v; and latitude of any point on a great circle, L_x.

2. **Mean latitude (Lm)**. Half the arithmetical sum of the latitudes of two places on the same side of the equator.

3. **Middle or mid latitude (Lm)**. The latitude at which the arc length of the parallel separating the meridians passing through two specific points is exactly equal to the departure in proceeding from one point to the other. The mean latitude is used when there is no practicable means of determining the middle latitude.

4. **Difference of latitude (l or DLat.)**.

5. **Meridional parts (M)**. The Meridional parts of the point of departure are designated M_I, and of the point of arrival or the destination, M_2.

6. **Meridional difference (m)**.

7. **Longitude (Lo)**. The longitude of the point of departure is designated Lo_1; that of the point of arrival or the destination, Lo_2; of the vertex of a great circle, l_v; and of any point on a great circle, Lo_x

8. **Difference of longitude (DLo)**.

9. **Departure (p or Dep.)**.

10. **Course** or **course angle (Cn or C)**.

11. **Distance (D or Dist.)**.

GREAT CIRCLE SAILING

Great Circle Sailing By Chart

Navigators can most easily solve great-circle sailing problems graphically. DMAHTC publishes several gnomonic projections covering the principal navigable waters of the world. On these **great circle charts**, any straight line is a great circle. The chart, however, is not conformal; therefore, the navigator cannot directly measure directions and distances as on a Mercator chart. The usual method of using a gnomonic chart is to plot the route and pick points along the track every 5° of longitude using the latitude and longitude scales in the immediate vicinity of each point. These points are then transferred to a Mercator chart and connected by rhumb lines. The course and distance for each leg is measured on the Mercator chart.

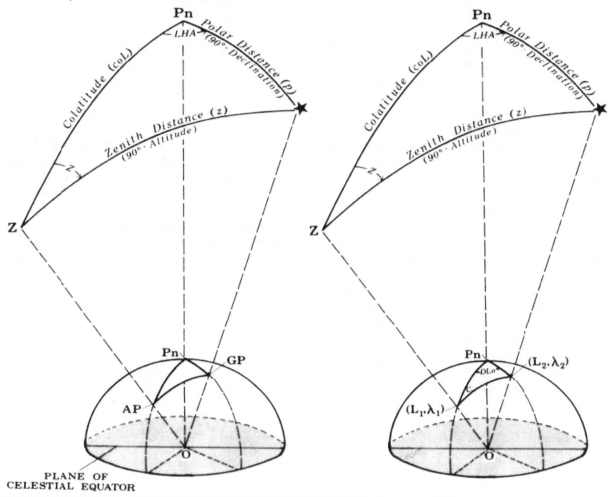

Figure 1 Adapting the astronomical triangle to the navigational triangle of great circle sailing.

Great Circle Sailing By Sight Reduction Tables

Any method of solving a celestial spherical triangle can be used for solving great circle sailing problems. The point of departure replaces the assumed position of the observer, the destination replaces the geographical position of the body, difference of longitude replaces meridian angle or local hour angle, initial course angle replaces azimuth angle, and great circle distance replaces zenith distance (90° - altitude). See Figure 1

Therefore, any table of azimuths (if the entering values are meridian angle, declination, and latitude) can be used for determining initial great-circle course. Tables which solve for altitude, such as *Pub. No. 229*, can be used for determining great circle distance. The required distance is 90°- altitude. In inspection tables such as *Pub. No. 229*, the given combination of L1, L2, and DLo may not be tabulated. In this case reverse the name of L2 and use 180° - DLo for entering the table. The required course angle is then 180° minus the tabulated azimuth, and distance is 90° plus the altitude. If neither combination can be found, solution cannot be made by that method. By interchanging L1 and L2, one can find the supplement of the final course angle. Solution by table often provides a rapid approximate check, but accurate results usually require triple interpolation. Except for *Pub. No. 229*, inspection tables do not provide a solution for points along the great circle. *Pub. No.229* provides solutions for these points only if interpolation is not required.

Great Circle Sailing By *Pub. No. 229*

By entering *Pub. No. 229* with the latitude of the point of departure as latitude, latitude of destination as declination, and difference of longitude as LHA, the tabular altitude and azimuth angle may be extracted and converted to great-circle distance and course. As in sight reduction, the tables are entered according to whether the name of the latitude of the point of departure is the same as or contrary to the name of the latitude of the destination (declination). If the values correspond to those of a celestial body above the celestial horizon, 90° minus the arc of the tabular altitude becomes the distance; the tabular azimuth angle becomes the initial great-circle course angle. If the respondents correspond to those of a celestial body below the celestial horizon, the arc of the tabular altitude plus 90° becomes the distance; the supplement of the tabular azimuth angle becomes the initial great-circle course angle. When the Contrary/Same (CS) Line is crossed in either direction, the altitude becomes negative; the body lies below the celestial horizon. For example: If the tables are entered with the LHA (DLo) at the bottom of a right-hand page and declination (L2) such that the respondents lie above the CS Line, the CS Line has been crossed. Then the distance is 90° plus the tabular altitude; the initial course angle is the

supplement of the tabular azimuth angle. Similarly, if the tables are entered with the LHA (DLo) at the top of a right-hand page and the respondents are found below the CS Line, the distance is 90° plus the tabular altitude; the initial course angle is the supplement of the tabular azimuth angle. If the tables are entered with the LHA (DLo) at the bottom of a right-hand page and the name of L2 is contrary to L1, the respondents are found in the column for L1 on the facing page. In this case, the CS Line has been crossed; the distance is 90° plus the tabular altitude; the initial course angle is the supplement of the tabular azimuth angle. The tabular azimuth angle, or its supplement, is prefixed N or S for the latitude of the point of departure and Figure 2405. Adapting the astronomical triangle to the navigational triangle of great circle sailing. suffixed E or W depending upon the destination being east or west of the point of departure. If all entering arguments are integral degrees, the distance and course angle are obtained directly from the tables without interpolation. If the latitude of the destination is non-integral, interpolation for the additional minutes of latitude is done as in correcting altitude for any declination increment; if the latitude of departure or difference of longitude is non-integral, the additional interpolation is done graphically. Since the latitude of destination becomes the declination entry, and all declinations appear on every page, the great circle solution can always be extracted from the volume which covers the latitude of the point of departure.

Great Circle Sailing By Computation

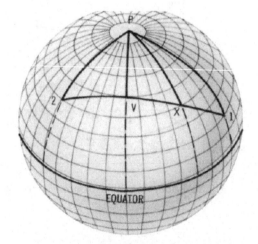

Figure 2. The navigational triangle and great circle sailing.

In Figure 2, 1 is the point of departure, 2 the destination, P the pole nearer 1, I-X-V-2 the great circle through 1 and 2, V the vertex, and X any point on the great circle. The arcs P1, PX, PV, and P2 are the colatitudes of points 1, X, V, and 2, respectively. If 1 and 2 are on opposite sides of the equator, P2 is 90°+L2. The length of arc 1-2 is the great circle distance between 1 and 2. Arcs 1-2, P1, and P2 form a spherical triangle. The angle at 1 is the initial great-circle course from 1 to 2, that at 2 the supplement of the final great-circle course (or the initial course from 2 to 1), and that at P the DLo between 1 and 2. Great circle sailing by computation usually involves solving for the initial great circle course; the distance; latitude and longitude, and sometimes the distance, of the vertex; and the latitude and longitude of various points (X) on the great circle. The computation for initial course and the distance involves solution of an oblique spherical triangle, and any method of solving such a triangle can be used. If 2 is the geographical position (GP) of a celestial body (the point at which the body is in the zenith), this triangle is solved in celestial navigation, except that 90° - D (the altitude) is desired instead of D. The solution for the vertex and any point X usually involves the solution of right spherical triangles.

Great Circle Formulae

$$\cos D = (\cos L_1 \times \cos L_2 \times \cos DLo) \pm (\sin L_1 \times \sin L_2)$$

- Distance x 60
- Subtract (-) when crossing the Equator

$$tan\ C =$$
$$\sin Dlo \div ((\cos L_1 \times \tan L_2) - (\sin L_1 \times \cos Dlo))$$

- Make L_2 (-) negative when crossing the Equator
- Label the initial course angle according the same name of L_1 and DLo
- Label the initial course angle according the same name of L_2 and DLo, when crossing the equator.

$$\cos L_v = \cos L_1 \times \sin C$$

- use Initial Course
- name L_v same name as L_1

$$\sin DLo_v = \cos C \div \sin L_v$$

- If the initial course angle is less than 90° then the vertex is ahead of you and in the direction of the original DLo.

- If the initial course angle is more than 90° then the vertex is behind you and in the direction of the away from original DLo

$$\tan L_x = \cos DLo_{vx} \times \tan L_v$$

Altering A Great Circle Track To Avoid Obstructions

Land, ice, or severe weather may prevent the use of great circle sailing for some or all of one's route. One of the principal advantages of solution by great circle chart is that the presence of any hazards is immediately apparent. The pilot charts are particularly useful in this regard. Often a relatively short run by rhumb line is sufficient to reach a point from which the great circle track can be followed. Where a choice is possible, the rhumb line selected should conform as nearly as practicable to the direct great circle. If the great circle route crosses a navigation hazard, change the track. It may be satisfactory to follow a great circle to the vicinity of the hazard, one or more rhumb lines along the edge of the hazard, and another great circle to the destination. Another possible solution is the use of composite sailing; still another is the use of two great circles, one from the point of departure to a point near the maximum latitude of unobstructed water and the second from this point to the destination.

Composite Sailing

When the great circle would carry a vessel to a higher latitude than desired, a modification of great circle sailing called **composite sailing** may be used to good advantage. The composite track consists of a great circle from the point of departure and tangent to the limiting parallel, a course line along the parallel, and a great circle tangent to the limiting parallel and through the destination. Solution of composite sailing problems is most easily made with a great circle chart. For this solution, draw lines from the point of departure and the destination, tangent to the limiting parallel. Then measure the coordinates of various selected points along the composite track and transfer them to a Mercator chart, as in great circle sailing. Composite sailing problems can also be solved by computation, using the equation:

cos DLovx + tanLx cot Lv

The point of departure and the destination are used successively as point X. Solve the two great circles at each end of the limiting parallel, and use parallel sailing along the limiting parallel. Since both great circles have vertices at the same parallel, computation for C, D, and DLo_{vx} can be made by considering them parts of the same great circle with L_1, L_2, and L_v as given and $DLo = DLo_{v1} + DLo_{v2}$. The total distance is the sum of the great circle and parallel distances.

THE SAILING BY COMPUTATION

Plane Sailing

In plane sailing the figure formed by the meridian through the point of departure, the parallel through the point of arrival, and the course line is considered a plane right triangle. This is illustrated in Figure 3. P_1 and P_2 are the points of departure and arrival, respectively. The course angle and the three sides are as labeled. From this triangle:

From the first two of these formulas the following relationships can be derived:

$$DLat = D \times \cos C \qquad D = DLat \div \cos C$$

$$p = D \times \sin C$$

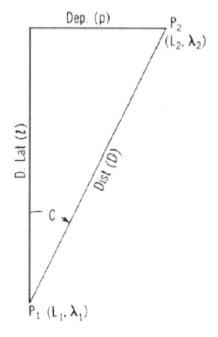

Figure 3. The plane sailing triangle.

Example 1

A ship has steamed 188.0 miles on a course of 005°
Required: (1)(a) Difference in Latitude and (b) departure

Solution:

(1) (a) DLat by computation:

$$Dlat = D \times \cos C$$

= 188.0 miles x cos (005°)
= 187.3 arc min / 60
= 3° 07.3' N

Draw the course vectors to determine the correct course. In this case the vessel has gone north 136 miles and west 203 miles. The course, therefore, must have been between 270° and 360°. No solution other than 304° is reasonable.

Parallel Sailing

Parallel sailing consists of the interconversion of departure and difference of longitude. It is the simplest form of spherical sailing. The formulas for these transformations are:

$$DLo = p \div \cos L \qquad p = DLo \times \cos L$$

Example 1: The DR latitude of a ship on course 090 is 49° 30' N. The ship steams on this course until the longitude changes 3° 30'.

Required: *The departure by (1) computation*

DLo = 3° 30' x 60
DLo = 210 arc min
$$p = DLo \times \cos L$$
p = 210 arc minutes x cos (49.5°)
p = 136.4 miles

Answer:
p = 136.4 miles

Example 2: *The DR latitude of a ship on course 270° is 38° 15' S. The ship steams on this course for a distance of 215.5 miles.*

Required: *The change in longitude by (1) computation*

$$DLo = p \div \cos L$$

3 - 9

Solution:
(1) Solution by computation

DLo = 215.5 arc min / cos (38.25°)
DLo = 215.5 arc min ÷ 0.7853
DLo = 274.4 minutes of arc (west)/ 60
DLo = 4° 34.4' W

Answer:
DLo = 4° 34.4' W

Middle-Latitude Sailing
Middle-latitude sailing combines plane sailing and parallel sailing. Plane sailing is used to find difference of latitude and departure when course and distance are known, or vice versa. Parallel sailing is used to interconvert departure and difference of longitude. The mean latitude (L_m) is normally used for want of a practicable means of determining the middle latitude, the latitude at which the arc length of the parallel separating the meridians passing through two specific points is exactly equal to the departure in proceeding from one point to the other. The formulas for these transformations are:

$$DLo = p \div \cos L_m \qquad p = DLo \times \cos L_m \, D$$

The mean latitude (L_m) is half the arithmetical sum of the latitudes of two places on the same side of the equator. It is labeled N or S to indicate its position north or south of the equator. If a course line crosses the equator, solve each course line segment separately.

Example 1: A vessel steams 1,253 miles on course 070° from lat. 15° 17.0' N, long. 151°37.0' E.

Required: Latitude and longitude of the point of arrival by (1) computation.

Solution:

(1) Solution by computation:

$$DLat = D \times \cos C \qquad p = D \times \sin C$$

$$DLo = p \div \cos L_m$$

D = 1253.0 miles.
C = 070°

p = 1177.4 miles E

L_1 = 15° 17.0' N
L_2 = 22° 25.6' N
DLat = 7° 08.6' N
Dlat = 428.6' N

L_m = 18° 51.3' N

Lo_1 = 151° 37.0' E
Lo_2 = 172° 21.2' E
DLo = 20° 44.2' E
DLo = 1244.2' E

Answer:
L_2 = 22° 25.6' N
L_2 = 172° 21.2' E

Example 2: A vessel at lat. 8° 48.9' S, long. 89° 53.3' W is to proceed to lat. 17° 06.9' S, long. 104° 51.6' W.

Required: Course and distance by (1) Solution by computation:

$$p = DLo \times \cos L_m \qquad \tan C = p \div DLat$$
$$D = DLat \div \cos C$$

DLo = 14° 58.3'
DLo = 898.3'

L_m = 12° 57.9' S
p = 898.3 arc min x cos (12° 57.9')
p = 875.4 arc min
DLat = 17.1° - 8.8'
DLat = 8.3°
DLat l = 498 arc min

C = Tan⁻¹(875.4 DLat 498)
C = S 60.4° W
C = 240.4°

D = 498 arc min x DLat cos (60.4°)
D = 1008.2 miles

Answer:
C = 240.4°
D = 1008.2 miles

The labels (N, S, E, W) of l, p, DLo, and C are determined by noting the direction of motion or the relative positions of the two places.

Mercator Sailing

Mercator sailing problems can be solved graphically on a Mercator chart. For mathematical solution, the formulas of Mercator sailing are:

$$\tan C = DLo \div m \qquad DLo = m \times \tan C$$

After solving for course angle by Mercator sailing, solve for distance using the plane sailing formula:

$$D = DLat \div \cos C.$$

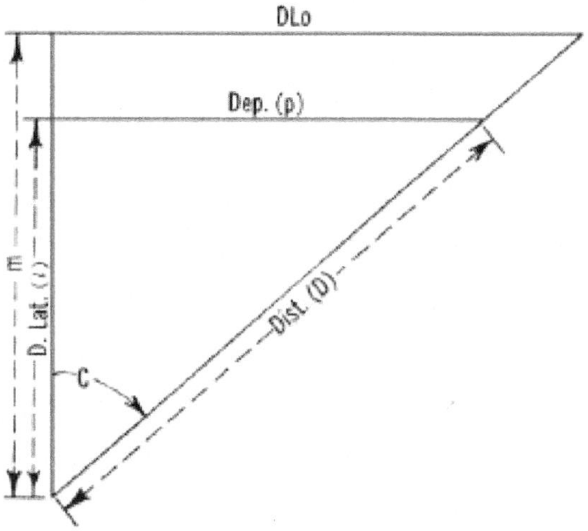

DLo

Dep. (p)

m

D. Lat. (l)

Dist (D)

C

Figure 4 Mercator and plane sailing relationships.

Example 1: *A ship at lat. 32°14.7' N, long. 66° 28.9' W is to head for a point near Chesapeake Light, lat. 36° 58.7' N, long. 75° 42.2' W.*

Required: *Course and distance by (1) computation*

Solution:
(1) Solution by computation:

First calculate the meridional difference by entering Table 6 and interpolating for the meridional parts for the original and final latitudes. The meridional difference is the difference between these two values. (Except when crossing the equator the values are added.) Having calculated the meridional difference, simply solve for course and distance from the equations above.

M_2 (36° 58.7' N) = 2377.5
M_1 (32° 14.7' N) = 2032.9
m = 344.6

L_2 = 075° 42.2' W
L_1 = 066° 28.9' W
DLo = 9° 13.3' W
DLo = 553.3' W

C = arctan (553.3 ÷ 344.6')
C = N 58.1° W
C = 301.9°

L_2 = 36° 58.7' N
L_1 = 32° 14.7' N

DLat = 4° 44.0' N
DLal = 284.0'
D = 284.0 arc min x sec (58.1°)
D = 537.4 miles

Answer:
C = 301.9°
D = 537.4 miles

Example 2: *A ship at lat. 75° 31.7' N, long. 79° 08.7' W, in Baffin Bay, steams 263.5 miles on course 155°.*

Required: *Latitude and longitude of point of arrival by (1) computation and (2) traverse table.*
Solution:

(1) Solution by computation:

$$DLat = D \times \cos C \qquad DLo = m \times \tan C$$

and DLo = m tan C

= (263.5 x cos 155)÷60
= 3°58.8'

L_1 = 75°31.7' N
DLat = 3° 58.8' S
L_2 = 71° 32.9' N

M_1 = 7072.4
M_2 = 6226.1
m = 846.3

3 - 11

= 846.3 x tan 155
DLo = 394.8' E÷60
DLo = 6° 34.8' E

L₁ = 79° 08.7' W
DLo = 6° 34.8' E
L₂ = 072° 34.3' W

The labels (N, S, E, W) of L, DLo, and C are determined by noting the direction of motion or the relative positions of the two places.

Answer:
L₂ = 71° 32.9'
L₂ = 072° 34.3'

Parallel Sailings

Deterring Distance and Course

1. (00526) Your vessel receives a distress call from a vessel reporting her position as LAT 35° 01.0' S, LONG 18° 51.0' W. Your position is LAT 35° 01.0' S, LONG 21° 42.0' W. Determine the true course and distance from your vessel to the vessel in distress by parallel sailing.

A. 090° T, 140.0 miles
B. 090° T, 189.2 miles
C. 270° T, 140.0 miles
D. 270° T, 189.2 miles

2. (00532) You depart LAT 26° 03' S, LONG 10° 28' E, for LAT 26° 03' S, LONG 01° 16' W. What are the course and distance?

A. 090° T, 547.2 miles
B. 090° T, 632.5 miles
C. 270° T, 547.2 miles
D. 270° T, 632.5 miles

3. (00533) You depart LAT 38° 14' N, LONG 12° 42' W, for LAT 38° 14' N, LONG 46° 09' W. What are the course and distance?

A. 090° T, 1576.5 miles
B. 090° T, 2879.0 miles
C. 270° T, 1576.5 miles
D. 270° T, 2868.5 miles

Deterring Longitude of Arrival.

1. (00527) You depart LAT 25° 54' N, LONG 9° 38' E and steam 592 miles on course 270°. What is the LONG of arrival?

A. 1° 20' E
B. 0° 40' E
C. 0° 40' W
D. 1° 20' W

2. (00528) You depart LAT 38° 12' S, LONG 12° 06' W and steam 1543 miles on course 270°. What is the LONG of arrival?

A. 44° 49' W
B. 45° 12' W
C. 45° 37' W
D. 45° 42' W

3. (00529) You depart LAT 51° 48.0' S, LONG 178° 35.0' W and steam 179 miles on course 270°. What is the LONG of arrival?

A. 173° 47' W
B. 174° 27' E
C. 176° 36' E
D. 179° 52' W

Required Course and Distance worked-out

PARALLEL SAILINGS Required Course and Distance				
1. (00526)				
Date:				
L_1	35° 01.0' S		Lo_1	21° 42.0' W
L_2	35° 01.0' S		Lo_2	18° 51.0' W
DLat	0		DLo	2° 51' E
		Formulae		171'
Distance	140.0	$p(D) = Dlo \times \cos L =$		
Course	090	$p(D) = 171 \times \cos 35° 01.0' = 140$		
Answer A				

2. (00532)					
Date:					
L$_1$	26° 03.0′ S			Lo$_1$	10° 28.0′ E
L$_2$	26° 03.0′ S			Lo	01° 16.0′ W
DLat	0			DLo	11° 44.0′ W
		Formulae			**704'**
Distance	632.5	$p(D) = Dlo \times \cos L =$			
Course	270	$p(D) = 704 \times \cos 26° 03.0' = 632.5$			
Answer D					

3. (00533)					
Date:					
L$_1$	38° 14.0′ N			Lo$_1$	12° 42.0' W
L$_2$	38° 14.0′ N			Lo	46° 09.0 W
DLat	0			DLo	33° 27.0' W
		Formulae			**2007'**
Distance	1576.5	$p(D) = Dlo \times \cos L =$			
Course	270	$p(D) = 2007 \times \cos 38° 14.0' = 1576.5$			
Answer C					

Required Longitude of Arrival problems worked-out

PARALLEL SAILINGS
Required Longitude of Arrival

1. (00527)					
Date:					
L$_1$	25° 54.0′ N			Lo$_1$	9° 38.0′ E
±DLat	0′			±DLo	10° 58.1′ W
L$_2$	25° 54.0′ N			Lo	1° 20.0′ W
		Formulae			
Distance	592	$Dlo = \dfrac{p(D)}{\cos L} = \dfrac{592}{\cos 25° 54.0} = 658.1011/60 = 10° 58.1'$			
Course	270				
Answer D					

2. (00528)					
Date:					
L$_1$	38° 12.0′ N			Lo$_1$	12° 06.0′ W
±DLat	0′			±DLo	32° 43.5′ W
L$_2$	38° 12.0′ N			Lo	44° 49.5′ W
		Formulae			
Distance	1543	$Dlo = \dfrac{p(D)}{\cos L} = \dfrac{1543}{\cos 38° 12.0} = 1963.46/60 = 32° 43.5'$			
Course	270				
Answer A					

3. (00529)				
Date:				
L_1	51° 48.0' S		Lo_1	178° 35.0' W
±DLat	0'		±DLo	4° 49.5' W
L_2	51° 48.0' S		Lo	183° 24.5'
			360 - 183° 24.5 = **176° 35.5' E**	

Formulae

$$Dlo = \frac{p(D)}{\cos L} = \frac{179}{\cos 51° 48.0'} = 289.45/60 = 4° \ 49.5'$$

Distance 179
Course 270
Answer C

MID-LATITUDE SAILINGS

Determining Course and Distance

1.
301. You depart LAT 28° 55.0' N, LONG 89° 10.0' W, enroute to LAT 24° 25.0' N, LONG 83° 00.0' W.
Determine the true course and distance by mid-latitude sailing.

A. 418 miles, 122° T
B. 427 miles, 129° T
C. 436 miles, 133° T
D. 442 miles, 122° T

2.
307.   A vessel at LAT 28° 00.0' N, LONG 116° 00.0' E is to proceed to LAT 34° 00.0' N, LONG 123° 40.0' E.

Required. -- Course and distance by Mid-latitude sailing.

A. 045.0° T, 530.1 miles
B. 049.5° T, 525.8 miles
C. 047.6° T, 533.9 miles
D. 042.1° T, 527.7 miles

3.
308.   A vessel at LAT 20° 00' N, LONG 107° 30' W is to proceed to LAT 24° 40' N, LONG 112° 30' W.

Required. -- Course and distance by Mid-latitude sailing.

A. 314.0° T, 389.0 miles
B. 315.3° T, 394.0 miles
C. 317.2° T, 397.0 miles
D. 318.3° T, 399.0 miles

4.
309.   A vessel at LAT 14° 10' N, LONG 61° 00' W is to proceed to LAT 10° 00' N, LONG 53° 23' W.

Required. -- Course and distance by mid-latitude sailing.

A. 117.3° T, 503.0 miles
B. 117.9° T, 504.0 miles
C. 118.6° T, 508.0 miles
D. 119.2° T, 512.0 miles

<table>
<tr><td colspan="7" align="center">**Mid-Latitude SAILINGS**
Required Course and Distance</td></tr>
<tr><td>Problem # 1</td><td>(301)</td><td></td><td colspan="2" align="center">Chapter</td><td></td><td></td></tr>
<tr><td>Date:</td><td></td><td></td><td colspan="2" align="center">Mid-Latitude</td><td></td><td></td></tr>
<tr><td>L_1</td><td>28° 55.0' N</td><td>L_1</td><td colspan="2">28° 55.0' N</td><td>Lo_1</td><td>89° 10.0' W</td></tr>
<tr><td>L_2</td><td>24° 25.0' N</td><td>±½ Dlat</td><td colspan="2">2° 15.0' S</td><td>Lo</td><td>83° 00.0' W</td></tr>
<tr><td>DLat</td><td>4° 30.0' S</td><td>MidLat</td><td colspan="2">26° 40'.0' N</td><td>DLo</td><td>6° 10.0' E</td></tr>
<tr><td>X 60</td><td>270</td><td></td><td colspan="2"></td><td>X 60</td><td>370</td></tr>
</table>

		Formulae		N

Distance 426.92
Course 129.23
Answer B

$$\tan C = \frac{p}{DLat} = \tan^{-1}\left(\frac{330.64}{270}\right) = 50.77 \quad \begin{array}{c|c} 360- & \text{Same} \\ \hline 180+ & 180- \end{array}$$

180- 50.77 = 129.23

$$p = DLo \times \cos L_m = 370 \times \cos 26° 40' = 330.64 \qquad D = \frac{DLat}{\cos C} = \left(\frac{270}{\cos 129.23}\right) = 426.92$$

<table>
<tr><td>Problem # 2</td><td>(307)</td><td></td><td colspan="2" align="center">Chapter</td><td></td><td></td></tr>
<tr><td>Date:</td><td></td><td></td><td colspan="2" align="center">Mid-Latitude</td><td></td><td></td></tr>
<tr><td>L_1</td><td>28° 00.0' N</td><td>L_1</td><td colspan="2">28° 00.0' N</td><td>Lo_1</td><td>116° 00.0' E</td></tr>
<tr><td>L_2</td><td>34° 00.0' N</td><td>±½ Dlat</td><td colspan="2">3° 00.0' N</td><td>Lo</td><td>123° 40.0' E</td></tr>
<tr><td>DLat</td><td>6° 00.0' N</td><td>MidLat</td><td colspan="2">31° 00.0' N</td><td>DLo</td><td>7° 40.0' E</td></tr>
<tr><td>X 60</td><td>360</td><td></td><td colspan="2"></td><td>X 60</td><td>460</td></tr>
</table>

Distance 533.8
Course 047.6
Answer C

$$\tan C = \frac{p}{DLat} = \tan^{-1}\left(\frac{394.3}{360}\right) = 47.6 \quad \begin{array}{c|c} 360- & \text{Same} \\ \hline 180+ & 180- \end{array}$$

$$p = DLo \times \cos L_m = 460 \times \cos 31 = 394.3 \qquad D = \frac{DLat}{\cos C} = \left(\frac{360}{\cos 047.6}\right) = 533.8$$

3 - 17

Problem # 3	(308)			Chapter			
Date:				Mid-Latitude			
L₁	20° 00.0' N	L₁		20° 00.0' N		Lo₁	107° 30.0' W
L₂	24° 40.0' N	±½ Dlat		2° 20.0' N		Lo	112° 30.0' W
DLat	4° 40.0' N	MidLat		22° 20.0' N		DLo	5° 00.0' W
X 60	280					X 60	300

		Formulae	N
Distance	393.9	$$tan\,C = \frac{p}{DLat} = tan^{-1}\left(\frac{277.5}{280}\right) = 44.7$$	360 - | Same
Course	315.3		180 + | 180 -
Answer B		$360 - 44.7 = 315.3$	S

$$p = DLo \times \cos L_m = 300 \times \cos 22° 20 = 277.5 \qquad D = \frac{DLat}{\cos C} = \left(\frac{280}{\cos 315.3}\right) = 393.9$$

Problem # 4	(309)			Chapter			
Date:				Mid-Latitude			
L₁	14° 10.0' N	L₁		14° 10.0' N		Lo₁	61° 00.0' W
L₂	10° 00.0' N	±½ Dlat		2° 05.0' S		Lo	53° 23.0' W
DLat	4° 10.0' S	MidLat		12° 05.0' N		DLo	7° 37.0' W
X 60	250					X 60	457

		Formulae	N
Distance	512.1	$$tan\,C = \frac{p}{DLat} = tan^{-1}\left(\frac{446.87}{250}\right) = 60.77$$	360 - | Same
Course	119.2		180 + | 180 -
Answer D		$180 - 60.8 = 119.22$	S

$$p = DLo \times \cos L_m = 457 \times \cos 12° 05' = 446.87 \qquad D = \frac{DLat}{\cos C} = \left(\frac{250}{\cos 119.22}\right) = 512.12$$

3 - 18

MID-LATITUDE SAILINGS
Chapter 1, Advanced Subjects for Master/Mate Unlimited

Determining Latitude and Longitude

1. 302. A vessel steams 720 miles on course 058° T from LAT 30° 06.0' S LONG 31° 42.0' E.

Required. -- Latitude and longitude of the point of arrival by Mid-latitude sailing.

A. LAT 23° 46' S,	LONG 43° 11' E
B. LAT 23° 42' S,	LONG 43° 07' E
C. LAT 23° 38' S,	LONG 43° 03' E
D. LAT 23° 34' S,	LONG 43° 00' E

3. 304. A vessel steams 580 miles on course 083° T from LAT 13° 12' N, LONG 71° 12' W.

Required. -- Latitude and longitude of the point of arrival by Mid-latitude sailing.

A. LAT 14° 17' N,	LONG 61° 23' W
B. LAT 14° 20' N,	LONG 61° 21' W
C. LAT 14° 23' N,	LONG 61° 19' W
D. LAT 14° 25' N,	LONG 61° 17' W

2. 303. A vessel steams 576 miles on course 260° T from LAT 40° 36' N, LONG 50° 24' W.

Required. -- Latitude and longitude of the point of arrival by Mid-latitude sailing.

A. LAT 39° 12' N,	LONG 62° 28' W
B. LAT 39° 06' N,	LONG 62° 34' W
C. LAT 39° 02' N,	LONG 62° 37' W
D. LAT 38° 56' N,	LONG 62° 42' W

4. 305. A vessel steams 666 miles on course 295° T from LAT 24° 24' N, LONG 83° 00' W.

Required. -- Latitude and longitude of the point of arrival by Mid-latitude sailing.

A. LAT 29° 01' N,	LONG 94° 18' W
B. LAT 29° 06' N,	LONG 94° 16' W
C. LAT 29° 10' N,	LONG 94° 10' W
D. LAT 29° 13' N,	LONG 94° 06' W

MID-LATITUDE SAILINGS					
Required Latitude and Longitude of Arrival					
Problem # 1	(00302)		Chapter		
Date:			Mid-Latitude		
L₁	30° 06.0' S	L₁	30° 06.0' S	Lo₁	31° 42.0' E
±DLat	6° 21.5' N	±½ Dlat	3° 10.5' N	±DLo	11° 24.8' E
L₂	23° 44.5' S	Lm	26° 55.5' S	Lo	43° 06.8 E

Distance 720	**Formulae**
Course 058	$DLat = D \times \cos C = 720 \times \cos 58 = 381.54 \div 60 = 6° 21.5'$
Answer B	

$$p = D \times \sin C = 720 \times \sin 58 = 610.59$$

$$DLo = \frac{p}{\cos L_m} = \frac{610.59}{\cos 26° 55.7'} = 684.85$$

$$\div 60 = 11° 24.8'$$

Problem # 2	(00303)		Chapter			
Date:			Mid-Latitude			
L_1	40° 36.0' N	L_1	40° 36.0' N		Lo_1	50° 24.0' W
±DLat	1° 40.0' S	±½ Dlat	00° 50.0' S		±DLo	12° 17.9' W
L_2	38° 56.1' N	Lm	39° 46.0' N		Lo_2	62°41.9' W

		Formulae	
Distance	576		
Course	260	$DLat = D \times \cos C = 576 \times \cos\ 260 = 100.02 \div 60 = 1°40'$	
Answer D			

$$p = D \times \sin C = 576 \times \sin 260 = 567.25$$

$$DLo = \frac{p}{\cos L_m} = \frac{567.25}{\cos 39° 46'} = 737.98$$

$$\div 60 = 12°17.9'$$

Problem # 3	(00304)		Chapter			
Date:			Mid-Latitude			
L_1	13° 12.0' N	L_1	13° 12.0' N		Lo_1	71° 12.0' W
±DLat	1° 11.0' N	±½ Dlat	36.0' N		±DLo	9° 53.0' E
L_2	14° 23.0' N	Lm	13° 48.0' N		Lo	61° 19.0' W

		Formulae	
Distance	580		
Course	083	$DLat = D \times \cos C = 580 \times \cos 83 = 70.68 \div 60 = 1°11'$	
Answer C			

$$p = D \times \sin C = 580 \times \sin 83 = 575.68$$

$$DLo = \frac{p}{\cos L_m} = \frac{575.68}{\cos 13° 48'} = 592.79$$

$$\div 60 = 9° 53'$$

Problem # 4	(00305)		Chapter			
Date:			Mid-Latitude			
L_1	24° 24.0' N	L_1	24° 24.0' N		Lo_1	83° 00.0' W
±DLat	4° 41.5' N	±½ Dlat	2° 20.5' N		±DLo	11° 15.9' W
L_2	29° 05.5' N	Lm	26° 44.5' N		Lo	94° 15.9' W

		Formulae	
Distance	666		
Course	295	$DLat = D \times \cos C = 666 \times \cos 295 = 281.46 \div 60 = 4° 41.5'$	
Answer B			

$$p = D \times \sin C = 666 \times \sin 295 = 603.60$$

$$DLo = \frac{p}{\cos L_m} = \frac{603.60}{\cos 26° 44.5'} = 675.89$$

$$\div 60 = 11°15.9'$$

Mercator Sailings,
Chapter 1, Advanced subjects for Master/Mate Unlimited

1. 376. You depart LAT 40° 42.0' N, LONG 74° 01.0' W, and steam 3365.6 miles on course 118°T. What is the longitude of your arrival?

A. 10° 46.0' W
B. 22° 58.0' W
C. 17° 41.0' W
D. 24° 29.0' W

2. 377. You depart LAT 22° 35.0'N, LONG 157° 30.0'W, and steam 4505.0 miles on course 135° T. What are the latitude and longitude of your arrival?

A. 30° 30.5' S, 102°35.3' W
B. 30° 30.5' S, 104° 30.0' W
C. 32° 20.0' S, 102° 35.3' W
D. 32° 20.0' S, 104° 30.0' W

3. 405. You depart LAT 33° 45.0' N, LONG 118° 30.0' W, and steam 2216 miles on course 250° T. What is the longitude of your arrival by Mercator sailing?

A. LONG 156° 08.0' W
B. LONG 156° 36.0' W
C. LONG 157° 21.0' W
D. LONG 157° 31.0' W

4. 406. You depart LAT 49° 45.0' N, LONG 06° 35.0' W, and steam 3599 miles on course 246.5° T. What is the longitude of your arrival by Mercator sailing?

A. LONG 76° 36.2' W
B. LONG 77° 02.8' W
C. LONG 78° 14.0' W
D. LONG 78° 22.6' W

MERCATOR SAILINGS					
Required Latitude and Longitude of Arrival					
Problem # 1 (00376)			Chapter		
Date:			Meridional Parts		
L_1	40° 42.0' N	M_1	2662.8	Lo_1	74° 01.0 'W
±DLat	26° 20.0' S			±DLo	56° 20.2' E
L_2	14° 22.0' N	M_2	865.5	Lo_2	17° 41.8' W
		m	1797.3		
			Formulae		
Distance	3365.6				
Course	118		$DLat = D \times \cos C = 3365.6 \times \cos 118 = 1580.05 \div 60 =$		
Answer C			$26° 20.0'S$		
Notes:			$DLo = m \times \tan C = 1797.3 \times \tan 118 = 3380.23 \div 60 =$		
			$56°20.2'E$		

Problem # 2 (00377)			Chapter		
Date:			Meridional Parts		
L_1	22° 35.0' N	M_1	1382.7	Lo_1	157° 30.0' W
±DLat	53° 05.5' S			±DLo	54° 55.3' E
L_2	30° 30.5' S	M_2	1912.0	Lo_2	102° 34.7' W
		m	3294.7		
			Formulae		
Distance	4505.0		$DLat = D \times \cos C = \times \cos = 4505 \times \cos 135 = 3185.5160$		
Course	135		$\div 60 = 53° 05.5'$		
Answer A					
Notes:			$DLo = m \times \tan C = \times \tan = 3294.7 \times \tan 135 = 3294.7 \div 60 =$		
			$54° 54.7'E$		

Problem # 3	(00405)		Chapter			
Date:			Meridional Parts			
L_1	33° 45.0' N	M_1	2140.6		Lo_1	118° 30.0' W
±DLat	12° 37.9' S				±DLo	39° 01.1' W
L_2	21° 07.1' N	M_2	1288.5		Lo_2	157° 31.1' W
		m	852.1			
			Formulae			
Distance	2216					
Course	250		$DLat = D \times \cos C = 2216 \times \cos 250 = 757.91 \div 60 = 12° 37.9\,S$			
Answer D						
Notes:			$DLo = m \times \tan C = 852.1 \times \tan 250 = 2341.13 \div 60 = 39° 01.1\,W$			

Problem # 4	(00406)		Chapter			
Date:			Meridional Parts			
L_1	49° 45.0' N	M_1	3433.6		Lo_1	6° 35.0' W
±DLat	23° 55'.1' S				±DLo	70° 28.0' W
L_2	25° 49.9' N	M_2	1595.2		Lo_2	77° 03.0' W
		m	1838.4			
			Formulae			
Distance	3599		$DLat = D \times \cos C = 3599 \times \cos 246.5 = 1435.1 \div 60 = 23° 55.1'\,S$			
Course	246.5					
Answer B						
Notes:			$DLo = m \times \tan C = 1838.4 \times \tan 246.5 = 4228.03 \div 60 = 70° 28.0'\,W$			

Mercator Sailings,
Chapter 1, Advanced subjects for Master/Mate Unlimited

1. 378. A vessel at LAT 37° 24.0' N, LONG 178° 15.0' W, heads for a destination at LAT 34° 18.0' N, LONG 178° 25.0' E. Determine the true course and distance by Mercator sailing.

A. 041° T, 273.9 miles
B. 047° T, 273.9 miles
C. 221° T, 247.2 miles
D. 227° T, 247.2 miles

2. 379. A vessel at LAT 32° 05.0' N, LONG 81° 06.0' W, heads for a destination at LAT 35° 57.0N, LONG 5° 45.0' W. Determine the distance by Mercator sailing.

A. 3128.2 miles
B. 3768.0 miles
C. 4126.1 miles
D. 4508.0 miles

3. 380. A vessel at LAT 21° 18.5' N, LONG 157° 52.2' W, heads for a destination at LAT 8° 53.0' N, LONG 79° 31.0' W. Determine the true course and distance by Mercator sailing.

A. 081° T, 4613.7 miles
B. 081° T, 4915.8 miles
C. 099° T, 4613.1 miles
D. 099° T, 4915.8 miles

4. 00390. A vessel at LAT 29° 38.0' N, LONG 93° 49.0' W heads for a destination at LAT 24° 38.0' N, LONG 82° 55.2' W. Determine the true course and distance by Mercator sailing.

A. 115° T, 637 miles
B. 117° T, 660 miles
C. 122° T, 648 miles
D. 126° T, 665 miles

MERCATOR SAILINGS
Required Course and Distance

Problem 1. (00378)			Chapter			
Date:			Meridional Parts			
L_1	37° 24.0' N	M_1	2408.8		Lo_1	178° 15.0' W
L_2	34° 18.0' N	M_2	2180.3		Lo_2	178° 25.0' E
DLat	3 ° 06.0' S	m	228.5		DLo	3° 20.0' W
X 60	186 S				X 60	200 W

	Formulae		N
Distance 247.2	$$\tan C = \frac{Dlo}{m} = \tan^{-1}\left(\frac{200}{228.5}\right) = 41.2$$		360 - | Same
Course 221.2			180 + | 180 -
Answer C	S41.2' W + 180 = 221.2		S

Notes: crossing the dateline we add the longitudes and subtract from 360. 178 ° 15' - 178° 25' = 356 ° 40' - 360 = 3° 20'	$$D = \frac{DLat}{\cos C} = \left(\frac{186}{\cos 221.2}\right) = 247.204$$

Problem 2. (00379)			Chapter			
Date:			Meridional Parts			
L_1	32° 05.0' N	M_1	2022.1		Lo_1	81° 06.0' W
L_2	35° 57.0' N	M_2	2300.8		Lo_2	5° 45.0' W
DLat	3° 52.0' N	m	278.7		DLo	75 ° 21.0' E
X 60	232 N				X 60	4521 E

	Formulae		N
Distance 3767.99	$$\tan C = \frac{Dlo}{m} = \tan^{-1}\left(\frac{4521}{278.7}\right) = 86.47$$	360 -	Same
Course 86.5		180 +	180 -
Answer B	N86.47E		S

Notes:	$$D = \frac{DLat}{\cos C} = \left(\frac{232}{\cos 86.47}\right) = 3767.99$$

Problem 3. (00380)			Chapter			
Date:			Meridional Parts			
L_1	21° 18.5' N	M_1	1300.5		Lo_1	157° 52.2' W
L_2	8° 53.0' N	M_2	531.6		Lo_2	79° 31.0' W
DLat	12° 25.5' S	m	768.9		DLo	78° 21.2' E
X 60	745.5 S				X 60	4701.2 E

	Formulae		N
Distance 4613.1	$$\tan C = \frac{Dlo}{m} = \tan^{-1}\left(\frac{4701.2}{768.9}\right) = 80.7$$	360 -	Same
Course 99.3		180 +	180 -
Answer C	180 − S80.7E = 99.3		S

Notes:	$$D = \frac{DLat}{\cos C} = \left(\frac{745.5}{\cos 99.3}\right) = 4613.1$$

Problem 4. (0390)			Chapter			
Date:			Meridional Parts			
L_1	29° 38.0' N	M_1	1851.6		Lo_1	93° 49.0' W
L_2	24° 38.0' N	M_2	1516.2		Lo_2	82° 55.2' W
DLat	5° 00.0' S	m	335.4		DLo	10° 53.8' E
X 60	300 S				X 60	653.8 E

	Formulae		N
Distance 117.2	$$\tan C = \frac{Dlo}{m} = \tan^{-1}\left(\frac{653.8}{335.4}\right) = 62.8421$$	360 -	Same
Course 656.3		180 +	180 -
Answer B	180 - S62.8E = 117.2		S

Notes:	$$D = \frac{DLat}{\cos C} = \left(\frac{300}{\cos 117.2}\right) = 656.3145056$$

GREAT CIRCLE SAILINGS
Chapter 1, Advanced Subjects for Master/Mate Unlimited

1. 451. Given the following information:

1. Latitude of departure (L1) 27° 51.0' N
2. Longitude of departure (LO1) 71° 41.0' W
3. Latitude of arrival   (L2) 49° 45.0' N
4. Longitude of arrival   (LO2) 06° 14.0' W

Determine the great circle distance (GCD) and initial course (Cn).

A. 3196 miles,   Cn 043.1° T
B. 3214 miles,   Cn 046.9° T
C. 3219 miles,   Cn 042.5° T
D. 3231 miles,   Cn 041.4° T

2. 452. Given the following information:

1. Latitude of departure (L1) 35° 17.6' N
2. Longitude of departure (LO1) 144° 23.0' E
3. Latitude of arrival   (L2) 47° 36.0' N
4. Longitude of arrival   (LO2) 124° 22.0' W

Determine the great circle distance (GCD) and initial course (Cn).

A. 3946 miles,   Cn 312 T
B. 3931 miles,   Cn 048° T
C. 3881 miles,   Cn 042° T
D. 3718 miles,   Cn 318° T

3. 453. Given the following information:

1. Latitude of departure (L1) 08° 36.0' N
2. Longitude of departure (LO1) 126° 17.0' E
3. Latitude of arrival   (L2) 02° 12.0' S
4. Longitude of arrival   (LO2) 81° 53.0' W

Determine the great circle distance (GCD) and initial course (Cn).

A. 9015 miles,   Cn 067° T
B. 9076 miles,   Cn 067° T
C. 9105 miles,   Cn 079° T
D. 9076 miles,   Cn 079° T

4. 454. Given the following information:

1. Latitude of departure (L1) 26° 00.0' S
2. Longitude of departure (LO1) 56° 00.0' W
3. Latitude of arrival   (L2) 34° 00.0' S
4. Longitude of arrival   (LO2) 18° 15.0' E

Determine the great circle distance (GCD) and initial course (Cn).

A. 3705 miles,   Cn 153° T
B. 3481 miles,   Cn 068° T
C. 3849 miles,   Cn 248° T
D. 3805 miles,   Cn 117° T

Great Circle

Problem 1.   451

L$_1$ 27° 51.0' N   Lo$_1$ 71° 41.0' W

L$_2$ 49° 45.0' N   Lo$_2$ 06° 14.0' W

                                                                               Dlo 65° 27.0' E

$$\cos D = (\cos L_1 \times \cos L_2 \times \cos DLo) + (\sin L_1 \times \sin L_2)$$

$$COS^{-1}\big((\cos 27° 51.0' \times \cos 49° 45.0' \times \cos 65° 27.0') + (\sin 27° 51.0' \times \sin 49° 45.0')\big)$$
$$= 53.56486287 \times 60 = 3213.891772$$

$$\tan C = \sin DLo \div ((\cos L_1 * \tan L_2) - (\sin L_1 * \cos DLo))$$

$$\tan^{-1}\big((\sin 65° 27.0' \div \big((\cos 27° 51.0' \times \tan 49° 45') - (\sin 27° 51.0' \times \cos 65° 27.0')\big)\big)$$
$$= 46.92882608$$

Course Angle $N46°.92882608E$

Rules to convert course angle to course:

IF:

L1 is N, DLo is E	CN = C
L1 is S, DLo is E	CN = 180 - C
L1 is S, DLo is W	CN = 180 + C
L1 is N, DLo is W	CN = 360 - C

Convert to True Course   N 46.9° E

Answer B

Problem 2. 452

L_1 35° 17.6' N Lo_1 144° 23.0' E
L_2 47° 36.0' N $\underline{Lo_2\ 124°\ 22.0'\ W}$
                                             Dlo 91° 15.0' E

144°23.0' + 124°22.0' = 268°45.0' = (360° - 268°45.0') = 91°15.0'

Note: when crossing the Date Line (180 E/W), We add Lo1 and Lo2 and Subtract the sum from 360 to find Dlo.

$$cos\ D\ =\ (cos\ L_1\ \times\ cos L_2\ \times\ cos\ DLo)\ +\ (sin\ L_1\ \times\ sin\ L_2)$$

$$COS^{-1}((\cos 35°\ 17.6'\ \times \cos 47°\ 36.0'\ \times \cos 91°\ 15.0')\ +\ (\sin 35°\ 17.6'\ \times \sin 47°\ 36.0'))$$
$$=\ 65.50299428\ \times\ 60\ =\ 3930.179657$$

$$tan\ C\ =\ sin\ DLo \div ((cos\ L_1\ *\ tan\ L_2)\ -\ (sin\ L_1\ *\ cos\ DLo))$$

$$tan^{-1}((Sin\ 91°\ 15.0'\ \div \left((\cos 35°\ 17.6'\ \times \tan 47°\ 36.0')\ -\ (\sin 35°\ 17.6'\ \times \cos 91°15.0')\right))$$
$$=\ 47.80209747$$

Course Angle $N47.80209747°E$

Rules to convert course angle to course:

IF:

L1 is N, DLo is E	CN = C
L1 is S, DLo is E	CN = 180 - C
L1 is S, DLo is W	CN = 180 + C
L1 is N, DLo is W	CN = 360 - C

Convert to True Course   N 47.8° E

Answer B

Problem 3. 453

L₁ 08° 36.0' N   Lo₁ 126° 17.0' E
L₂ 02° 12.0' S   Lo₂ 081° 53.0' W
                                                    Dlo 151° 50.0' E

L_1 08° 36.0' N $\qquad$ Lo_1 126° 17.0' E

126° 17.0' + 081° 53.0' = 208° 10.0' = (360° - 208° 10.0') = 151° 50.0'

Note: when crossing the Date Line (180 E/W), We add Lo1 and Lo2 and Subtract the sum from 360 to find Dlo.

$$cos\ D\ =\ (cos\ L_1\ \times\ cosL_2\ \times\ cos\ DLo)\ +\ (sin\ L_1\ \times\ sin\ L_2)$$

$$COS^{-1}((\cos\ 08°\ 36.0' \times \cos 2°\ 12.0' \times \cos 151°\ 50.0') - (\sin 08°\ 36.0'\ \times \sin 2°\ 12.0'))$$
$$=\ 151.2544292 \times 60\ =\ 9075.265753$$

$$tan\ C\ =\ sin\ DLo \div ((cos\ L_1\ *\ tan\ L_2) - (sin\ L_1\ *\ cos\ DLo))$$

$$tan^{-1}((Sin\ 151°\ 50.0' \div ((\cos 8°\ 36.0' \times tan - 2°\ 12.0') - (\sin 8°\ 36.0' \times \cos 151°\ 50.0')))$$
$$=\ 78.75598702$$

Course Angle $N78.5598702°E$

Rules to convert course angle to course:

IF:

L1 is N, DLo is E   CN = C
L1 is S, DLo is E   CN = 180 - C
L1 is S, DLo is W   CN = 180 + C
L1 is N, DLo is W   CN = 360 - C

Convert to True Course   N 78.6° E

Answer D

Problem 4. 454

L$_1$ 26° 00.0' S Lo$_1$ 56° 00.0' W
L$_2$ 34° 00.0' S Lo$_2$ 18° 15.0' E
Dlo 74° 15.0' E

56° 00.0' + 18° 15.0' = 74° 15.0'

Note: when crossing Greenwich (000 E/W), We add Lo1 and Lo2 and the sum is Dlo.

$$cos\,D = (cos\,L_1 \times cosL_2 \times cos\,DLo) + (sin\,L_1 \times sin\,L_2)$$

$COS^{-1}((cos\,26°\,00.0' \times cos\,34°\,00.0' \times cos\,74°\,15.0') + (sin\,26°\,00.0' \times sin\,34°\,00.0'))$
$= 6342342048 \times 60 = 3805.405229$

$$tan\,C = sin\,DLo \div ((cos\,L_1 * tan\,L_2) - (sin\,L_1 * cos\,DLo))$$

$tan^{-1}((Sin\,74°15.0' \div ((cos\,26°\,00.0' \times tan\,34°\,00.0') - (sin\,26°\,00.0' \times cos\,74°\,15.0')))$
$= 63.14873112$

Course Angle $S63.14873112E$

Rules to convert course angle to course:

IF:
L1 is N, DLo is E CN = C
L1 is S, DLo is E CN = 180 - C
L1 is S, DLo is W CN = 180 + C
L1 is N, DLo is W CN = 360 - C

Convert to True Course 180 – 63.14 = S 116.86° E

Answer D

Great Circle
Example 1
Determine the parallel of latitude (L_x)

4002212.
Given the following information:

1. L1 25°50.0' N LO_1 77° 00.0' W
2. L2 36°56.0' N LO_2 06° 15.0' W
3. Great circle distance (CGD)   3616 Miles
4. Initial great circle course (Cn)   61.7° T
5. Latitude of upper vertex (L_v) (V1)   37° 35.6' N
6. Longitude of upper vertex (LO_v) (V1)   25° 57.8' W
7. Difference of longitude from the upper vertex (V_1) to a point (X) on the great circle track (DLO_{vx}) 10°0' W.

Determine the parallel of latitude (L_x) which intersects the great circle track at point (X).

A. LAT 37° 02.5' N
B. LAT 37° 10.2' N
C. LAT 37° 15.0' N
D. LAT 37° 21.0' N

Formula:

$$tan\, L_x \; = \; cos\, DLo_{vx} \; \times \; tan\, L_v$$

Note: If Dlovx is given in Nautical Miles East or West of Vertex convert it to Degrees by dividing the distance by 60.

$$cos\, 10° \; \times \; tan\, 37°\, 35.6' \; = \; tan\, 0.7582215386$$

$$tan^{-1}\, 0.7582215386 \times 37.17018789 \; = \; 37°\, 10'\, 12.68''\; or$$

<u>Ans. B   37°10.2'</u>

<u>Great Circle</u>
Example 2
Determine the longitude of the upper vertex (LO$_v$) (V1).

4002200.
Given the following information:

1. L1 35° 57.2' N	LO$_1$	05° 45.7' W
2. L2 24° 25.3' N	LO$_2$	83° 02.6' W
3. Great circle distance (GCD)		3966.5 miles
4. Initial great circle course (Cn)		076° 16.5' T
5. Latitude of upper vertex (L$_v$) (V1)		38° 09.4' N

Determine the longitude of the upper vertex (LO$_v$) (V1).

A. LONG 28° 12.6' W
B. LONG 28° 24.5' W
C. LONG 28° 36.3' W
D. LONG 28° 47.7' W

Formula:

$$sin\ Dlov\ =\ cos\ C\ \div\ sin\ L_v$$

$$cos\ 76°\ 16.5'\ \div\ sin\ 38°\ 09.4'\ =\ 0.3844922011\ sin^{-1}\ =\ 22.58383420\ =\ 22°\ 35.1$$

Lo$_1$	05° 45.7'
+ Dlo$_v$	22° 35.1'
	28° 20.8'

Great Circle
Example 3
Determine the distance in miles (Dv)

4002203.

Given the following information:

1. Latitude of departure (L$_1$)		25° 50.0' N
2. Longitude of departure (LO$_1$)		77° 00.0' W
3. Latitude of vertex (Lv)		37° 35.6' N
4. Longitude of vertex (LOv)		25° 57.8' W
5. Initial course (Cn)		061.7° T

Determine the distance in miles (Dv) along the great circle track (GCT) between the point of departure (L$_1$, LO$_1$) and the vertex (V$_1$).

A. 2735.1 miles
B. 2664.9 miles
C. 2583.2 miles
D. 2420.0 miles

Formula:

$$sin\ Dv\ =\ cos\ L_1\ \times\ sin\ Dlov$$

$$cos\ 25°\ 50'\ \times\ sin\ 51°02.2\ =\ 0.701650631 sin^{-1}\ =\ 44.4145332$$

$$44.4145332\ \times\ 60\ =\ 2664.871992\ NM$$

Great Circle

Example 4

Determine the latitude of the upper vertex (V_1)

4002204.

Given the following information:

1. L1 35° 08.0' S	LO_1	19° 26.0' E
2. L2 33° 16.0' S	LO_2	115° 36.0' E
3. Great circle distance (GCD)		4559 miles
4. Initial great circle course (Cn)		121° 02.4' T

Determine the latitude of the upper vertex (V_1).

A. LAT 44° 29.1' S
B. LAT 45° 30.9' S
C. LAT 46° 18.2' S
D. LAT 43° 41.8' S

Formula:

$$cos\ Lvx\ =\ cos\ L_1\ \times\ sin\ C$$

$$cos\ 35°08'\ \times\ sin\ 121°02.4'\ =\ 0.7007710094\ cos^{-1}\ =\ 45.5159972$$

$$45°30.9'\ S$$

Additional USCG problems worked-out for this chapter can be found in **Celestial Navigation Calculations (Upon Oceans Endorsement) Worked-Out for Master 500 GT through 2nd Mate Unlimited, Volume 3, part 1, Chapter2, The Sailings.**

Alexander F. Hickethier MBA © 1990-2020

ESTIMATED TIME OF ARRIVAL PROBLEMS
Chapter 4

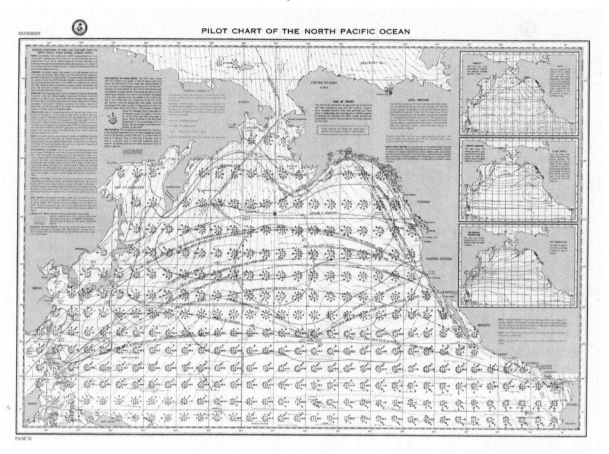

by
Alexander F. Hickethier, MBA

ESTIMATED TIME OF ARRIVAL (ETA)

In Marine Navigation, we are continually determining our ETA to insure safe navigation. We use the: time, speed, distance calculation **(ETA = Distance/Speed)** to find our DR position, the time we will sight a light or the time of an upcoming turn. These ETA's are normally for a few minutes to several hours, but with Ocean going vessels that make world voyages we must determine ETA's taking into consideration great distances which may cross several time zones.

As in the other chapters of this textbook we will use an actual U.S.C.G. question below to explain a method of calculating this type of ETA.

You are on a voyage from Valdez, AK to Panama Canal Zone. The distance from pilot to pilot is 4950 miles. The speed of advance is 15.0 knots. You estimate a layover in San Francisco, CA of 36.0 hours. If you take departure at 0800 (ZD +10) 29, October, what is your ETA (ZD +5) at Panama Canal Zone.

    A. 1900, 13 November
    B. 1400, 13 November
    C. 1400, 14 November
    D. 0900, 13 November

Our first step is to change our departure time from local zone time to Greenwich Mean Time (GMT). (For more information on Time Zones see chapter 7)

0800 (ZD + 10) = 1800 29 October

Next, we calculate the time required to transit the 4950 miles between Valdez, AK to the Panama Canal Zone at 15 knots with a 36 hour layover in San Francisco.

First, we divide the distance to be traveled (4950 NM) by our speed of 15 kts.

    4950/15 = 330 hours

Then, we convert this to days by dividing the 330 hours by 24.

    330/24 = 13.75 Days

Next, we multiply the .75 of a day back to hours by 24.

    .75 x 24 = 18 Hours.

This gives us the number of days and hours for our transit not including our 36 hour layover.

To 13 days 18 hours of transit we add the 1 day 12 hours of layover. Thus we have 15 day and 06 hours. Adding this to our departure time of 29 October, 1800 we have an arrival date and time of November 14, 0000 GMT. **(Remember: October has 31 days)**

We must now convert this to local time in Panama (ZD + 5). This is done by applying the reverse of the destination zone description (ZD - 5).

November 14, 0000 – 5 Hours = <u>November 13, 1900 or answer A</u>

End of chapter USCG problems
Estimated Time of Arrival

00601. At 1210 zone time on 1 December 1981, you depart Seattle, LAT 47° 36.0' N, LONG 122° 22.0' W (ZD +8). You are bound for Guam, LAT 13° 27.0' N, LONG 144° 37.0' E, and you estimate your speed of advance at 20 knots. The distance is 4,948 miles. What is your estimated zone time of arrival at Guam?

A. 1734, 11 December
B. 1934, 11 December
C. 0334, 12 December
D. 1334, 12 December

00602. At 1845 zone time on 24 October 1981, you depart Bimini Island, LAT 25° 50.0' N, LONG 77° 00.0' W (ZD +5). You are bound for Bishop Rock, LAT 49° 40.0' N, LONG 6° 34.0' W, and you estimate your speed of advance at 13.6 knots. The distance is 3,491 miles. What is your estimated zone time of arrival at Bishop Rock?

A. 0627, 3 November
B. 1642, 3 November
C. 0939, 4 November
D. 1627, 4 November

00603. At 0915 zone time on 7 November 1981, you depart Seattle, LAT 47° 36.0' N, LONG 122° 22.0' W (ZD +8). You are bound for Kobe, LAT 34° 40.0' N, LONG 135° 12.0' E, and you estimate your speed of advance at 18.5 knots. The distance is 4,527 miles. What is your estimated zone time of arrival at Kobe?

A. 1257, 17 November
B. 0657, 18 November
C. 1857, 18 November
D. 0657, 19 November

00604. At 1820 zone time on 21 March 1981, you depart San Francisco, LAT 37° 48.5' N, LONG 122° 24.0' W (ZD +8). You are bound for Melbourne, LAT 37° 49.2' S, LONG 144° 56.0' E, and you estimate your speed of advance at 21 knots. The distance is 6,970 miles. What is your estimated zone time of arrival at Melbourne?

A. 1214, 4 April
B. 2214, 4 April
C. 0814, 5 April
D. 1314, 5 April

00605. At 0915 zone time on 26 July 1981, you depart Yokohoma, LAT 35° 27.0' N, LONG 139° 39.0' E (ZD -9). You are bound for Seattle, LAT 47° 36.0' N, LONG 122° 22.0' W, and you estimate your speed of advance at 14 knots. The distance is 4,245 miles. What is your estimated zone time of arrival at Seattle?

A. 0728, 7 August
B. 1528, 7 August
C. 0028, 8 August
D. 1528, 8 August

ETA PROBLEMS WORKED-OUT

0601 (1)	Month	day	Hour	Minutes
Departure ZT	12	01	12	10
ZD			+8	
Departure GMT	12	01	20	10
Dist. Run + Lay		10	07	24
Arrival GMT	12	12	03	34
Rev. ZD			+10	
Arrival ZT	12	12	13	34

0602 (2)	Month	day	Hour	Minutes
Departure ZT	10	24	18	45
ZD			+5	
Departure GMT	10	24	23	45
Dist. Run + Lay		10	16	41
Arrival GMT	11	04	16	26
Rev. ZD			0	
Arrival ZT	11	04	16	26

Distance Run plus lay time Calculations

$$\frac{4948}{20} = \frac{247.4}{24} = 10 \; Days$$

$$.30833333 \quad \times 24 = 07 \; Hours$$

$$.4 \times 60 = 24 \; Minutes$$

Distance Run plus lay time Calculations

$$\frac{3491}{13.6} = \frac{256.6911765}{24} = 10 \; Days$$

$$.69546569 \times 24 = 16 \; Hours$$

$$.69117647 \times 60 = 41 \; Minutes$$

0603 (3)	Month	day	Hour	Minutes
Departure ZT	11	07	09	15
ZD			+8	
Departure GMT	11	07	17	15
Dist. Run + Lay		10	04	42
Arrival GMT	11	17	21	57
Rev. ZD			+9	
Arrival ZT	11	18	06	57

0604 (4)	Month	day	Hour	Minutes
Departure ZT	03	21	18	20
ZD			+8	
Departure GMT	03	22	02	20
Dist. Run + Lay		13	19	54
Arrival GMT	04	04	22	14
Rev. ZD			+10	
Arrival ZT	040	05	08	14

Distance Run plus lay time Calculations

$$\frac{4527}{18.5} = \frac{244.7527027}{24} = 10 \quad Days$$

$$.1959459459 \times 24 = 04 \ Hours$$

$$..7027027027 \times 60 = 42 \ Minutes$$

Distance Run plus lay time Calculations

$$\frac{6970}{21} = \frac{331.9047619}{24} = 13 \ Days$$

$$.82936508 \times 24 = 19 \ Hours$$

$$.9047619 \times 60 = 54 \ Minutes$$

0605 (5)	Month	day	Hour	Minutes
Departure ZT	07	26	09	15
ZD			-9	
Departure GMT	07	26	00	15
Dist. Run + Lay		12	15	13
Arrival GMT	08	07	15	28
Rev. ZD			-8	
Arrival ZT	08	07	07	28

Distance Run plus lay time Calculations

$$\frac{4245}{14} = \frac{303.2142857}{24} = 12 \ Days$$

$$.63392857 \times 24 = 15 \ Hours$$

$$.2142857143 \times 60 = 13 \ Minutes$$

Additional USCG problems worked-out for this chapter can be found in **Celestial Navigation Calculations (Upon Oceans Endorsement) Worked-Out for Master 500 GT through 2nd Mate Unlimited, Volume 3, part 2, Chapter 3, Estimated Time of Arrival.**

NAUTICAL ASTRONOMY
Chapter 5

Although we know that the Earth is not a perfect sphere, we consider it to be so for many navigational purposes. All problems in celestial navigation involve the use of two spheres. One such body is the Earth itself, and the other is an imaginary celestial sphere.

Let's go back again and the use the lighted transparent sphere with which we illustrated a chart projection. Assume the sphere is the size of a tennis ball, with the Earth's meridians and parallels laid out on it in black. Assume further that it is suspended in the exact center of another sphere, made of glass, about the size of a basketball.

The basketball-sized sphere, on which the meridians and parallels are projected from the smaller one, represents the imaginary celestial sphere on which all the heavenly bodies are presumed to be located. The entire system of navigation by the stars is founded upon the fact that angular distances on the celestial sphere can be reduced to fit the Earth (terrestrial sphere).This system makes it possible for a navigator to locate objects on the Earth with reference to the locations of heavenly bodies on the celestial sphere.

As previously discussed in **Volume III, Practical Navigation**, objects are located on the terrestrial sphere by a system of coordinates called latitude and longitude. Latitude lines (parallels) are parallel to the equator and are used to indicate distance north or south of the equator. On the Mercator chart, longitude lines (meridians) cross the equator at right angles and are used to indicate distance east or west of the Greenwich meridian. Objects on the celestial sphere are located in a similar manner, but the horizontal lines are called declination, and the vertical lines are called Greenwich hour angle (GHA).

Longitude is measured on the terrestrial sphere east and west from the Greenwich meridian (G) along the equator. The **GHA** of a body on the celestial sphere is measured **westward** from the projected Greenwich meridian to the body's hour circle.

What is an hour circle? It is half of a great circle on the surface of the celestial sphere which passes through a celestial body and terminates at the celestial poles. The hour circle, contrasted to the celestial meridian, moves with the celestial body progressively with time from east to west (since we consider apparent motion), while the position of the celestial meridian remains fixed. With knowledge of the Earth's rotation (one turn upon its axis per 24 hours), we realize that each celestial body crosses our meridian once each 24 hours. **Dividing 360 degrees (number of degrees in a circle) by 24 hours**, we find that an hour circle advances **15 degrees per hour**.

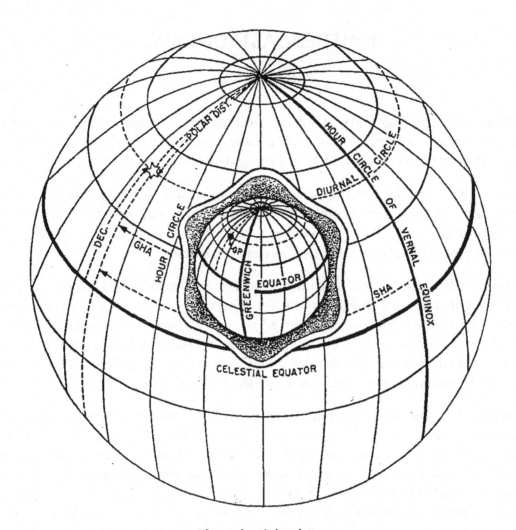

The celestial sphere

The GHA of any body is the degrees, minutes, and tenths of minutes of arc of the celestial equator intercepted at a given instant between that body's hour circle and the celestial meridian of Greenwich, measured westward from Greenwich through 360 degrees. Whether measured on the celestial or the terrestrial sphere, the amount of arc is the same. The figure above shows you GHA of a star as measured on the terrestrial sphere.

Notice that the star's position on the terrestrial sphere' is indicated by GP. The letters GP stand for geographic position and represent the point where a line drawn from the center of the Earth to the body would intersect the Earth's surface. Depending on whether the body in question is the Sun, the Moon, or a star, a GP may be variously a subsolar, sublunar, or substellar point.

You can see from the figure how closely GHA corresponds to longitude. Remember, however, that GHA of any body increases continuously as the body moves westward. The GHA is always measured westward from Greenwich (0 degrees) through 360 degrees. Longitude is measured east or west from Greenwich through 180 degrees.

The GHA of any navigational body of the solar system {Sun; moon; and planets) and of the first point of Aries (T}, sometimes called vernal equinox, is listed in the Nautical Almanac for every hour of GMT, for any date. The first point of Aries **(T)** is the zero point on the celestial equator from which the westward distance of the stars is measured. The **GHA of any navigational star** may be determined from the Nautical Almanac by **adding GHA of Aries to the tabulated sidereal hour angle (SHA) of the star**. Let's see what all these explanations mean.

SIDEREAL HOUR ANGLE

Referring to the figure on **page 5-2**, the marking "hour circle of vernal equinox" is the line from which sidereal hour angle is measured. The SHA of any star is measured westward through 360 degrees like GHA; but measurement is from the vernal equinox or first point of Aries, instead of from Greenwich.

GHA of the vernal equinox, like GHA of any other body, is increasing continuously westward. But the sidereal hour angle of any star (measured westward from the vernal equinox to the body's hour circle) remains relatively constant. Why? Because all the stars move westward along with the vernal equinox. The SHA of any body changes slightly, and its tabulated value in the Nautical Almanac varies slightly throughout the year. The reasons for the changes are beyond the scope of this course.

You will see later that the SHA and GHA of the vernal equinox are factors used in star observations. However, neither is applicable in observations of navigational planets.

DECLINATION

The GP you see on the small sphere in the figure on **page 5-2** corresponds to the star's location on the celestial sphere. The latitude of a point on the terrestrial sphere is measured from the equator northward or southward along the point's meridian to a maximum of 90 degrees. Declination of a body on the celestial sphere is measured in exactly the same way-from the celestial equator (equinoctial) northward or southward along the body's hour circle. The polar distance is the number of degrees, minutes, and tenths of minutes of arc between the heavenly body and the elevated pole. The elevated pole is the one above the horizon; in other words, the one with the same name as your latitude.

From the foregoing description, it follows that the polar distance of a body whose declination has the same name (north or south) as the elevated pole is always 90 degrees minus its declination (d). Polar distance of a body whose declination has a different name from that of the elevated pole is always 90 degrees plus d.

Declination of any navigational star is listed in the Nautical Almanac for each date. Declination of each body of the solar system is listed for every hour GMT.

5-3

TIME DIAGRAM

So far you have learned that a heavenly body is located on the celestial sphere by its Greenwich hour angle (corresponding to longitude) and its declination (corresponding to latitude). You have seen how both of these coordinates are measured and how, from them, the GP of a heavenly body can be located on the terrestrial sphere.

Before going further into nautical astronomy, you should acquire a knowledge of the use of the diagram of the plane of the celestial equator (time diagram), which not only will make it easier for you to understand the ensuing discussion but will simplify the solution of celestial navigation problems.

In the time diagram the observer is theoretically located outside the celestial sphere, over its South Pole. The diagram consists of a circle representing the celestial equator. The center of the circle is the South celestial Pole. Counterclockwise direction is westerly. The local meridian is drawn in as a vertical line, thus placing the upper branch (M), which is the arc of a celestial meridian between the poles at the top of the diagram and the lower branch (m) at the bottom. To avoid confusion, the lower meridian is shown by a dashed line.

You locate the Greenwich meridian by means of your longitude. You were in 90 degrees W longitude, G would appear on your diagram 90 degrees clockwise from M because you're counterclockwise or west of G. A glance at the figure will confirm this location. What you really do, then, is count from M toward Greenwich, the direction depending upon whether you are in east or west longitude.

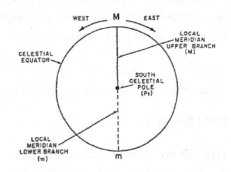

The second figure shows another time diagram on which GHA of the Sun is indicated. The upper branch of the Sun's hour circle is shown as a solid line. The angle, or arc, of the celestial equator between the Greenwich meridian and the Sun's hour circle is 90 degrees.

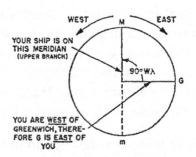

Therefore, GHA of the Sun GHA or the Sun on a time diagram at this instant is 90 degrees. Remember, GHA is always measured westward from G. The GHA of a star is measured in the same direction from Greenwich to the star. Because the SHA enters the picture here, however, your method of locating a star on the time diagram is somewhat different. First, you must locate the vernal equinox by its tabulated GHA. Let's say GHA of the vernal equinox for the time of your observation is 45 degrees. You locate the vernal equinox 45 degrees W from Greenwich, as shown in the figure. The symbol that resembles a pair of ram's horns represents the vernal equinox.

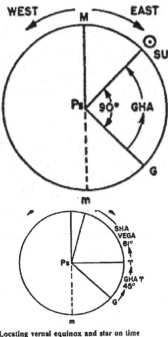

From the Nautical Almanac you find SHA of the star in question. You already know that SHA is measured to the west from the vernal equinox (first point of Aries).All you have to do here is find the SHA of this star, measure SHA westward from the vernal equinox, and you have the star located on the time diagram. Let's say it's the star Vega whose SHA is approximately 81 degrees. The figure on page 5-5 shows you Vega located on the time diagram.

Locating vernal equinox and star on time diagram.

It's easy to see here that GHA of Vega must be equal to GHA of the vernal equinox plus SHA of Vega. GHA (Vega) = GHA (T) = SHA (Vega). In this example GHA of Vega is 81 degrees plus 45 degrees, or 126 degrees.

Now let's use the time diagram to explain some more facts about nautical astronomy.

LOCAL HOUR ANGLE (LHA)

Local hour angle is the name given to the angle of arc (expressed in degrees, minutes, and tenths of minutes) of the celestial equator between the celestial meridian of a point on the celestial sphere place and the hour circle of a heavenly body. It is always measured westward from the local meridian through 360 degrees.

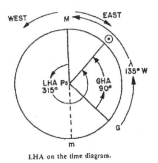

LHA on the time diagram.

Let's work this problem of LHA on a time diagram. Say you're in 135 degrees W longitude. You know your own meridian is represented by M. Measure approximately 135 degrees from M toward Greenwich, which means, of course, that Greenwich will be shown east of M. Think it over for a moment you're to the west of Greenwich, therefore Greenwich is to the east of you.

Now that we know where Greenwich is and where you are, let's take the Sun as we had it in the figure and try to figure out its LHA. The figure shows us that the Sun is 90 degrees west of Greenwich. We know that LHA is always measured westward from your local meridian (M) to the hour circle of the body (in this example, the Sun).

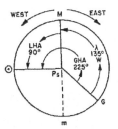

LHA, with Sun west of your celestial meridian.

5-5

Therefore, LHA here is the whole 360 degrees around, minus the 45 degrees between the Sun's hour circle and M. This 45 degrees may be found by inspecting the figure or by subtracting 90 degrees from 135 degrees. Let's think this over -we're 135 degrees W of Greenwich, therefore G is 135 degrees clockwise of us. The Sun is 90 degrees W or counter clockwise of G. The difference is the 45 degrees we mentioned. Subtract this 45 degrees from 360 degrees and we get 315 degrees, the LHA.

Look again at the figure on **page 5-5**. As you can see, the Sun was east (clockwise on the diagram) of your local meridian (M). Now let's suppose that you're in the same longitude (135 degrees W) but GHA of the Sun is 225 degrees instead of 90 degrees.

The time diagram will appear as in the figure. The Sun is now west of your meridian (M). The LHA is always measured westward from the local celestial meridian to the hour circle of the body. Therefore, LHA is the 90 degrees from M to the Sun's hour circle.

Here are two general rules that will help you in finding LHA when GHA and longitude are known:

LHA =   GHA   - W

LHA =   GHA   + E

In west longitude it may be necessary to add 360 degrees to GHA before the subtraction can be made. In east longitude 360 degrees is subtracted from LHA if it exceeds this amount. Be sure, however, to check the accuracy of your work by referring to a time diagram. It offers a graphic means of obtaining the data you need.

TIME ZONES
ZONE (STANDARD) TIME
Chapter 6

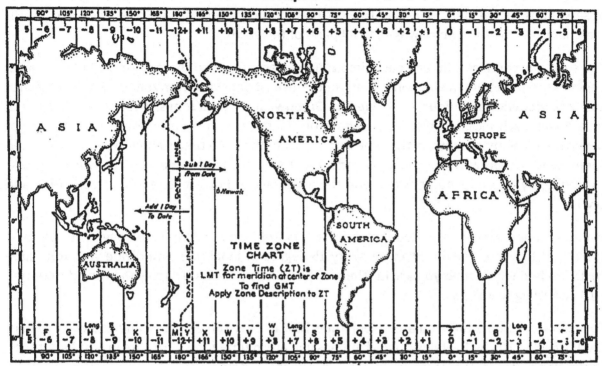

Standard time zones have been established within which all clocks are set to the same time. A difference of 1 hour takes place between one time zone and the next. Because **1h is equal to 15°,** you can see that each time zone comprises 15° of longitude. The standard time zones begin at the **Greenwich meridian (0°).** Every **meridian east and west of Greenwich** that is a **multiple of 15°** (15°, 30°, 45°, 60°, 75°, and so on) is a standard time meridian. Each standard time meridian is at the center of its time zone, and the zone extends 7° 30' (half of 15°) on either side of the meridian. Certain standard time zones on land vary somewhat from this procedure to give adjacent populated areas the same time, and for other reasons of convenience.

Local mean time along each standard time meridian is zone (standard) time for the entire time zone. Zone time in navigation is abbreviated ZT.

Daylight saving time is simple zone time set ahead 1hour (sometimes 2 hours) to extend the time of daylight in the evening. **Daylight saving time is ignored in navigation.**

ZONE TIME AND GMT (UTC)

If GMT, is the time at the Greenwich meridian, measured by the mean sun, and the Greenwich meridian is the standard time meridian for the time zone, it follows that zone time anywhere in the zone is the same as GMT. Most of the information in navigational tables relates to GMT; hence, you must know how to convert the time in any zone to GMT.

NOTE ON GREENWICH TIME: Since accurate marine chronometers have been available, mariners have come to accept the **Greenwich meridian as the prime meridian**. The meridian passes through the **Royal Observatory in Greenwich, England**. This observatory, located on the Thames River near London, was once the best source of time available to seafarers. Its observations of the stars were used to set the chronometers of the Royal Navy and British merchantmen, whose ships voyaged to all parts of the earth.

The solar day contains 24h, and each time zone represents 1h, so there must be 24 time zones, beginning with the Greenwich zone. Time zones run east and west from zone 1 to zone 12. Zones **east of Greenwich are minus**; those **west of Greenwich are plus zones**. (Note that +12 and -12 time zones each include only 7 1/2 degree of longitude.) In other words, in zones **east of Greenwich**, you must **subtract** the zone number from the zone time to find Greenwich Time. In zones **west of Greenwich**, you must **add** the two. The zone time at Greenwich is GMT; consequently, the zone number tells you the difference in hours between your zone time and GMT.

Standard time zones are also designated by letters (refer to the diagram on page 7-1). Because there is a standard time meridian for every 15 degree of longitude, **you divide your longitude by 15° to find which zone you are in**. Then, to find GMT, you merely apply the zone description (ZD) according to its sign.

To illustrate, assume that you are in longitude 105° E, ZT is 16h 23m 14s, and you want to find GMT. Dividing 105 by 15 yields 7, which means you are in time zone 7. You are in **East longitude**, so the **sign is minus**. Therefore, your ZD is -7h. The minus sign means that you subtract ZD from ZT to find GMT. Thus:

ZT	16h 23m 14s
ZD	- 7h
GMT	09h 23m 14s

Or, suppose you're in longitude 75°W, ZT is 7h13m57s, and you want to find GMT. Divide 75 by 15 and your answer is 5. Therefore, you are in zone 5, and **it must be plus 5h because your longitude is west**. Consequently:

ZT	07h 13m 57s
ZD	+ 5h
GMT	12h 13m 57s

Alexander F. Hickethier MBA © 1988-2019

In both examples; your Longitude coincides with a standard time meridian which simplifies the solution somewhat. If you are not located on one of these meridians, you can figure out which zone you're in by dividing your longitude by 15 and observing the size of the remainder. You must bear in mind that each standard time meridian is at the center of its time zone, and the zone extends **7° 30' on either side of the meridian**. For example, say your longitude is 142° 41' W, and you want to know ZD. **Dividing 142° 41' by 15**, you have **9, with 7° 41' left over**. But **7° 41' is more than 7° 30'**, so you must be in the next zone beyond 9, **meaning zone 10.**

TIME AND DATE

In the first diagram on page 7-3 illustrates, the mean sun is over the Greenwich meridian, meaning that it is noon, 1 May, GMT. Because it is noon, GMT, it must be 12 hours later (midnight) at the 180th meridian on the other side of the earth. In other words, the sun is just starting its 24 hour cruise; it is the same day all the way around the earth, but a new day is about to begin at the 180th meridian.

When you refer to **GMT in the Nautical Almanac**, you must know what the **date is at Greenwich**. Frequently, the date there differs from what it is in your longitude. Assume that on 1May you are in longitude 176°41' W and ZT is 16h 00m 00s. Divide 176° by 15. The nearest whole number is 12, the ZD. Longitude is west; therefore, ZD is + 12h. Adding ZD to ZT, we obtain the following data:

ZT	16h 00m 00s (1 May)
ZD	+ 12
GMT	**28h 00m 00s (1 May)**

What have we here, 28 o'clock? Time **2800 on 1 May** is the same as **0400 on 2 May**. Therefore, **GMT is 4h 0m 0s on 2 May**.

Suppose that, at the same ZT, you were in longitude 176° 41' E on the other side of 180° where it is 2 May. In this example, **ZD is -12** but GMT comes out the same; the date where you are is the same as the date at Greenwich. In the former problem, it has already become a day later at Greenwich.

ZT	16h 00m 00s (2 May)
ZD	- 12
GMT	**04h 00m 00s (2 May)**

Here is a problem with a new twist. Suppose you're in longitude 47° 53'E, ZT is 2h 0m 0s, and the date is **2 May**. The **ZD is -3h**. (You should. know why by now.) How can you subtract 3 from 2h 0m 0s? Time 0200 on 2 May is the same as **2600 on 1 May**. The figuring goes like this:

ZT	26h 00m 00s (1 May)
ZD	- 3
GMT	**23h 00m 00s (1 May)**

6-3

THE CHRONOMETER

Chief among navigational timepieces is the chronometer. It is considered one of the most accurate mechanical time machines devised by man. If a ship does not have a chronometer and still must navigate by celestial observations, the ship is provided with a timepiece that reasonably approximates the chronometers accuracy.

The chronometer is a clock of unusually fine construction. It is designed for extreme accuracy and dependability and is built to withstand shock, vibration, and variations of temperature. The magnetic compass, it is mounted in gimbals to offset ship's motion. It must be handled with the greatest care because its accuracy and regularity are essential in determining GMT, the basic time used in fixing position by celestial navigation.

The ship's chronometer is the principal navigation timepiece aboard ship. It can easily be identified by its 4-inch dial and the jerky motion of its second hand, which jumps 1/2 second every other tick.

The quartz crystal chronometer does not require winding because it is battery operated. Frequent checking of the battery should be avoided because of increased battery load during testing. Batteries must be checked once a month by using the built-in battery test meter. Regardless of the condition of the batteries, they must be replaced annually or sooner if test results warrant replacement. The quartz crystal chronometer has a limitation on deviation of daily rate of not more than 0.02 second, and significant error, such as 0.5 second should not occur for a month. This chronometer is equipped with a means of regulating long-term drift (deviation).

The quartz crystal chronometer does not require periodic overhaul since it is designed for a minimum life of 5 years.

Error and Rate

Even a chronometer cannot keep exact time indefinitely. Sooner or later the chronometer time gradually begins to draw away from GMT. The difference between chronometer time and GMT, at any instant, is called **chronometer error**. Error direction is identified with a sign or letter (**+ or F = Fast**) or (**- or S = Slow**) to indicate that the chronometer is either fast or slow in relation to the correct *GMT*.

Chronometer rate, on the other hand, is the amount the instrument gains or losses in a specified time. For example, a chronometer whose rate is **+1.5 seconds will gain 1.5 seconds every 24 hours**. Chronometer rate is usually expressed as seconds and tenths of seconds per day and is labeled "gaining" or "losing". Chronometer rate is determined by comparing errors obtained several days apart and dividing the difference by the number of days between readings.

Determining Chronometer Error

Inasmuch as chronometers **are never reset aboard ship**, an accumulated error may become quite large. Such an error is unimportant, though, if an accurate record is kept of the error.

The most accurate check on the chronometer and other timepieces is the radio time signal broadcast by radio station NSS and other stations listed in Radio Navigational Aids (Pub No. 117).

Since **1 January 1973**, the broadcast time signals have **differed from GMT** by amounts up to **+ 0.7s**. The difference arises because the times given in the navigational tables depend on the variable rate of rotation of the earth, while the broadcast time signals are now based on an atomic time scale. Step adjustments of exactly 1 second are made to the time signals as required (normally at 24h on December 31 and June 30 so that the difference between the time signals and GMT may not exceed 0.9s. For those who require GMT to accuracy better than 0l s, a correction (DUT) is coded into the transmitted time signal. GMT accurate to 0.ls is obtained by applying DUT to the transmitted time signal; i.e.

GMT = GMT + DUT

Naval radio stations transmit time signals (on seven different frequencies) for the 5 minutes immediately preceding certain hours GMT. The DUT correction is given in Morse code in the final 9-second pause prior to the long dash.

Each second in the time signal is marked by the beginning of a dash; the end of the dash has no significance. Beginning at 5 minutes before the hour, every second is transmitted except the 51st second of the 1st minute, 52nd second of the 2nd minute, 53 seconds of the 3rd minute, 54th second of the 4th minute, 29th second of each minute, the last 4 seconds of each of the first 4 minutes, and the last 9 seconds of the last minute. The hour signal after the 9-second break (59m 60s) consists of a longer dash than the others.

All other time signal transmissions,· e.g., WWV (Ft. Collins, Colo.), WWVH (Honolulu), CHU (Ottawa, Can.), are broadcast on **2.5, 5, 10, 15, 20, and 25 megahertz** and consist of dashes at the beginning of each second (commencing with the zero second of each minute). DUT is coded into the first 16 seconds by doubling of the dashes in seconds 1 to 8 for +0.1s to +0.8s, and in seconds 9 to 16.for -0.1s to -0.8s. For example: If DU = + 0.4s, the dashes for seconds 1, 2, 3, 4 would be double; if DUT = -0.6s, the dashes for seconds 9, 10, 11, 12, 13, 14 would be double.

The upcoming time is announced during the interruption of the audio frequency. The exact time is taken the instant the audio frequency is resumed. An example of the voice announcement might be: This is radio station WWV. **At the tone, the time will be eight hours, fifty minutes, coordinated universal time."**

The most accurate timepiece on board is checked against the time signal, and its error is recorded. Errors of the other chronometers can be calculated by referring to the chronometer just checked.

Chronometers checked against the transmitted time signal will show a jump of + 1 second on 31 Dec. 23h 59m (and possibly 30 June 23h 59m when a leap second is introduced. This adjustment, which is required to keep the broadcast time signals in step with the variable rate of rotation of the earth, is accompanied by a change in the sign of DUT.

The **CT** is the **chronometer time** of the observation. Apply CE to CT to find GMT.

If CE is slow add the error and if CE is fast subtract the error.

Another problem encountered in reading a chronometer arises when it has a 12 hour face because if the clock reads 1 o'clock we cannot tell by looking outside if it is 0100 or 1300 in England, if it is a 12 hour clock as many are onboard ship.

In Coast Guard problems, we solve this problem by first using the longitude to find ZD and then applying it to the ZT. Once you have found the approximate GMT, you apply CT and CE to calculate the exact time of the sight. Referring to the GMT you calculated using the ZD, you establish the hour of GMT that you read from the Chronometer.

Do not worry if the minutes in the GMT established by ZD do not match the chronometer. **The calculation is only used to find the hour of GMT**. The **corrected chronometer time (CCT)** is the time of the sight and the time used to enter the almanac.

Example 1

25 January 1982, ZT 1721, CT 01 29-30, CE 1m 25s fast, DR 24° 19.0' N   121° 35'W

ZT	17:21	25 Jan
ZD	+ 8	
GMT	25:21	25 Jan
	01:21	**26 Jan**

CT	01:29:30
CE	-. 1:25
CCT	01:28:05
GMT	**01:28:05**

Example 2

15 October 1981, ZT 1215, CT 04:15:10, CE 00m 30s slow, DR Lat 21° 47.2' S   Long 060° 15' W

ZT	12:15	15 Oct
ZD	+ 4	
GMT	**16:15**	**15 Oct**

CT	04:15:10
CE	-+ :30
CCT	04:15:40
GMT	**16:15:40**

PROBLEMS

Find GMT of the sight:

1.　　　April 21, 1981, ZT 1542, CT 04-44-11, CE 1m 54s fast,　　DR 28° 54.0' S　019° 07.0' W.

GMT_____

2.　　　May 22, 1981, ZT 0437, CT 07-40-40, CE 3m 24s.fast　　DR° 25-18.5' N　51° 18.0' W.
GMT_____

3.　　　March 21, 1981, ZT 1832,　　　　　　　　　　　　DR 26° 18.0' S, 10° 18.0' W

GMT_____

4.　　　Sep 28, 1981, ZT 0523, CT 11-29-42, CE 3m 30s slow　　DR 24° 12.0' S,　085° 25.0' E

GMT_____

5.　　　June 16, 1981, ZT 0850, CT 00-53-19, CE 2m 43s fast,　　DR 27° 23.0' S　56°-22.0' W

GMT_____

6.　　　February 22, 1981, ZT 1148　　　　　　　　　　DR 24°-16.0' S　095°-37.0'E

GMT_____

7.　　　March 6, 1981, ZT 1854, CT 11-52-40, CE 1m 56s slow　　DR 23° 51.5' S　073° 14.0' W

GMT_____

8.　　　July 22, 1981, ZT 1759, CT 06-01-31, CE 2m 15s fast,　　DR 24° 50.2' S　005° 16.0' E

GMT_____

9.   June 30, 1981, ZT 1742   DR 24° 55.0' S   008° 19.6' E

GMT_____

10.   February 10, 1981, ZT 0639, CT 09-43-25, CE 3m 20s fast   DR 25° 32.0' N   135° 15.0'E.

GMT_____

Answers

1.	21 April	16h 42m 17s
2.	22 May	07h 37m 16s
3.	21 March	1932
4.	27 Sept	23h 33m 12s
5.	16 Jun	12h 50m 36s
6.	22 Feb	0548
7.	6 Mar	23h 54m 36s
8.	22 July	17h 59m 16s
9.	30 June	1642
10.	9 Feb	2lh 40m 05s

Below are questions 1 and 2 worked out:

1.

Apr 21	28° 54.0' S		19° 07.0' W

ZT 1542		CT	04-44-11
ZD +1		CE	- 1-54
GMT 1642		CCT	04-42-17
GMT			16-42-17

2.

May 22	25° 18.5' N		51° 18.0' W

ZT 0437		CT	07-40-40
ZD +3		CE	-3.24
GMT 0737		CCT	07-37-16
GMT			07-37-16

Chronometer time (CT) is time indicated by a chronometer. Since a chronometer is set approximately to GMT and not reset until it is overhauled and cleaned about every 3 years, there is nearly always a **chronometer error (CE)**, either **fast (F)** or **slow (S).** The change in **chronometer error in 24** hours is called **chronometer rate**, or **daily rate**, and designated gaining or losing. With a consistent rate of 1s per day for three years, the chronometer error would total approximately 18m. Since chronometer error is subject to change, it should be determined from time to time, preferably daily at sea. Chronometer error is found by radio time signal, by comparison with another timepiece of known error, or by applying chronometer rate to previous readings of the same instrument. It is recorded to the nearest whole or half second. Chronometer rate is recorded to the nearest **0.1 second.**

Chronometer Error (TIME TICK)
Upon Oceans for Master Limited

1. 02578. On 12 November, you are taking a time tick using the 1600 GMT BBC Broadcast. You hear four pulses followed by a longer pulse. At the start of the longer pulse you start a stopwatch. You stop the stopwatch at the same time reading the chronometer with the following results: stopwatch 03m 19s, chronometer 15h 59m 46s. What is the chronometer error?

A. 01m 14s slow
B. 3m 19s fast
C. 3m 33s slow
D. 6m 54s slow

2. 02579. You take a time tick using the 2000 signal from Montevideo, Uruguay. You hear a 10 second dash, a 5 second silent period, and then six dots. At the sixth dot, your comparing watch reads 08h 00m 12s. When compared to the chronometer, the comparing watch reads 08h 01m 22s, and the 0hronometer reads 07h 59m 39s. What is the chronometer error?

A. 0m 12s fast
B. 1m 10s fast
C. 0m 21s slow
D. 1m 31s slow

3. 02580. You take a time tick using the 2000 GMT signal from Montevideo, Uruguay. You hear a 10 second dash, a 5 second silent period, and then six dots. At the sixth dot your comparing watch reads 07h 58m 18s. When compared to the chronometer, the watch reads 07h 59m 56s, and the chronometer reads 08h 00m 02s. What is the chronometer error?

A. 1m 42s slow
B. 1m 36s slow
C. 0m 02s fast
D. 1m 38s fast

4. 02582. You take a time tick using the 2000 GMT signal from Montevideo, Uruguay. You hear a 10 second dash, a 5 second silent period, and then six dots. At the sixth dot, your comparing watch reads 7h 57m 38s. When compared to the chronometer, the comparing watch reads 7h 59m 18s and the chronometer reads 8h 00m 02s. What is the chronometer error?

A. 1m 38s slow
B. 2m 22s slow
C. 0m 02s fast
D. 1m 40s fast

5. 02583. You take a time tick using the 2000 GMT signal from Montevideo, Uruguay. You hear a 10 second dash, a 5 second silent period, and then six dots. At the sixth dot, your comparing watch reads 8h 01m 16s. When compared to the chronometer, the comparing watch reads 8h 02m 48s and the chronometer reads 8h 02 48s. What is the chronometer error?

A. 1m 16s slow
B. 1m 32s slow
C. 1m 16s fast
D. 2m 48s fast

Answers to the Chronometer Questions

1. 02578 C
2. 02579 D
3. 02580 B
4. 02582 A
5. 02583 C

1. USCG # 02578 12 Nov	
GMT	16-00-00
Stop Watch	+03-19
GMT	16-03-19
CT	15-59-46
CE	(Slow) 3-33

2. USCG # 02579	
GMT	20-00-00
CWatch	20-00-12
WE	(Fast) 0-12
CWatch	20-01-22
WE	-12
GMT	20-01-10
CT	19-59-39
CE	(Slow) 1-31

3. USCG # 02580	
GMT	20-00-00
CWatch	19-58-18
WE	(Slow) 1-42
CWatch	19-59-56
WE	+1-42
GMT	20-01-38
CT	20-00-02
CE	(Slow) 1-36

4. USCG # 02582	
GMT	20-00-00
CWatch	19-57-38
WE	(Slow) 2-22
CWatch	19-59-18
WE	+2-22
GMT	20-01-40
CT	20-00-02
CE	(Slow) 1-38

5. USCG # 02583	
GMT	20-00-00
CWatch	20-01-16
WE	(Fast) 1-16
CWatch	20-02-48
WE	-1-16
GMT	20-01-32
CT	20-02-48
CE	(Fast) 1-16

THE SEXTANT AND COMPUTING Ho
Chapter 7

The instrument of chief importance in celestial navigation is the sextant. It is used to measure the altitude of a heavenly body above the visible horizon. Sextant altitude is corrected for various factors to determine the body's true (or corrected) altitude above the celestial horizon. Before going into the correction problem the definition of these terms must be thoroughly understood:

The sextant altitude, or altitude of a body above the visible horizon, is the sextant reading without correction. (**Hs**)

The observed altitude (true altitude) is the altitude of the center of the observed body above the celestial horizon. It is obtained by applying certain corrections to the sextant altitude. (**Ho**)

ALTITUDE CORRECTIONS

Of the following five altitude corrections, the first three apply to observations of all celestial bodies. The last two corrections are applicable only when the observed body belongs to the solar system. The **figure on page 7-2** illustrates the correction problem. To obtain the true altitude, then, the sextant altitude of any celestial body must be corrected for-

1. **Index error**, which is the constant amount of which the sextant angle between two objects differs from the true angle.

2. **Refraction**, which is the deviation of rays of light from a straight line caused by the earth's atmosphere.

3. **Dip of the horizon**, which is the difference in direction between the visible and celestial horizons caused by the observer's height above the surface.

If the observed body belongs to the solar system, corrections must also be made for:

4. **Parallax**, which is caused by the proximity of bodies to the earth, resulting in a difference in altitudes measured from the surface of the earth and from the center of the earth. Such an occurrence is not true of other heavenly bodies whose distance from the earth is considered infinite.

5. **Semidiameter**, which results from the nearness of bodies of the solar system, makes it necessary to consider the observed bodies as appreciable size instead of as mere points of light; for example, stars. The sextant altitude of such a body is obtained by bringing its disk tangent to the horizon. Semidiameter correction must be applied to find the altitude of the center.

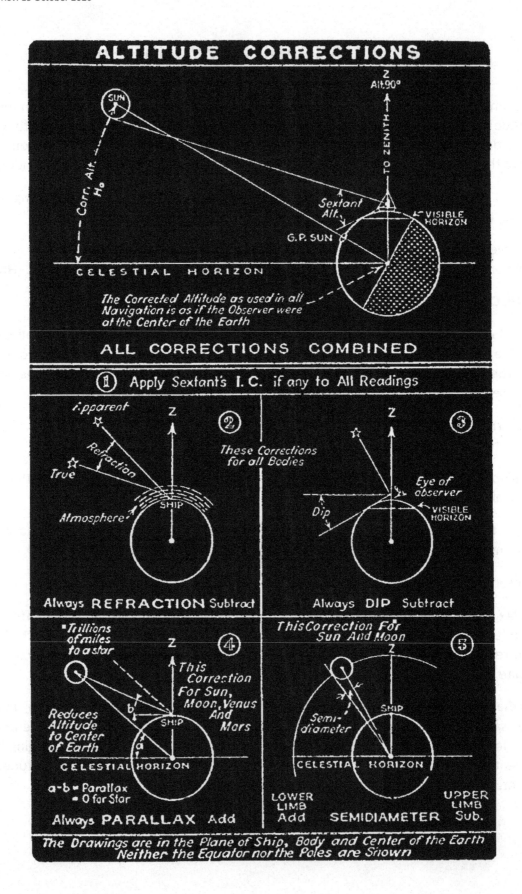

ALTITUDE CORRECTIONS

The Corrected Altitude as used in all Navigation is as if the Observer were at the Center of the Earth

ALL CORRECTIONS COMBINED

① Apply Sextant's **I.C.** if any to All Readings

② These Corrections for all Bodies

Always **REFRACTION** Subtract

③ Always **DIP** Subtract

④ This Correction For Sun, Moon, Venus And Mars
Reduces Altitude to Center of Earth
a−b = Parallax = 0 for Star
Always **PARALLAX** Add

⑤ This Correction For Sun And Moon
LOWER LIMB Add   **SEMIDIAMETER**   UPPER LIMB Sub.

The Drawings are in the Plane of Ship, Body and Center of the Earth
Neither the Equator nor the Poles are Shown

Index Correction

An error, known as the index error, is introduced if there is a small lack of parallelism of the horizon glass. Index correction is resolved by the following procedures:

Set the sextant near zero. Hold the sextant vertical and sight toward the horizon. Use the micrometer drum to bring the direct horizon and reflected horizon exactly in line as shown in the diagram to the right. If the sextant reading is zero, there is no error. If the reading is not zero, the amount of error is the index correction. If the index mark is to the **left of the zero (on the arc)** of the limb, the reading is too large, and this index correction must be **subtracted** from the sextant altitude. If the index mark is to **the right of zero, (off the arc)** of the limb, the reading is too low; and this amount must be **added** to the sextant altitude.

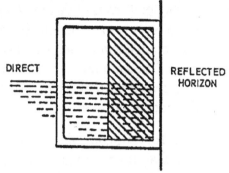

DIRECT   REFLECTED HORIZON

THE ALTITUDE OF THE HORIZON = 0

The amount of index correction is obtained as follows:

If the index mark is on the arc, the sextant is read in the usual way. The reading is the index correction to be subtracted. Always read the degree graduation mark of the limb to the right of the index mark, whether the index mark is on or off the mark. **In the figure to the right** the index mark points to the right of the 0 mark (off the arc) to a spot between the **1° and 2°** mark. The **2°** mark must be used. On the drum the 16 mark lies below the 0 mark on the vernier, hence the reading in **minutes is 16**. The mark above the 0 mark on the vernier that coincides most nearly with a mark on the drum is the·**3 mark**. Thus, the remainder of the reading is **0.3** minute. The combined drum and vernier reading tells you how much the index mark is to the left of the **2°** mark on the arc of the limb.

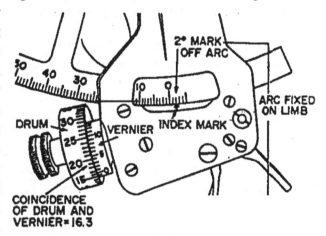

COINCIDENCE OF DRUM AND VERNIER = 16.3

The result obtained by **subtracting 16.3'** from **2°** is your index correction of 1° 43.7'. Because the reading is **off the arc**, **1° 43.7' must be added** to the sextant altitude. **(NOTE: This index correction is abnormally large and is used here for illustrative purposes only.)**

Refraction

The earth is wrapped in a blanket of atmosphere more than 50 miles deep. Density of the atmosphere, like that of the ocean, increases with depth and is greatest at the bottom, next to the earth's surface. Light rays do not follow a straight line when passing through atmosphere of different densities, but are slightly bent into a gentle arc. This phenomenon is called refraction. Refraction is defined as the deviation of light rays from a straight line caused by their passage obliquely through mediums of different density. The measure of refraction is the angular difference between the apparent rays of light from an observed celestial body and its true direction.

The effect of refraction is always to make the observed altitude greater than the true altitude. Consequently, **refraction correction is always subtracted** from the sextant altitude. Since refraction is caused by the oblique passage of rays through the atmosphere, rays from a body in the observer's zenith, intersecting the atmosphere at right angles, are not refracted. Maximum refraction occurs when a body is on the horizon, amounting then to between 34 and 39 minutes of arc. The amount of refractions depends on atmospheric conditions. Density of the atmosphere varies with barometric pressure and temperature. Refraction varies with density and also with the body's altitude:

Because refraction varies with atmospheric conditions, and the effect of atmospheric conditions at low altitudes cannot be estimated with complete accuracy, **observations of bodies below 10° should be regarded with suspicion**. Refraction has no effect on the azimuth of a celestial body because it takes place entirely in the vertical plane of passage of the light rays.

Dip of the Horizon

The higher an observer's position is above the surface, the more he must lower (or dip) the line of vision to see the horizon. Logically, then, all altitude observations must be corrected for the height of eye. Refer again to page 7-2, and you will see why a dip correction is always subtracted.

Failure to correct for dip from a height of 10 feet will result in an error of 3 miles in a line of position. From the bridge of the average ship, the resulting error would be approximately 10 miles.

Parallax

Parallax is the difference between the altitude of a body, as measured from the earth's center, and its altitude (corrected for refraction and dip) as measured from the earth's surface. Altitude from the center of the earth is bound to be greater than from the surface. Consequently, parallax is always a plus correction.

Parallax increases from 0° for a body directly overhead to a maximum for a body on the horizon. In the latter instance, it is called horizontal parallax (HP). Parallax of the moon is both extreme and varied because of its changing distance from the earth in its passage through its orbit. Parallax of the sun is small; parallax of the planets is even smaller. For the stars, parallax is so tiny it is negligible.

Semidiameter

The true altitude of a body is measured to the center of that body. Because the **sun and moon** are of appreciable size, the usual practice is to observe the **lower limb**. Therefore, semidiameter correction **must be added**. It follows, then that if the **upper limb** of either body is observed, the semidiameter **correction is subtractive**. **Semidiameter** correction amounts to about **16 minutes** of arc for either the sun or moon. **Stars** are considered as points, and, as such, they **require no semidiameter correction**.

When observing a planet, the center of the planet is visually estimated by the observer, so there is never a semidiameter correction.

In concluding the subject of altitude corrections, mention should be made that some· tables for altitude corrections (the Nautical Almanac, for example) combine two or more of the corrections for refraction, parallax, and semidiameter. The correction for height of eye (dip) appears in a separate table for use with all bodies. **Index error** which is impossible to include in such tables should always be determined, recorded, marked plus or minus, and applied before any of the tabulated corrections.

Observing the sun

At this point, a few words on the general technique of observing the sun with a sextant is appropriate. **Experience, of course, is the only way to gain real proficiency in shooting the sun or any other body.**

First, either one or both of your eyes may be left open while observing the sun. Some navigators feel that there is less eye strain if both eyes are open; however, if it is easier for you, you may close one eye and aim as if firing a gun. No loss of accuracy will result. Focus the telescope properly before you start. This adjustment is accomplished by observing a distant object and moving the eyepiece in or out until the image is clears. Then, check the index correction.

Next, select the shade glasses you want to use, and turn them into position in front of the index glass. Sometime, they are slightly prismatic, so it would be well for you to recheck the index error after they are set. If the telescope is equipped with polarizing fitters instead of shade glasses, adjust the filters as necessary.

Hold the sextant vertical, and train the line of sight on that point of the horizon just below the sun. Beginning with zero position, move the index arm slowly outward until the image of the sun appears in the mirror of the horizon glass. Continue moving the arm until the sun's lower limb in nearly tangent to the horizon (as shown in the illustration) and set the clamp.

Before moving the micrometer drum to bring the sun's lower limb exactly tangent to the horizon, you must ascertain whether you actually are holding the sextant vertical. Rotate the sextant slowly through a small arc about the line of sight. As you do so, the sun's image moves in a small arc convex to the horizon. At the point where the image is lowest, the sextant is held vertically. This procedure, called swinging the arc, should be followed every time an observation is taken. If the sextant is not held vertically, the angle measured will be between the observed body and a point on the horizon that is not exactly below it; therefore the altitude measured will be inaccurate.

If you have an assistant taking the time, warn the assistant to stand by with the watch. Move the micrometer drum until the sun's lower limb is in contact with the horizon, and, at the instant of contact, sing out **"mark!"** At this word, your helper notes the time to the second.

Observing Stars and Planets

The technique of bringing down or pulling down a star or planet is similar to shooting the sun, except that no shade glasses are required. Usually, a telescope is needed to increase the body's size and ensure against losing sight of it. Use of the telescope reduces the field-of vision somewhat, making it harder to "pick up" stars originally; but, because the stars are magnified, fixes obtained are normally more accurate.

Once you identify the star you want, the chief difficulty in pulling down the star sterns from the likelihood of losing sight of it when you direct your line of sight to the horizon. Often the star is a dim one whose reflection may not be easy to identify. Besides, during early morning or late twilight, more than one star may appear in the field of the telescope, and you may be unable to tell which one you intended to observe.

To keep track of your star, the following procedure is recommended. Set the sextant at approximately zero, and direct the line of sight toward the sta. The star should then be nearly coincident with its image. Hold the sextant approximately in the plane of the star's vertical circle, and move the index arm slowly outward, which causes the star's image to move downward. As you move the arm outward, move the horizon glass downward to keep the star's image in the glass. When the index arm moves to the reading of the star's approximate altitude, the horizon shows up in the clear half of the horizon glass. Set the index arm clamp, and proceed as described for the sun. To avoid bringing down the wrong star, you should keep both eyes open while observing.

Many navigators prefer a second method of bringing down a star. It consists essentially of bring the horizon up instead. For this method set the arm near the zero mark, invert the sextant, and direct the line of sight at the star. You will see the star in the clear part of the horizon glass. Move the index arm until you bring the horizon up to the star, then clamp the arm·

With the index arm set at the approximate altitude, the sextant is turned right side up, and the altitude is observed in the usual manner. In this method, the desired star is kept constantly in direct view as opposed to reflected view. You may have some slight difficulty picking up the star again after you right the sextant; but if you train on the proper bearing, it should appear in the horizon mirror. Most navigational stars are far enough apart so that no other bright star is likely to show up near the same. Azimuth at the approximate altitude set.

Brightness of the reflection from the horizon glass may be varied by moving the telescope toward or away from the plane of the instrument; Slacken the set screw of the telescope carrier, adjust the telescope as desired, and set up the screw again. Moving the telescope away from the plane of the limb causes more light to enter from the un-silvered part of the horizon glass and less light from the mirrored part. This movement, in turn, makes the horizon relatively brighter and the reflected celestial body dimmer. This is helpful in the darker twilight, when the horizon is difficult to see but the stars are bright.

Moving the telescope toward the plane of the limb reverses the effect just described. As a result, more light is reflected from the mirrored part of the horizon glass. This procedure is desirable during the brighter twilight, when the horizon is clear but the stars remain faint.

Whenever possible, you should plan the order of taking sights so that you can take maximum advantage of horizon conditions. During morning sights, for example, you should observe dimmer stars to the east before the horizon becomes too bright, and then observe stars to the west while that horizon is good.

COMPUTING HO OF THE SUN:

Now that we have learned the theory behind taking celestial sights and the factors that affect them, we will learn how to use the **Altitude Correction Tables found on the back of the front cover in the Almanac or on the first few pages of the reproduction of the Almanac for training.**

Example:

You observe the lower limb **(L/L)** of the sun at a sextant altitude **(hs)** of **57° 16.4'** on **December 29, 1981**. The index error **(IE)** is **1.2'** off the arc. The height of eye **(Dip)** is **49.9** feet. What is the observed altitude **(Ho)?**

1. Using our work form to the right bottom, we enter our sextant altitude (Hs) of **57° 16.4'**.

2. Then since they said that we have an IE of **1.2** off the Arc we will **ADD** it back on.

3. Next we determine dip by taking the height of eye **49.9** feet and entering the altitude correction tables of the Nautical Almanac. These tables are located inside the front cover. From the reprint on **page 7-8** we find this correction to be **-6.9.**

4. Ha is then calculated by applying the algebra sum of IE and Dip. **(57° 10.7')**

5. Using **Ha**, we enter the altitude correction table, once again, under the heading for the lower limb and **October-March**. The apparent altitude correction is **+15.6'**. Corrections found in these tables include the effects of semidiameter, parallax, and mean refraction.

6. The sixth step is to apply the apparent altitude correction to the **Ha**. The result is the corrected altitude **(Ho) 57° 26.3'**.

Ho SUN	
USCG #	
Date	29 Dec
Obj	Sun L/L
Hs	57° 16.4'
I.C.	+ 1.2'
Dip(49.9)	- 6.9'
Sum	-5.7'
Ha	57° 10.7'
Alt (Sun)	+ 15.6'
Ho	57° 26.3'

A2 ALTITUDE CORRECTION TABLES 10°–90°—SUN, STARS, PLANETS

SUN

OCT.—MAR.			APR.—SEPT.		
App. Alt.	Lower Limb	Upper Limb	App. Alt.	Lower Limb	Upper Limb
9 34	+10·8	−21·5	9 39	+10·6	−21·2
9 45	+10·9	−21·4	9 51	+10·7	−21·1
9 56	+11·0	−21·3	10 03	+10·8	−21·0
10 08	+11·1	−21·2	10 15	+10·9	−20·9
10 21	+11·2	−21·1	10 27	+11·0	−20·8
10 34	+11·3	−21·0	10 40	+11·1	−20·7
10 47	+11·4	−20·9	10 54	+11·2	−20·6
11 01	+11·5	−20·8	11 08	+11·3	−20·5
11 15	+11·6	−20·7	11 23	+11·4	−20·4
11 30	+11·7	−20·6	11 38	+11·5	−20·3
11 46	+11·8	−20·5	11 54	+11·6	−20·2
12 02	+11·9	−20·4	12 10	+11·7	−20·1
12 19	+12·0	−20·3	12 28	+11·8	−20·0
12 37	+12·1	−20·2	12 46	+11·9	−19·9
12 55	+12·2	−20·1	13 05	+12·0	−19·8
13 14	+12·3	−20·0	13 24	+12·1	−19·7
13 35	+12·4	−19·9	13 45	+12·2	−19·6
13 56	+12·5	−19·8	14 07	+12·3	−19·5
14 18	+12·6	−19·7	14 30	+12·4	−19·4
14 42	+12·7	−19·6	14 54	+12·5	−19·3
15 06	+12·8	−19·5	15 19	+12·6	−19·2
15 32	+12·9	−19·4	15 46	+12·7	−19·1
15 59	+13·0	−19·3	16 14	+12·8	−19·0
16 28	+13·1	−19·2	16 44	+12·9	−18·9
16 59	+13·2	−19·1	17 15	+13·0	−18·8
17 32	+13·3	−19·0	17 48	+13·1	−18·7
18 06	+13·4	−18·9	18 24	+13·2	−18·6
18 42	+13·5	−18·8	19 01	+13·3	−18·5
19 21	+13·6	−18·7	19 42	+13·4	−18·4
20 03	+13·7	−18·6	20 25	+13·5	−18·3
20 48	+13·8	−18·5	21 11	+13·6	−18·2
21 35	+13·9	−18·4	22 00	+13·7	−18·1
22 26	+14·0	−18·3	22 54	+13·8	−18·0
23 22	+14·1	−18·2	23 51	+13·9	−17·9
24 21	+14·2	−18·1	24 53	+14·0	−17·8
25 26	+14·3	−18·0	26 00	+14·1	−17·7
26 36	+14·4	−17·9	27 13	+14·2	−17·6
27 52	+14·5	−17·8	28 33	+14·3	−17·5
29 15	+14·6	−17·7	30 00	+14·4	−17·4
30 46	+14·7	−17·6	31 35	+14·5	−17·3
32 26	+14·8	−17·5	33 20	+14·6	−17·2
34 17	+14·9	−17·4	35 17	+14·7	−17·1
36 20	+15·0	−17·3	37 26	+14·8	−17·0
38 36	+15·1	−17·2	39 50	+14·9	−16·9
41 08	+15·2	−17·1	42 31	+15·0	−16·8
43 59	+15·3	−17·0	45 31	+15·1	−16·7
47 10	+15·4	−16·9	48 55	+15·2	−16·6
50 46	+15·5	−16·8	52 44	+15·3	−16·5
54 49	+15·6	−16·7	57 02	+15·4	−16·4
59 23	+15·7	−16·6	61 51	+15·5	−16·3
64 30	+15·8	−16·5	67 17	+15·6	−16·2
70 12	+15·9	−16·4	73 16	+15·7	−16·1
76 26	+16·0	−16·3	79 43	+15·8	−16·0
83 05	+16·1	−16·2	86 32	+15·9	−15·9
90 00			90 00		

STARS AND PLANETS

App. Alt.	Corrⁿ	App. Alt.	Additional Corrⁿ
9 56	−5·3		**1981**
10 08	−5·2		**VENUS**
10 20	−5·1		Jan. 1–Sept. 27
10 33	−5·0		
10 46	−4·9	42	+0·1
11 00	−4·8		Sept. 28–Nov. 13
11 14	−4·7		
11 29	−4·6	47	+0·2
11 45	−4·5		
12 01	−4·4		Nov. 14–Dec. 10
12 18	−4·3		
12 35	−4·2	46	+0·3
12 54	−4·1		
13 13	−4·0		Dec. 11–Dec. 26
13 33	−3·9		
13 54	−3·8	11	+0·4
14 16	−3·7	41	+0·5
14 40	−3·6		
15 04	−3·5		Dec. 27–Dec. 31
15 30	−3·4		
15 57	−3·3	6	+0·5
16 26	−3·2	20	+0·6
16 56	−3·1	31	+0·7
17 28	−3·0		
18 02	−3·0		
18 38	−2·8		**MARS**
19 17	−2·7		Jan. 1–Dec. 31
19 58	−2·6		
20 42	−2·5	60	+0·1
21 28	−2·4		
22 19	−2·3		
23 13	−2·2		
24 11	−2·1		
25 14	−2·0		
26 22	−1·9		
27 36	−1·8		
28 56	−1·7		
30 24	−1·6		
32 00	−1·5		
33 45	−1·4		
35 40	−1·3		
37 48	−1·2		
40 08	−1·1		
42 44	−1·0		
45 36	−0·9		
48 47	−0·8		
52 18	−0·7		
56 11	−0·6		
60 28	−0·5		
65 08	−0·4		
70 11	−0·3		
75 34	−0·2		
81 13	−0·1		
87 03	0·0		
90 00			

DIP

Ht. of Eye (m)	Corrⁿ	Ht. of Eye (ft.)	Ht. of Eye (m)	Corrⁿ
2·4	−2·8	8·0	1·0	−1·8
2·6	−2·9	8·6	1·5	−2·2
2·8	−3·0	9·2	2·0	−2·5
3·0	−3·1	9·8	2·5	−2·8
3·2	−3·2	10·5	3·0	−3·0
3·4	−3·3	11·2	See table	←
3·6	−3·4	11·9		
3·8	−3·5	12·6	(m)	
4·0	−3·6	13·3	20	−7·9
4·3	−3·7	14·1	22	−8·3
4·5	−3·8	14·9	24	−8·6
4·7	−3·9	15·7	26	−9·0
5·0	−4·0	16·5	28	−9·3
5·2	−4·1	17·4		
5·5	−4·2	18·3	30	−9·6
5·8	−4·3	19·1	32	−10·0
6·1	−4·4	20·1	34	−10·3
6·3	−4·5	21·0	36	−10·6
6·6	−4·6	22·0	38	−10·8
6·9	−4·7	22·9		
7·2	−4·8	23·9	40	−11·1
7·5	−4·9	24·9	42	−11·4
7·9	−5·0	26·0	44	−11·7
8·2	−5·1	27·1	46	−11·9
8·5	−5·2	28·1	48	−12·2
8·8	−5·3	29·2	ft.	
9·2	−5·4	30·4	2	−1·4
9·5	−5·5	31·5	4	−1·9
9·9	−5·6	32·7	6	−2·4
10·3	−5·7	33·9	8	−2·7
10·6	−5·8	35·1	10	−3·1
11·0	−5·9	36·3	See table	←
11·4	−6·0	37·6		
11·8	−6·1	38·9	ft.	
12·2	−6·2	40·1	70	−8·1
12·6	−6·3	41·5	75	−8·4
13·0	−6·4	42·8	80	−8·7
13·4	−6·5	44·2	85	−8·9
13·8	−6·6	45·5	90	−9·2
14·2	−6·7	46·9	95	−9·5
14·7	−6·8	48·4	100	−9·7
15·1	−6·9	49·8	105	−9·9
15·5	−7·0	51·3	110	−10·2
16·0	−7·1	52·8	115	−10·4
16·5	−7·2	54·3	120	−10·6
16·9	−7·3	55·8	125	−10·8
17·4	−7·4	57·4	130	−11·1
17·9	−7·5	58·9	135	−11·3
18·4	−7·6	60·5	140	−11·5
18·8	−7·7	62·1	145	−11·7
19·3	−7·8	63·8	150	−11·9
19·8	−7·8	65·4	155	−12·1
20·4	−8·0	67·1		
20·9	−8·1	68·8		
21·4		70·5		

App. Alt. = Apparent altitude = Sextant altitude corrected for index error and dip.
For daylight observations of Venus, see page 260.

Observed Altitude (Ho) of the other celestial bodies is calculated in the same way with the only difference being the Altitude (Alt) correction.

Apparent Altitude (Ha): Apply the correction determined to the measured altitude and enter the result as the apparent altitude.

> **Altitude Correction:** Every observation requires an altitude correction. This correction is a function of the apparent altitude of the body and is the algebraic sum of Parallax, Refraction and Semidiameter. The Almanac contains tables for determining these corrections. For the Sun, planets, and stars, these tables are located on the inside front cover and facing page. For the Moon, these tables are located on the back inside cover and preceding page.

> **Mars or Venus Additional Correction:** As the name implies, this correction is applied to sights of Mars and Venus. The correction is a function of the planet measured, the time of year, and the apparent altitude. The inside front cover of the Almanac lists these corrections.

> **Correction to Apparent Altitude:** Sum the altitude correction, the Mars or Venus additional correction, the additional correction, the horizontal parallax correction, and the Moon's upper limb correction. Be careful to determine and carry the algebraic sign of the corrections and their sum correctly. Enter this sum as the correction to the apparent altitude.

> **Moon Upper Limb Correction:** Enter **- 30'** for this correction if the sight was of the upper limb of the Moon.

Observed Altitude: Apply the Correction to Apparent Altitude algebraically to the apparent altitude. The result is the observed altitude (**Ho**).

Ho Star	
USCG #	
Date	
Obj	
Hs	
I.C.	
Dip( )	_____
Sum	
Ha	
Alt (Star)	_____
Ho	

Ho Planet	
USCG #	
Date	
Obj	
Hs	
I.C.	
Dip( )	_____
Sum	
Ha	
Alt (Star)	
Add't Corr	
Ho	

Ho Moon	
USCG #	
Date	
Obj	
Hs	
I.C.	
Dip( )	_____
Sum	
Ha	
Alt Moon	
HP U/L	
Upper Limb	- 30'
Ho	

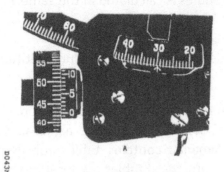
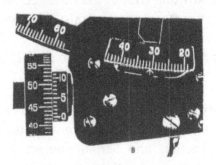
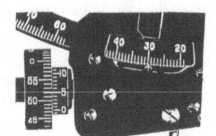
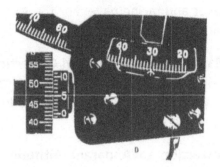

D043NG

1. 1219 Which sextant in illustration D043NG reads 29°42.5'?

    A. A
    B. B
    C. C
    D. D

2. 1537 Which sextant in illustration D043NG reads 29°47.5'?

    A. A
    B. B
    C. C
    D. D

3. 1552 Which sextant in illustration D043NG reads 30°42.5'?

    A. A
    B. B
    C. C
    D. D

4. 1571 Which sextant in illustration D043NG reads 29°42.7'?

    A. A
    B. B
    C. C
    D. D

5. 1582 Sextant C in illustration D043NG reads _____.

    A. 30°45.9'
    B. 29°56.0'
    C. 29°52.0'
    D. 29°47.5'

6. 1601 Sextant B in illustration D043NG reads _____.

    A. 30°51.0'
    B. 30°42.5'
    C. 30°47.5'
    D. 31°00.0'

7. 1639 Sextant D in illustration D043NG reads
_____.

    A. 30°47.5'
    B. 29°47.5'
    C. 29°42.5'
    D. 29°41.6'

Answers to Sextant Readings:

    1. 1219 D
    2. 1537 C
    3. 1552 B
    4. 1571 A
    5. 1582 D
    6. 1601 B
    7. 1339 C

CALCULATING HO
Chapter 8, Upon Oceans for Master Limited

1.   02275. You observe the lower limb of the Sun at a sextant altitude (hs) of 24° 00.7' on 10 January 1981. The index error is 2.6' off the arc. The height of eye is 55 feet. What is the observed altitude (Ho)?

A. 24° 07.4'
B. 24° 08.9'
C. 24° 10.2'
D. 24° 11.8'

2.   02276. You observe the lower limb of the Sun at a sextant altitude (hs) of 46° 20.3' on 1 April 1981. The index error is 4.5' off the arc. The height of eye is 57 feet. What is the observed altitude (Ho)?

A. 46° 24.2'
B. 46° 27.9'
C. 46° 30.1'
D. 46° 32.6'

3.   02277. You observe the lower limb of the Sun at a sextant altitude (hs) of 41° 29.8' on 11 January 1981. The index error is 2.4' off the arc. The height of eye is 68 feet. What is the observed altitude (Ho)?

A. 41° 36.4'
B. 41° 39.4'
C. 41° 42.0'
D. 41° 44.5'

4.   02278. You observe the lower limb of the Sun at a sextant altitude (hs) of 31° 31.5' on 6 March 1981. The index error is 2.5' on the arc. The height of eye is 76 feet. What is the observed altitude (Ho)?

A. 31° 35.3'
B. 31° 36.7'
C. 31° 38.2'
D. 31° 39.5'

5.   02279. You observe the lower limb of the Sun at a sextant altitude (hs) of 58° 06.6' on 5 April 1981. The index error is 1.0' off the arc. The height of eye is 55 feet. What is the observed altitude (Ho)?

A. 58° 14.2'
B. 58° 15.8'
C. 58° 16.9'
D. 58° 18.1'

Answers tom Ho Problems

1. 02275 C
2. 02276 D
3. 02277 B
4. 02278 A
5. 02279 B

Celestial Problems
Calculating Ho worked-out

Ho	
USCG #	2275
Date	10 Jan
Obj	Sun L/L
Hs	24° 00.7'
I.C.	+2.6'
Sum	24° 03.3'
Dip (55)	-7.2'
Ha	23° 56.1'
alt	+14.1'
Ho	24° 10.2'
Answer C	

Ho	
USCG #	2276
Date	1 Apr
Obj	Sun L/L
Hs	46° 20.3'
I.C.	+4.5'
Sum	46° 24.8'
Dip (57)	-7.3'
Ha	46° 17.5'
alt	+15.1'
Ho	46° 32.6'
Answer D	

Ho	
USCG #	2277
Date	11 Jan
Obj	Sun L/L
Hs	41° 29.8'
I.C.	+2.4'
Sum	41° 32.2'
Dip (68)	-8.0'
Ha	41° 24.2'
alt	+15.2'
Ho	41° 39.4'
Answer B	

Ho	
USCG #	2278
Date	6 Mar
Obj	Sun L/L
Hs	31° 31.5'
I.C.	-2.5'
Sum	31° 29.0'
Dip (76)	-8.4'
Ha	31° 20.6'
alt	+14.7'
Ho	31° 35.3'
Answer B	

Ho	
USCG #	2279
Date	5 Mar
Obj	Sun L/L
Hs	58° 06.6'
I.C.	+1.0'
Sum	58° 07.6'
Dip (55)	-7.2'
Ha	58° 00.4'
alt	+15.4'
Ho	58° 15.8'
Answer B	

Additional USCG problems worked-out for this chapter can be found in **Celestial Navigation Calculations (Upon Oceans Endorsement) Worked-Out for Master 500 GT through 2nd Mate Unlimited, Volume 3, part 2, Chapter 6, Determining Position by Sight Reduction.**

GREENWICH HOUR ANGLE (GHA)
Chapter 8

Longitude is measured on the terrestrial sphere east and west from the Greenwich meridian along the equator. **The GHA of a body on the celestial sphere is measured westward from the projected Greenwich meridian to the body's hour circle**.

What is an hour circle? It is half of a great circle on the surface of the celestial sphere that passes through a celestial body and terminates at the celestial poles. The hour circle contrasted to the celestial meridian, moves with the celestial body progressively with the time from east to west (since we consider apparent motion}, while the position of the celestial meridian remains fixed. With knowledge of the: earth's rotation (one tum upon its axis per 24 hours), we realize that each Celestial body crosses our meridian once each 24 hours. Dividing 360 degrees (number of degrees in a circle) by 24 hours, we find that an hour circle advances 15 degrees per hour.

The **GHA of any body is the degrees, minutes, and tenths of minutes** of arc of the celestial equator intercepted at a given instant between that body's hour circle and the celestial meridian of Greenwich, measured westward from **Greenwich through 360 degrees**. Whether measured on the celestial or the terrestrial sphere, the amount of arc is the same.

The GHA of any navigational body of the solar system (sun, moon, and planets) and of the **first point of Aries sometimes called the vernal equinox** is listed in the Nautical Almanac for every hour of GMT, for any date. The **first point of Aries is the zero point on the celestial** equator from which **the westward distance of the stars is measured**. The GHA of any navigational star may be determined from the Nautical Almanac by adding **GHA of Aries to the tabulated sidereal hour angle (SHA) of the star.**

The latitude of a point on the terrestrial sphere is measured from the equator northward or southward along the point's meridian to a maximum of 90 degrees. Declination of a body on the celestial sphere is measured in exactly the same way from the celestial equator northward or southward along the body's hour circle. The polar distance is the number of degrees, minutes and tenths of minutes of arc between the heavenly body and the elevated pole. The elevated pole is the one above the horizon; in other words, the one with the same name as your latitude.

From the foregoing description, it follows that the polar distance of a body whose declination has the same name (north or south) as the elevated pole is always 90 degrees minus its declination (d). Polar distance of a body whose declination has a different name from that of the elevated pole is always 90 plus d.

Declination of any navigational star is listed in the Nautical Almanac for each date. Declination of each body of the solar system is listed for every hour of **Greenwich Mean Time (GMT).**

1984 MAR. 31, APRIL 1, 2 (SAT., SUN., MON.)

G.M.T.	SUN G.H.A.	Dec.	MOON G.H.A.	v	Dec.	d	H.P.
31 00	178 56.0 N 4 08.6		192 11.2 16.4 S 6 53.2	12.4	54.1		
01	193 56.2	09.6	206 46.6 16.3	6 40.8	12.6	54.1	
02	208 56.3	10.5	221 21.9 16.4	6 28.2	12.5	54.1	
03	223 56.5 ··	11.5	235 57.3 16.4	6 15.7	12.6	54.1	
04	238 56.7	12.5	250 32.7 16.4	6 03.1	12.6	54.1	
05	253 56.9	13.4	265 08.1 16.4	5 50.5	12.6	54.1	
06	268 57.1 N 4 14.4		279 43.5 16.5 S 5 37.9	12.6	54.1		
07	283 57.3	15.4	294 19.0 16.4	5 25.3	12.7	54.1	
S 08	298 57.5	16.3	308 54.4 16.4	5 12.6	12.7	54.1	
A 09	313 57.7 ··	17.3	323 29.8 16.5	4 59.9	12.7	54.1	
T 10	328 57.8	18.3	338 05.3 16.5	4 47.2	12.7	54.1	
U 11	343 58.0	19.2	352 40.8 16.5	4 34.5	12.8	54.1	
R 12	358 58.2 N 4 20.2		7 16.3 16.4 S 4 21.7	12.7	54.1		
D 13	13 58.4	21.2	21 51.7 16.5	4 09.0	12.8	54.1	
A 14	28 58.6	22.1	36 27.2 16.5	3 56.2	12.9	54.1	
Y 15	43 58.8 ··	23.1	51 02.7 16.5	3 43.3	12.8	54.2	
16	58 59.0	24.1	65 38.2 16.5	3 30.5	12.8	54.2	
17	73 59.1	25.0	80 13.7 16.5	3 17.7	12.9	54.2	
18	88 59.3 N 4 26.0		94 49.2 16.5 S 3 04.8	12.9	54.2		
19	103 59.5	27.0	109 24.8 16.5	2 51.9	12.9	54.2	
20	118 59.7	27.9	124 00.3 16.5	2 39.0	12.9	54.2	
21	133 59.9 ··	28.9	138 35.8 16.5	2 26.1	12.9	54.2	
22	149 00.1	29.9	153 11.3 16.5	2 13.2	13.0	54.2	
23	164 00.3	30.8	167 46.8 16.5	2 00.2	12.9	54.2	
1 00	179 00.4 N 4 31.8		182 22.3 16.5 S 1 47.3	13.0	54.2		
01	194 00.6	32.8	196 57.8 16.5	1 34.3	12.9	54.2	
02	209 00.8	33.7	211 33.3 16.5	1 21.4	13.0	54.3	
03	224 01.0 ··	34.7	226 08.8 16.5	1 08.4	13.0	54.3	
04	239 01.2	35.7	240 44.3 16.5	0 55.4	13.0	54.3	
05	254 01.4	36.6	255 19.8 16.5	0 42.4	13.0	54.3	
06	269 01.6 N 4 37.6		269 55.3 16.4 S 0 29.4	13.1	54.3		
07	284 01.7	38.6	284 30.7 16.5	0 16.3	13.0	54.3	
08	299 01.9	39.5	299 06.2 16.4 S 0 03.3	13.0	54.3		
S 09	314 02.1	40.5	313 41.6 16.5 N 0 09.7	13.0	54.3		
U 10	329 02.3	41.5	328 17.1 16.4	0 22.7	13.1	54.3	
N 11	344 02.5	42.4	342 52.5 16.4	0 35.8	13.0	54.3	
D 12	359 02.7 N 4 43.4		357 27.9 16.4 N 0 48.8	13.1	54.4		
A 13	14 02.8	44.3	12 03.3 16.4	1 01.9	13.0	54.4	
Y 14	29 03.0	45.3	26 38.7 16.4	1 14.9	13.1	54.4	
15	44 03.2 ··	46.3	41 14.1 16.3	1 28.0	13.0	54.4	
16	59 03.4	47.2	55 49.4 16.3	1 41.0	13.0	54.4	
17	74 03.6	48.2	70 24.8 16.3	1 54.0	13.1	54.4	
18	89 03.8 N 4 49.2		85 00.1 16.3 N 2 07.1	13.0	54.4		
19	104 04.0	50.1	99 35.4 16.3	2 20.1	13.1	54.4	
20	119 04.1	51.1	114 10.7 16.2	2 33.2	13.0	54.4	
21	134 04.3 ··	52.0	128 45.9 16.3	2 46.2	13.0	54.5	
22	149 04.5	53.0	143 21.2 16.2	2 59.2	13.1	54.5	
23	164 04.7	54.0	157 56.4 16.2	3 12.3	13.0	54.5	
2 00	179 04.9 N 4 54.9		172 31.6 16.1 N 3 25.3	13.0	54.5		
01	194 05.1	55.9	187 06.7 16.2	3 38.3	13.0	54.5	
02	209 05.2	56.9	201 41.9 16.1	3 51.3	13.0	54.5	
03	224 05.4 ··	57.8	216 17.0 16.1	4 04.3	13.0	54.5	
04	239 05.6	58.8	230 52.1 16.0	4 17.3	13.0	54.5	
05	254 05.8 4 59.7		245 27.1 16.1	4 30.3	12.9	54.6	
06	269 06.0 N 5 00.7		260 02.2 16.0 N 4 43.2	13.0	54.6		
07	284 06.2	01.7	274 37.2 16.0	4 56.2	12.9	54.6	
08	299 06.4	02.6	289 12.2 15.9	5 09.1	13.0	54.6	
M 09	314 06.5 ··	03.6	303 47.1 15.9	5 22.1	12.9	54.6	
O 10	329 06.7	04.5	318 22.0 15.9	5 35.0	12.9	54.6	
N 11	344 06.9	05.5	332 56.9 15.8	5 47.9	12.8	54.6	
D 12	359 07.1 N 5 06.5		347 31.7 15.9 N 6 00.7	12.9	54.7		
A 13	14 07.3	07.4	2 06.6 15.7	6 13.6	12.9	54.7	
Y 14	29 07.5	08.4	16 41.3 15.8	6 26.5	12.8	54.7	
15	44 07.6 ··	09.3	31 16.1 15.7	6 39.3	12.8	54.7	
16	59 07.8	10.3	45 50.8 15.6	6 52.1	12.8	54.7	
17	74 08.0	11.3	60 25.4 15.7	7 04.9	12.8	54.7	
18	89 08.2 N 5 12.2		75 00.1 15.5 N 7 17.7	12.7	54.7		
19	104 08.4	13.2	89 34.6 15.6	7 30.4	12.7	54.7	
20	119 08.6	14.1	104 09.2 15.5	7 43.1	12.7	54.8	
21	134 08.7 ··	15.1	118 43.7 15.4	7 55.8	12.7	54.8	
22	149 08.9	16.1	133 18.1 15.5	8 08.5	12.7	54.8	
23	164 09.1	17.0	147 52.6 15.3	8 21.2	12.6	54.8	
	S D 16.0 d 1.0		S.D. 14.8	14.8		14.9	

Lat.	Twilight Naut.	Civil	Sunrise	Moonrise 31	1	2	3
N 72	01 36	03 40	04 55	06 32	06 07	05 43	05 14
N 70	02 20	03 57	05 03	06 25	06 07	05 49	05 29
68	02 48	04 09	05 09	06 18	06 06	05 54	05 40
66	03 09	04 20	05 14	06 13	06 06	05 58	05 50
64	03 25	04 29	05 18	06 09	06 05	06 02	05 58
62	03 38	04 36	05 22	06 05	06 05	06 05	06 05
60	03 49	04 42	05 25	06 01	06 04	06 08	06 12
N 58	03 58	04 48	05 28	05 58	06 04	06 10	06 17
56	04 06	04 52	05 30	05 55	06 04	06 12	06 22
54	04 13	04 57	05 33	05 53	06 04	06 15	06 26
52	04 19	05 00	05 35	05 51	06 03	06 16	06 30
50	04 24	05 04	05 37	05 49	06 03	06 18	06 34
45	04 36	05 11	05 41	05 44	06 03	06 22	06 42
N 40	04 44	05 17	05 44	05 40	06 02	06 25	06 48
35	04 51	05 21	05 47	05 37	06 02	06 28	06 54
30	04 57	05 25	05 49	05 34	06 02	06 30	06 59
20	05 06	05 31	05 54	05 29	06 01	06 34	07 08
N 10	05 12	05 36	05 57	05 25	06 01	06 38	07 16
0	05 16	05 40	06 01	05 20	06 01	06 41	07 23
S 10	05 18	05 43	06 04	05 16	06 00	06 48	07 31
20	05 19	05 45	06 07	05 12	06 00	06 49	07 39
30	05 19	05 47	06 11	05 07	06 00	06 53	07 48
35	05 18	05 48	06 13	05 04	05 59	06 56	07 53
40	05 17	05 48	06 15	05 00	05 59	06 59	07 59
45	05 14	05 48	06 18	04 56	05 59	07 02	08 06
S 50	05 11	05 49	06 21	04 52	05 58	07 06	08 15
52	05 09	05 49	06 22	04 49	05 58	07 08	08 19
54	05 07	05 49	06 24	04 47	05 58	07 10	08 23
56	05 05	05 48	06 25	04 44	05 58	07 12	08 28
58	05 03	05 48	06 27	04 42	05 58	07 15	08 34
S 60	04 59	05 48	06 29	04 38	05 58	07 18	08 40

Lat.	Sunset	Twilight Civil	Naut.	Moonset 31	1	2	3
N 72	19 15	20 32	22 43	16 57	18 48	20 44	22 54
N 70	19 08	20 14	21 54	17 02	18 45	20 32	22 27
68	19 01	20 01	21 24	17 06	18 43	20 22	22 08
66	18 56	19 50	21 03	17 09	18 41	20 14	21 52
64	18 51	19 41	20 46	17 12	18 39	20 07	21 40
62	18 48	19 34	20 32	17 14	18 37	20 02	21 29
60	18 44	19 27	20 21	17 16	18 36	19 57	21 20
N 58	18 41	19 22	20 12	17 18	18 35	19 52	21 12
56	18 39	19 17	20 03	17 20	18 34	19 48	21 05
54	18 36	19 12	19 56	17 21	18 33	19 45	20 59
52	18 34	19 08	19 50	17 23	18 32	19 42	20 54
50	18 32	19 05	19 45	17 24	18 31	19 39	20 49
45	18 28	18 58	19 33	17 26	18 29	19 33	20 38
N 40	18 24	18 52	19 24	17 29	18 28	19 28	20 29
35	18 21	18 47	19 17	17 31	18 26	19 23	20 22
30	18 19	18 43	19 11	17 32	18 25	19 19	20 15
20	18 14	18 36	19 02	17 35	18 23	19 13	20 04
N 10	18 11	18 32	18 56	17 38	18 22	19 07	19 54
0	18 07	18 28	18 52	17 40	18 20	19 01	19 44
S 10	18 04	18 25	18 49	17 42	18 19	18 56	19 35
20	18 00	18 22	18 48	17 44	18 17	18 50	19 25
30	17 56	18 20	18 48	17 47	18 15	18 43	19 14
35	17 54	18 19	18 49	17 49	18 14	18 40	19 07
40	17 52	18 19	18 50	17 50	18 13	18 35	19 00
45	17 49	18 18	18 52	17 52	18 11	18 30	18 52
S 50	17 46	18 18	18 55	17 55	18 09	18 25	18 41
52	17 44	18 18	18 57	17 56	18 09	18 22	18 37
54	17 43	18 18	18 59	17 57	18 08	18 19	18 31
56	17 41	18 18	19 01	17 58	18 07	18 16	18 26
58	17 39	18 18	19 04	18 00	18 06	18 12	18 19
S 60	17 37	18 18	19 07	18 01	18 05	18 08	18 12

Day	SUN Eqn. of Time 00ʰ	12ʰ	Mer. Pass.	MOON Mer. Pass. Upper	Lower	Age	Phase
31	04 16	04 08	12 04	11 30	23 50	29	
1	03 59	03 50	12 04	12 10	24 31	30	●
2	03 41	03 32	12 04	12 51	00 31	01	

14ᵐ INCREMENTS AND CORRECTIONS 15ᵐ

14	SUN PLANETS	ARIES	MOON	v or Corrⁿ d	v or Corrⁿ d	v or Corrⁿ d	15	SUN PLANETS	ARIES	MOON	v or Corrⁿ d	v or Corrⁿ d	v or Corrⁿ d
s	° '	° '	° '	' '	' '	' '	s	° '	° '	° '	' '	' '	' '
00	3 30·0	3 30·6	3 20·4	0·0 0·0	6·0 1·5	12·0 2·9	00	3 45·0	3 45·6	3 34·8	0·0 0·0	6·0 1·6	12·0 3·1
01	3 30·3	3 30·8	3 20·7	0·1 0·0	6·1 1·5	12·1 2·9	01	3 45·3	3 45·9	3 35·0	0·1 0·0	6·1 1·6	12·1 3·1
02	3 30·5	3 31·1	3 20·9	0·2 0·0	6·2 1·5	12·2 2·9	02	3 45·5	3 46·1	3 35·2	0·2 0·1	6·2 1·6	12·2 3·2
03	3 30·8	3 31·3	3 21·1	0·3 0·1	6·3 1·5	12·3 3·0	03	3 45·8	3 46·4	3 35·5	0·3 0·1	6·3 1·6	12·3 3·2
04	3 31·0	3 31·6	3 21·4	0·4 0·1	6·4 1·5	12·4 3·0	04	3 46·0	3 46·6	3 35·7	0·4 0·1	6·4 1·7	12·4 3·2
05	3 31·3	3 31·8	3 21·6	0·5 0·1	6·5 1·6	12·5 3·0	05	3 46·3	3 46·9	3 35·9	0·5 0·1	6·5 1·7	12·5 3·2
06	3 31·5	3 32·1	3 21·9	0·6 0·1	6·6 1·6	12·6 3·0	06	3 46·5	3 47·1	3 36·2	0·6 0·2	6·6 1·7	12·6 3·3
07	3 31·8	3 32·3	3 22·1	0·7 0·2	6·7 1·6	12·7 3·1	07	3 46·8	3 47·4	3 36·4	0·7 0·2	6·7 1·7	12·7 3·3
08	3 32·0	3 32·6	3 22·3	0·8 0·2	6·8 1·6	12·8 3·1	08	3 47·0	3 47·6	3 36·7	0·8 0·2	6·8 1·8	12·8 3·3
09	3 32·3	3 32·8	3 22·6	0·9 0·2	6·9 1·7	12·9 3·1	09	3 47·3	3 47·9	3 36·9	0·9 0·2	6·9 1·8	12·9 3·3
10	3 32·5	3 33·1	3 22·8	1·0 0·2	7·0 1·7	13·0 3·1	10	3 47·5	3 48·1	3 37·1	1·0 0·3	7·0 1·8	13·0 3·4
11	3 32·8	3 33·3	3 23·1	1·1 0·3	7·1 1·7	13·1 3·2	11	3 47·8	3 48·4	3 37·4	1·1 0·3	7·1 1·8	13·1 3·4
12	3 33·0	3 33·6	3 23·3	1·2 0·3	7·2 1·7	13·2 3·2	12	3 48·0	3 48·6	3 37·6	1·2 0·3	7·2 1·9	13·2 3·4
13	3 33·3	3 33·8	3 23·5	1·3 0·3	7·3 1·8	13·3 3·2	13	3 48·3	3 48·9	3 37·9	1·3 0·3	7·3 1·9	13·3 3·4
14	3 33·5	3 34·1	3 23·8	1·4 0·3	7·4 1·8	13·4 3·2	14	3 48·5	3 49·1	3 38·1	1·4 0·4	7·4 1·9	13·4 3·5
15	3 33·8	3 34·3	3 24·0	1·5 0·4	7·5 1·8	13·5 3·3	15	3 48·8	3 49·4	3 38·3	1·5 0·4	7·5 1·9	13·5 3·5
16	3 34·0	3 34·6	3 24·3	1·6 0·4	7·6 1·8	13·6 3·3	16	3 49·0	3 49·6	3 38·6	1·6 0·4	7·6 2·0	13·6 3·5
17	3 34·3	3 34·8	3 24·5	1·7 0·4	7·7 1·9	13·7 3·3	17	3 49·3	3 49·9	3 38·8	1·7 0·4	7·7 2·0	13·7 3·5
18	3 34·5	3 35·1	3 24·7	1·8 0·4	7·8 1·9	13·8 3·3	18	3 49·5	3 50·1	3 39·0	1·8 0·5	7·8 2·0	13·8 3·6
19	3 34·8	3 35·3	3 25·0	1·9 0·5	7·9 1·9	13·9 3·4	19	3 49·8	3 50·4	3 39·3	1·9 0·5	7·9 2·0	13·9 3·6
20	3 35·0	3 35·6	3 25·2	2·0 0·5	8·0 1·9	14·0 3·4	20	3 50·0	3 50·6	3 39·5	2·0 0·5	8·0 2·1	14·0 3·6
21	3 35·3	3 35·8	3 25·4	2·1 0·5	8·1 2·0	14·1 3·4	21	3 50·3	3 50·9	3 39·8	2·1 0·5	8·1 2·1	14·1 3·6
22	3 35·5	3 36·1	3 25·7	2·2 0·5	8·2 2·0	14·2 3·4	22	3 50·5	3 51·1	3 40·0	2·2 0·6	8·2 2·1	14·2 3·7
23	3 35·8	3 36·3	3 25·9	2·3 0·6	8·3 2·0	14·3 3·5	23	3 50·8	3 51·4	3 40·2	2·3 0·6	8·3 2·1	14·3 3·7
24	3 36·0	3 36·6	3 26·2	2·4 0·6	8·4 2·0	14·4 3·5	24	3 51·0	3 51·6	3 40·5	2·4 0·6	8·4 2·2	14·4 3·7
25	3 36·3	3 36·8	3 26·4	2·5 0·6	8·5 2·1	14·5 3·5	25	3 51·3	3 51·9	3 40·7	2·5 0·6	8·5 2·2	14·5 3·7
26	3 36·5	3 37·1	3 26·6	2·6 0·6	8·6 2·1	14·6 3·5	26	3 51·5	3 52·1	3 41·0	2·6 0·7	8·6 2·2	14·6 3·8
27	3 36·8	3 37·3	3 26·9	2·7 0·7	8·7 2·1	14·7 3·6	27	3 51·8	3 52·4	3 41·2	2·7 0·7	8·7 2·2	14·7 3·8
28	3 37·0	3 37·6	3 27·1	2·8 0·7	8·8 2·1	14·8 3·6	28	3 52·0	3 52·6	3 41·4	2·8 0·7	8·8 2·3	14·8 3·8
29	3 37·3	3 37·8	3 27·4	2·9 0·7	8·9 2·2	14·9 3·6	29	3 52·3	3 52·9	3 41·7	2·9 0·7	8·9 2·3	14·9 3·8
30	3 37·5	3 38·1	3 27·6	3·0 0·7	9·0 2·2	15·0 3·6	30	3 52·5	3 53·1	3 41·9	3·0 0·8	9·0 2·3	15·0 3·9
31	3 37·8	3 38·3	3 27·8	3·1 0·7	9·1 2·2	15·1 3·6	31	3 52·8	3 53·4	3 42·1	3·1 0·8	9·1 2·4	15·1 3·9
32	3 38·0	3 38·6	3 28·1	3·2 0·8	9·2 2·2	15·2 3·7	32	3 53·0	3 53·6	3 42·4	3·2 0·8	9·2 2·4	15·2 3·9
33	3 38·3	3 38·8	3 28·3	3·3 0·8	9·3 2·2	15·3 3·7	33	3 53·3	3 53·9	3 42·6	3·3 0·9	9·3 2·4	15·3 4·0
34	3 38·5	3 39·1	3 28·5	3·4 0·8	9·4 2·3	15·4 3·7	34	3 53·5	3 54·1	3 42·9	3·4 0·9	9·4 2·4	15·4 4·0
35	3 38·8	3 39·3	3 28·8	3·5 0·8	9·5 2·3	15·5 3·7	35	3 53·8	3 54·4	3 43·1	3·5 0·9	9·5 2·5	15·5 4·0
36	3 39·0	3 39·6	3 29·0	3·6 0·9	9·6 2·3	15·6 3·8	36	3 54·0	3 54·6	3 43·3	3·6 0·9	9·6 2·5	15·6 4·0
37	3 39·3	3 39·9	3 29·3	3·7 0·9	9·7 2·3	15·7 3·8	37	3 54·3	3 54·9	3 43·6	3·7 1·0	9·7 2·5	15·7 4·1
38	3 39·5	3 40·1	3 29·5	3·8 0·9	9·8 2·4	15·8 3·8	38	3 54·5	3 55·1	3 43·8	3·8 1·0	9·8 2·5	15·8 4·1
39	3 39·8	3 40·4	3 29·7	3·9 0·9	9·9 2·4	15·9 3·8	39	3 54·8	3 55·4	3 44·1	3·9 1·0	9·9 2·6	15·9 4·1
40	3 40·0	3 40·6	3 30·0	4·0 1·0	10·0 2·4	16·0 3·9	40	3 55·0	3 55·6	3 44·3	4·0 1·0	10·0 2·6	16·0 4·1
41	3 40·3	3 40·9	3 30·2	4·1 1·0	10·1 2·4	16·1 3·9	41	3 55·3	3 55·9	3 44·5	4·1 1·1	10·1 2·6	16·1 4·2
42	3 40·5	3 41·1	3 30·5	4·2 1·0	10·2 2·5	16·2 3·9	42	3 55·5	3 56·1	3 44·8	4·2 1·1	10·2 2·6	16·2 4·2
43	3 40·8	3 41·4	3 30·7	4·3 1·0	10·3 2·5	16·3 3·9	43	3 55·8	3 56·4	3 45·0	4·3 1·1	10·3 2·7	16·3 4·2
44	3 41·0	3 41·6	3 30·9	4·4 1·1	10·4 2·5	16·4 4·0	44	3 56·0	3 56·6	3 45·2	4·4 1·1	10·4 2·7	16·4 4·2
45	3 41·3	3 41·9	3 31·2	4·5 1·1	10·5 2·5	16·5 4·0	45	3 56·3	3 56·9	3 45·5	4·5 1·2	10·5 2·7	16·5 4·3
46	3 41·5	3 42·1	3 31·4	4·6 1·1	10·6 2·6	16·6 4·0	46	3 56·5	3 57·1	3 45·7	4·6 1·2	10·6 2·7	16·6 4·3
47	3 41·8	3 42·4	3 31·6	4·7 1·1	10·7 2·6	16·7 4·0	47	3 56·8	3 57·4	3 46·0	4·7 1·2	10·7 2·8	16·7 4·3
48	3 42·0	3 42·6	3 31·9	4·8 1·2	10·8 2·6	16·8 4·1	48	3 57·0	3 57·6	3 46·2	4·8 1·2	10·8 2·8	16·8 4·3
49	3 42·3	3 42·9	3 32·1	4·9 1·2	10·9 2·6	16·9 4·1	49	3 57·3	3 57·9	3 46·4	4·9 1·3	10·9 2·8	16·9 4·4
50	3 42·5	3 43·1	3 32·4	5·0 1·2	11·0 2·7	17·0 4·1	50	3 57·5	3 58·2	3 46·7	5·0 1·3	11·0 2·8	17·0 4·4
51	3 42·8	3 43·4	3 32·6	5·1 1·2	11·1 2·7	17·1 4·1	51	3 57·8	3 58·4	3 46·9	5·1 1·3	11·1 2·9	17·1 4·4
52	3 43·0	3 43·6	3 32·8	5·2 1·3	11·2 2·7	17·2 4·2	52	3 58·0	3 58·7	3 47·2	5·2 1·3	11·2 2·9	17·2 4·4
53	3 43·3	3 43·9	3 33·1	5·3 1·3	11·3 2·7	17·3 4·2	53	3 58·3	3 58·9	3 47·4	5·3 1·4	11·3 2·9	17·3 4·5
54	3 43·5	3 44·1	3 33·3	5·4 1·3	11·4 2·8	17·4 4·2	54	3 58·5	3 59·2	3 47·6	5·4 1·4	11·4 2·9	17·4 4·5
55	3 43·8	3 44·4	3 33·6	5·5 1·3	11·5 2·8	17·5 4·2	55	3 58·8	3 59·4	3 47·9	5·5 1·4	11·5 3·0	17·5 4·5
56	3 44·0	3 44·6	3 33·8	5·6 1·4	11·6 2·8	17·6 4·3	56	3 59·0	3 59·7	3 48·1	5·6 1·4	11·6 3·0	17·6 4·5
57	3 44·3	3 44·9	3 34·0	5·7 1·4	11·7 2·8	17·7 4·3	57	3 59·3	3 59·9	3 48·4	5·7 1·5	11·7 3·0	17·7 4·6
58	3 44·5	3 45·1	3 34·3	5·8 1·4	11·8 2·9	17·8 4·3	58	3 59·5	4 00·2	3 48·6	5·8 1·5	11·8 3·0	17·8 4·6
59	3 44·8	3 45·4	3 34·5	5·9 1·4	11·9 2·9	17·9 4·3	59	3 59·8	4 00·4	3 48·8	5·9 1·5	11·9 3·1	17·9 4·6
60	3 45·0	3 45·6	3 34·8	6·0 1·5	12·0 2·9	18·0 4·4	60	4 00·0	4 00·7	3 49·1	6·0 1·6	12·0 3·1	18·0 4·7

COMPUTING GHA AND DECLINATION OF THE SUN

Example:

Determine the GHA and declination for a sight of the lower limb of the sun taken at 09h 15m 38s on the 31of March 1984.

This series of steps involves the use of the Nautical Almanac. On **page 8-2** is a reprint of the right-hand daily page for 31 March and 1 and 2 April 1984. Notice that for each day there are hourly entries for the GHA and the declination (Dec.) of the sun.

The entry of **09 hours on 31 March** is found and information is entered on the work form as follows:

The GHA for 09 hours **(313° 57.7')** is entered in the work form.

The Dec. for 09 hours **(N 4° 17.3')** and is entered work from.

Remain on this page and move down the Sun Dec. column to the bottom of the page. Determine as you move down this column whether the Dec. increases or decreases toward the bottom of the page. In a box the bottom of the column is a small (italicized) letter d followed by 1.0; this is called the d# and is entered as follows:

The value of d (+1.0) is entered on the right side of d# in the brackets, leaving room to enter the d correction (corr) later. The d value **IS NOT** the correction itself, but it will be used later to locate the correction in the increment and correction pages. The d value is assigned a positive (+) or a negative (-) sign according to whether the Dec. increases (+) or decreases (-) as you move toward the bottom of the page. Dec. values in our example increase so a plus (+) has been assigned to the reading. (+ 1.0)

Remember that GHA (h) and Dec. have been entered for the even hour of 0900, but GMT has **15m 38s remaining**. An increment of arc for GHA and a d corr are necessary to account for the remaining minutes and seconds of time. The increments and corrections page showing, 15 minutes in shown on **page 8-3**. Notice that the page also contains increments and corrections for 14 minutes.

Using the 15 minute table, follow down the seconds' column (at the far left margin) to the line for 38 seconds. In the first column to the right of 38 seconds (the Sun/Planets column) is the increment of GHA for 15 minutes, 38 seconds. This datum is entered on the work form as follows:

The increment **(3° 54.5')** is entered in work form.

Still using the 15 minute table look to the right at the three columns labeled v or d corr. Each of these columns has two sub-columns. The left sub-column (using smaller print) contains d#'s. The right sub-column (using larger print) contains d corrections. **Look down the d# sub-column to 1.0 and you will find a corresponding d correction of 0.3.**· The d correction, 0.3 will have a positive (+) sign because the d# is positive. This table provides a tabulated ratio of d.

The d correction **(+0.3)** is entered on the right side d# (+10) in our work form.

We now **add .3** to the Dec and the results is entered in space below **(N 4° 17.6)**

The next step is to add the GHA (h) and increment in space to obtain the total GHA). Remember **the increment (m/s)·is always added to the GHA (h).**

The next line on our form is left blank. We will use this space when we work a star sight later. The total **GHA 317° 52.2'** is entered below.

Almanac (Sun)			
GHA	313° 57.7'	**DEC**	N 4° 17.3'
M/S	+ 3° 54.5'	**d (+ 1.0)**	+ 0.3'
GHA	317° 52.2'	**DEC**	N 4° 17.6'

SIDEREAL HOUR ANGLE (SHA) AND GHA OF STARS

Aries **"hour circle of vernal equinox** is the line from which sidereal hour angle is measured. The SHA of any star is measured westward through 360 degrees like GHA; but measurement is from the vernal equinox or first point of Aries, instead of from Greenwich.

GHA of the vernal equinox, like GHA of any other body, is increasing continuously westward. But the sidereal hour angle of any star (measured westward from the vernal equinox to the body's hour circle) remains relatively constant. Why? Simply all the stars move westward along with the vernal equinox. The SHA of any body changes slightly, and its tabulated value in the Nautical Almanac varies slightly throughout the year. The reasons for the changes are beyond the scope of this course.

You will see later that the SHA and GHA of the vernal equinox are factors used in star observations. However, neither is applicable in observations of navigational planets.

72   APRIL 4, 5, 6 (SAT., SUN., MON.)

G.M.T.	ARIES G.H.A.	VENUS −3.5 G.H.A.	Dec.	MARS +1.4 G.H.A.	Dec.	JUPITER −2.0 G.H.A.	Dec.	SATURN +0.7 G.H.A.	Dec.	STARS Name	S.H.A.	Dec.
4 00	192 13.3	179 30.9 N 4	03.0	179 15.0 N 4	52.4	7 35.1 S 0	16.5	5 49.2 N 0	07.4	Acamar	315 37.3	S40 23.1
01	207 15.8	194 30.5	04.3	194 15.7	53.1	22 37.9	16.3	20 51.9	07.5	Achernar	335 45.6	S57 20.1
02	222 18.3	209 30.1	05.5	209 16.4	53.9	37 40.6	16.2	35 54.5	07.5	Acrux	173 36.1	S62 59.7
03	237 20.7	224 29.7 ··	06.8	224 17.1 ··	54.6	52 43.4 ··	16.1	50 57.2 ··	07.6	Adhara	255 31.8	S28 57.1
04	252 23.2	239 29.3	08.0	239 17.8	55.4	67 46.1	16.0	65 59.8	07.7	Aldebaran	291 17.8	N16 28.2
05	267 25.7	254 29.0	09.3	254 18.5	56.2	82 48.9	15.9	81 02.4	07.8			
06	282 28.1	269 28.6 N 4	10.5	269 19.2 N 4	56.9	97 51.6 S 0	15.7	96 05.1 N 0	07.8	Alioth	166 41.6	N56 03.7
07	297 30.6	284 28.2	11.7	284 19.9	57.7	112 54.4	15.6	111 07.7	07.9	Alkaid	153 17.8	N49 24.4
S 08	312 33.0	299 27.8	13.0	299 20.6	58.5	127 57.1	15.5	126 10.4	08.0	Al Na'ir	28 14.8	S47 03.1
A 09	327 35.5	314 27.4 ··	14.2	314 21.3 4	59.2	142 59.9 ··	15.4	141 13.0 ··	08.1	Alnilam	276 11.4	S 1 13.0
T 10	342 38.0	329 27.0	15.5	329 22.0 5	00.0	158 02.6	15.2	156 15.6	08.1	Alphard	218 20.0	S 8 34.8
U 11	357 40.4	344 26.6	16.7	344 22.7	00.8	173 05.4	15.1	171 18.3	08.2			
R 12	12 42.9	359 26.3 N 4	18.0	359 23.4 N 5	01.5	188 08.1 S 0	15.0	186 20.9 N 0	08.3	Alphecca	126 31.5	N26 46.5
D 13	27 45.4	14 25.9	19.2	14 24.1	02.3	203 10.9	14.9	201 23.6	08.4	Alpheratz	358 09.3	N28 59.0
A 14	42 47.8	29 25.5	20.4	29 24.8	03.1	218 13.7	14.7	216 26.2	08.4	Altair	62 32.2	N 8 48.9
Y 15	57 50.3	44 25.1 ··	21.7	44 25.5 ··	03.8	233 16.4 ··	14.6	231 28.8 ··	08.5	Ankaa	353 40.3	S42 24.6
16	72 52.8	59 24.7	22.9	59 26.2	04.6	248 19.2	14.5	246 31.5	08.6	Antares	112 56.2	S26 23.4
17	87 55.2	74 24.3	24.2	74 26.9	05.3	263 21.9	14.4	261 34.1	08.7			
18	102 57.7	89 23.9 N 4	25.4	89 27.6 N 5	06.1	278 24.7 S 0	14.3	276 36.8 N 0	08.8	Arcturus	146 17.8	N19 16.7
19	118 00.2	104 23.5	26.7	104 28.3	06.9	293 27.4	14.1	291 39.4	08.8	Atria	108 19.8	S68 59.4
20	133 02.6	119 23.2	27.9	119 29.0	07.6	308 30.2	14.0	306 42.1	08.9	Avior	234 27.9	S59 27.3
21	148 05.1	134 22.8 ··	29.1	134 29.7 ··	08.4	323 32.9 ··	13.9	321 44.7 ··	09.0	Bellatrix	278 58.5	N 6 19.8
22	163 07.5	149 22.4	30.4	149 30.4	09.2	338 35.7	13.8	336 47.3	09.1	Betelgeuse	271 28.0	N 7 24.1
23	178 10.0	164 22.0	31.6	164 31.1	09.9	353 38.4	13.6	351 50.0	09.1			
5 00	193 12.5	179 21.6 N 4	32.9	179 31.8 N 5	10.7	8 41.2 S 0	13.5	6 52.6 N 0	09.2	Canopus	264 07.1	S52 41.5
01	208 14.9	194 21.2	34.1	194 32.5	11.4	23 43.9	13.4	21 55.3	09.3	Capella	281 11.0	N45 58.8
02	223 17.4	209 20.8	35.3	209 33.2	12.2	38 46.7	13.3	36 57.9	09.4	Deneb	49 48.4	N45 12.5
03	238 19.9	224 20.4 ··	36.6	224 33.9 ··	13.0	53 49.4 ··	13.2	52 00.5 ··	09.4	Denebola	182 58.4	N14 40.6
04	253 22.3	239 20.1	37.8	239 34.6	13.7	68 52.2	13.0	67 03.2	09.5	Diphda	349 20.8	S18 05.6
05	268 24.8	254 19.7	39.1	254 35.3	14.5	83 54.9	12.9	82 05.8	09.6			
06	283 27.3	269 19.3 N 4	40.3	269 36.0 N 5	15.3	98 57.7 S 0	12.8	97 08.5 N 0	09.7	Dubhe	194 21.1	N61 51.3
07	298 29.7	284 18.9	41.5	284 36.7	16.0	114 00.4	12.7	112 11.1	09.7	Elnath	278 43.8	N28 35.5
08	313 32.2	299 18.5	42.8	299 37.4	16.8	129 03.2	12.5	127 13.7	09.8	Eltanin	90 57.4	N51 29.2
S 09	328 34.7	314 18.1 ··	44.0	314 38.1 ··	17.5	144 05.9 ··	12.4	142 16.4 ··	09.9	Enif	34 11.4	N 9 47.1
U 10	343 37.1	329 17.7	45.3	329 38.8	18.3	159 08.7	12.3	157 19.0	10.0	Fomalhaut	15 51.3	S29 43.4
N 11	358 39.6	344 17.3	46.5	344 39.5	19.1	174 11.4	12.2	172 21.6	10.0			
D 12	13 42.0	359 17.0 N 4	47.7	359 40.2 N 5	19.8	189 14.2 S 0	12.1	187 24.3 N 0	10.1	Gacrux	172 27.8	S57 00.5
A 13	28 44.5	14 16.6	49.0	14 40.9	20.6	204 16.9	11.9	202 26.9	10.2	Gienah	176 17.3	S17 26.3
Y 14	43 47.0	29 16.2	50.2	29 41.6	21.3	219 19.7	11.8	217 29.6	10.3	Hadar	149 22.2	S60 16.9
15	58 49.4	44 15.8 ··	51.5	44 42.3 ··	22.1	234 22.4 ··	11.7	232 32.2 ··	10.3	Hamal	328 28.9	N23 22.2
16	73 51.9	59 15.4	52.7	59 43.0	22.9	249 25.2	11.6	247 34.8	10.4	Kaus Aust.	84 16.3	S34 23.5
17	88 54.4	74 15.0	53.9	74 43.7	23.6	264 27.9	11.5	262 37.5	10.5			
18	103 56.8	89 14.6 N 4	55.2	89 44.4 N 5	24.4	279 30.7 S 0	11.3	277 40.1 N 0	10.5	Kochab	137 18.0	N74 13.9
19	118 59.3	104 14.2	56.4	104 45.1	25.1	294 33.4	11.2	292 42.8	10.6	Markab	14 03.1	N15 06.0
20	134 01.8	119 13.8	57.6	119 45.8	25.9	309 36.2	11.1	307 45.4	10.7	Menkar	314 41.0	N 4 00.8
21	149 04.2	134 13.4 4	58.9	134 46.5 ··	26.7	324 38.9 ··	11.0	322 48.0 ··	10.8	Menkent	148 36.2	S36 16.6
22	164 06.7	149 13.1 5	00.1	149 47.2	27.4	339 41.7	10.8	337 50.7	10.8	Miaplacidus	221 44.4	S69 38.7
23	179 09.1	164 12.7	01.4	164 47.9	28.2	354 44.4	10.7	352 53.3	10.9			
6 00	194 11.6	179 12.3 N 5	02.6	179 48.6 N 5	28.9	9 47.2 S 0	10.6	7 56.0 N 0	11.0	Mirfak	309 16.0	N49 47.7
01	209 14.1	194 11.9	03.8	194 49.3	29.7	24 49.9	10.5	22 58.6	11.1	Nunki	76 28.7	S26 19.2
02	224 16.5	209 11.5	05.1	209 50.0	30.5	39 52.7	10.4	38 01.2	11.1	Peacock	53 58.0	S56 47.6
03	239 19.0	224 11.1 ··	06.3	224 50.7 ··	31.2	54 55.4 ··	10.2	53 03.9 ··	11.2	Pollux	243 57.7	N28 04.3
04	254 21.5	239 10.7	07.5	239 51.4	32.0	69 58.2	10.1	68 06.5	11.3	Procyon	245 25.4	N 5 16.3
05	269 23.9	254 10.3	08.8	254 52.1	32.7	85 00.9	10.0	83 09.2	11.4			
06	284 26.4	269 09.9 N 5	10.0	269 52.8 N 5	33.5	100 03.7 S 0	09.9	98 11.8 N 0	11.4	Rasalhague	96 29.1	N12 34.3
07	299 28.9	284 09.5	11.2	284 53.4	34.3	115 06.4	09.8	113 14.4	11.5	Regulus	208 09.4	N12 03.5
08	314 31.3	299 09.1	12.5	299 54.1	35.0	130 09.2	09.6	128 17.1	11.6	Rigel	281 35.8	S 8 13.6
M 09	329 33.8	314 08.8 ··	13.7	314 54.8 ··	35.8	145 11.9 ··	09.5	143 19.7 ··	11.7	Rigil Kent.	140 24.8	S60 45.3
O 10	344 36.3	329 08.4	14.9	329 55.5	36.5	160 14.7	09.4	158 22.4	11.7	Sabik	102 40.6	S15 42.1
N 11	359 38.7	344 08.0	16.2	344 56.2	37.3	175 17.4	09.3	173 25.0	11.8			
D 12	14 41.2	359 07.6 N 5	17.4	359 56.9 N 5	38.0	190 20.2 S 0	09.2	188 27.6 N 0	11.9	Schedar	350 09.2	N56 25.9
A 13	29 43.6	14 07.2	18.6	14 57.6	38.8	205 22.9	09.0	203 30.3	12.0	Shaula	96 55.1	S37 05.3
Y 14	44 46.1	29 06.8	19.9	29 58.3	39.6	220 25.7	08.9	218 32.9	12.0	Sirius	258 55.4	S16 41.7
15	59 48.6	44 06.4 ··	21.1	44 59.0 ··	40.3	235 28.4 ··	08.8	233 35.5 ··	12.1	Spica	158 56.9	S11 03.8
16	74 51.0	59 06.0	22.3	59 59.7	41.1	250 31.2	08.7	248 38.2	12.2	Suhail	223 10.3	S43 21.7
17	89 53.5	74 05.6	23.6	75 00.4	41.8	265 33.9	08.6	263 40.8	12.3			
18	104 56.0	89 05.2 N 5	24.8	90 01.1 N 5	42.6	280 36.7 S 0	08.4	278 43.5 N 0	12.3	Vega	80 55.5	N38 45.7
19	119 58.4	104 04.8	26.0	105 01.8	43.3	295 39.4	08.3	293 46.1	12.4	Zuben'ubi	137 32.4	S15 57.8
20	135 00.9	119 04.4	27.3	120 02.5	44.1	310 42.2	08.2	308 48.7	12.5		S.H.A.	Mer. Pass.
21	150 03.4	134 04.0 ··	28.5	135 03.2 ··	44.9	325 44.9 ··	08.1	323 51.4 ··	12.6		° '	h m
22	165 05.8	149 03.6	29..	150 03.9	45.6	340 47.7	08.0	338 54.0	12.6	Venus	346 09.1	12 03
23	180 08.3	164 03.2	31.0	165 04.6	46.4	355 50.4	07.8	353 56.7	12.7	Mars	346 19.3	12 01
Mer. Pass. 11 05.3		v −0.4 d 1.2		v 0.7 d 0.8		v 2.8 d 0.1		v 2.6 d 0.1		Jupiter	175 28.7	23 21
										Saturn	173 40.1	23 28

8-6

INCREMENTS AND CORRECTIONS

18ᵐ

18	SUN PLANETS	ARIES	MOON	v or Corrⁿ d	v or Corrⁿ d	v or Corrⁿ d
00	4 30·0	4 30·7	4 17·7	0·0 0·0	6·0 1·9	12·0 3·7
01	4 30·3	4 31·0	4 17·9	0·1 0·0	6·1 1·9	12·1 3·7
02	4 30·5	4 31·2	4 18·2	0·2 0·1	6·2 1·9	12·2 3·8
03	4 30·8	4 31·5	4 18·4	0·3 0·1	6·3 1·9	12·3 3·8
04	4 31·0	4 31·7	4 18·7	0·4 0·1	6·4 2·0	12·4 3·8
05	4 31·3	4 32·0	4 18·9	0·5 0·2	6·5 2·0	12·5 3·9
06	4 31·5	4 32·2	4 19·1	0·6 0·2	6·6 2·0	12·6 3·9
07	4 31·8	4 32·5	4 19·4	0·7 0·2	6·7 2·1	12·7 3·9
08	4 32·0	4 32·7	4 19·6	0·8 0·2	6·8 2·1	12·8 3·9
09	4 32·3	4 33·0	4 19·8	0·9 0·3	6·9 2·1	12·9 4·0
10	4 32·5	4 33·2	4 20·1	1·0 0·3	7·0 2·2	13·0 4·0
11	4 32·8	4 33·5	4 20·3	1·1 0·3	7·1 2·2	13·1 4·0
12	4 33·0	4 33·7	4 20·6	1·2 0·4	7·2 2·2	13·2 4·1
13	4 33·3	4 34·0	4 20·8	1·3 0·4	7·3 2·3	13·3 4·1
14	4 33·5	4 34·2	4 21·0	1·4 0·4	7·4 2·3	13·4 4·1
15	4 33·8	4 34·5	4 21·3	1·5 0·5	7·5 2·3	13·5 4·2
16	4 34·0	4 34·8	4 21·5	1·6 0·5	7·6 2·3	13·6 4·2
17	4 34·3	4 35·0	4 21·8	1·7 0·5	7·7 2·4	13·7 4·2
18	4 34·5	4 35·3	4 22·0	1·8 0·6	7·8 2·4	13·8 4·3
19	4 34·8	4 35·5	4 22·2	1·9 0·6	7·9 2·4	13·9 4·3
20	4 35·0	4 35·8	4 22·5	2·0 0·6	8·0 2·5	14·0 4·3
21	4 35·3	4 36·0	4 22·7	2·1 0·6	8·1 2·5	14·1 4·3
22	4 35·5	4 36·3	4 22·9	2·2 0·7	8·2 2·5	14·2 4·4
23	4 35·8	4 36·5	4 23·2	2·3 0·7	8·3 2·6	14·3 4·4
24	4 36·0	4 36·8	4 23·4	2·4 0·7	8·4 2·6	14·4 4·4
25	4 36·3	4 37·0	4 23·7	2·5 0·8	8·5 2·6	14·5 4·5
26	4 36·5	4 37·3	4 23·9	2·6 0·8	8·6 2·7	14·6 4·5
27	4 36·8	4 37·5	4 24·1	2·7 0·8	8·7 2·7	14·7 4·5
28	4 37·0	4 37·8	4 24·4	2·8 0·9	8·8 2·7	14·8 4·6
29	4 37·3	4 38·0	4 24·6	2·9 0·9	8·9 2·7	14·9 4·6
30	4 37·5	4 38·3	4 24·9	3·0 0·9	9·0 2·8	15·0 4·6
31	4 37·8	4 38·5	4 25·1	3·1 1·0	9·1 2·8	15·1 4·7
32	4 38·0	4 38·8	4 25·3	3·2 1·0	9·2 2·8	15·2 4·7
33	4 38·3	4 39·0	4 25·6	3·3 1·0	9·3 2·9	15·3 4·7
34	4 38·5	4 39·3	4 25·8	3·4 1·0	9·4 2·9	15·4 4·7
35	4 38·8	4 39·5	4 26·1	3·5 1·1	9·5 2·9	15·5 4·8
36	4 39·0	4 39·8	4 26·3	3·6 1·1	9·6 3·0	15·6 4·8
37	4 39·3	4 40·0	4 26·5	3·7 1·1	9·7 3·0	15·7 4·8
38	4 39·5	4 40·3	4 26·8	3·8 1·2	9·8 3·0	15·8 4·9
39	4 39·8	4 40·5	4 27·0	3·9 1·2	9·9 3·1	15·9 4·9
40	4 40·0	4 40·8	4 27·2	4·0 1·2	10·0 3·1	16·0 4·9
41	4 40·3	4 41·0	4 27·5	4·1 1·3	10·1 3·1	16·1 5·0
42	4 40·5	4 41·3	4 27·7	4·2 1·3	10·2 3·1	16·2 5·0
43	4 40·8	4 41·5	4 28·0	4·3 1·3	10·3 3·2	16·3 5·0
44	4 41·0	4 41·8	4 28·2	4·4 1·4	10·4 3·2	16·4 5·1
45	4 41·3	4 42·0	4 28·4	4·5 1·4	10·5 3·2	16·5 5·1
46	4 41·5	4 42·3	4 28·7	4·6 1·4	10·6 3·3	16·6 5·1
47	4 41·8	4 42·5	4 28·9	4·7 1·4	10·7 3·3	16·7 5·1
48	4 42·0	4 42·8	4 29·2	4·8 1·5	10·8 3·3	16·8 5·2
49	4 42·3	4 43·0	4 29·4	4·9 1·5	10·9 3·4	16·9 5·2
50	4 42·5	4 43·3	4 29·6	5·0 1·5	11·0 3·4	17·0 5·2
51	4 42·8	4 43·5	4 29·9	5·1 1·6	11·1 3·4	17·1 5·3
52	4 43·0	4 43·8	4 30·1	5·2 1·6	11·2 3·5	17·2 5·3
53	4 43·3	4 44·0	4 30·3	5·3 1·6	11·3 3·5	17·3 5·3
54	4 43·5	4 44·3	4 30·6	5·4 1·7	11·4 3·5	17·4 5·4
55	4 43·8	4 44·5	4 30·8	5·5 1·7	11·5 3·5	17·5 5·4
56	4 44·0	4 44·8	4 31·1	5·6 1·7	11·6 3·6	17·6 5·4
57	4 44·3	4 45·0	4 31·3	5·7 1·8	11·7 3·6	17·7 5·5
58	4 44·5	4 45·3	4 31·5	5·8 1·8	11·8 3·6	17·8 5·5
59	4 44·8	4 45·5	4 31·8	5·9 1·8	11·9 3·7	17·9 5·5
60	4 45·0	4 45·8	4 32·0	6·0 1·9	12·0 3·7	18·0 5·6

19ᵐ

19	SUN PLANETS	ARIES	MOON	v or Corrⁿ d	v or Corrⁿ d	v or Corrⁿ d
00	4 45·0	4 45·8	4 32·0	0·0 0·0	6·0 2·0	12·0 3·9
01	4 45·3	4 46·0	4 32·3	0·1 0·0	6·1 2·0	12·1 3·9
02	4 45·5	4 46·3	4 32·5	0·2 0·1	6·2 2·0	12·2 4·0
03	4 45·8	4 46·5	4 32·7	0·3 0·1	6·3 2·0	12·3 4·0
04	4 46·0	4 46·8	4 33·0	0·4 0·1	6·4 2·1	12·4 4·0
05	4 46·3	4 47·0	4 33·2	0·5 0·2	6·5 2·1	12·5 4·1
06	4 46·5	4 47·3	4 33·4	0·6 0·2	6·6 2·1	12·6 4·1
07	4 46·8	4 47·5	4 33·7	0·7 0·2	6·7 2·2	12·7 4·1
08	4 47·0	4 47·8	4 33·9	0·8 0·3	6·8 2·2	12·8 4·2
09	4 47·3	4 48·0	4 34·2	0·9 0·3	6·9 2·2	12·9 4·2
10	4 47·5	4 48·3	4 34·4	1·0 0·3	7·0 2·3	13·0 4·2
11	4 47·8	4 48·5	4 34·6	1·1 0·4	7·1 2·3	13·1 4·3
12	4 48·0	4 48·8	4 34·9	1·2 0·4	7·2 2·3	13·2 4·3
13	4 48·3	4 49·0	4 35·1	1·3 0·4	7·3 2·4	13·3 4·3
14	4 48·5	4 49·3	4 35·4	1·4 0·5	7·4 2·4	13·4 4·4
15	4 48·8	4 49·5	4 35·6	1·5 0·5	7·5 2·4	13·5 4·4
16	4 49·0	4 49·8	4 35·8	1·6 0·5	7·6 2·5	13·6 4·4
17	4 49·3	4 50·0	4 36·1	1·7 0·6	7·7 2·5	13·7 4·5
18	4 49·5	4 50·3	4 36·3	1·8 0·6	7·8 2·5	13·8 4·5
19	4 49·8	4 50·5	4 36·6	1·9 0·6	7·9 2·6	13·9 4·5
20	4 50·0	4 50·8	4 36·8	2·0 0·7	8·0 2·6	14·0 4·6
21	4 50·3	4 51·0	4 37·0	2·1 0·7	8·1 2·6	14·1 4·6
22	4 50·5	4 51·3	4 37·3	2·2 0·7	8·2 2·7	14·2 4·6
23	4 50·8	4 51·5	4 37·5	2·3 0·7	8·3 2·7	14·3 4·6
24	4 51·0	4 51·8	4 37·7	2·4 0·8	8·4 2·7	14·4 4·7
25	4 51·3	4 52·0	4 38·0	2·5 0·8	8·5 2·8	14·5 4·7
26	4 51·5	4 52·3	4 38·2	2·6 0·8	8·6 2·8	14·6 4·7
27	4 51·8	4 52·5	4 38·5	2·7 0·9	8·7 2·8	14·7 4·8
28	4 52·0	4 52·8	4 38·7	2·8 0·9	8·8 2·9	14·8 4·8
29	4 52·3	4 53·1	4 38·9	2·9 0·9	8·9 2·9	14·9 4·8
30	4 52·5	4 53·3	4 39·2	3·0 1·0	9·0 2·9	15·0 4·9
31	4 52·8	4 53·6	4 39·4	3·1 1·0	9·1 3·0	15·1 4·9
32	4 53·0	4 53·8	4 39·7	3·2 1·0	9·2 3·0	15·2 4·9
33	4 53·3	4 54·1	4 39·9	3·3 1·1	9·3 3·0	15·3 5·0
34	4 53·5	4 54·3	4 40·1	3·4 1·1	9·4 3·1	15·4 5·0
35	4 53·8	4 54·6	4 40·4	3·5 1·1	9·5 3·1	15·5 5·0
36	4 54·0	4 54·8	4 40·6	3·6 1·2	9·6 3·1	15·6 5·1
37	4 54·3	4 55·1	4 40·8	3·7 1·2	9·7 3·2	15·7 5·1
38	4 54·5	4 55·3	4 41·1	3·8 1·2	9·8 3·2	15·8 5·1
39	4 54·8	4 55·6	4 41·3	3·9 1·3	9·9 3·2	15·9 5·2
40	4 55·0	4 55·8	4 41·6	4·0 1·3	10·0 3·3	16·0 5·2
41	4 55·3	4 56·1	4 41·8	4·1 1·3	10·1 3·3	16·1 5·2
42	4 55·5	4 56·3	4 42·0	4·2 1·4	10·2 3·3	16·2 5·3
43	4 55·8	4 56·6	4 42·3	4·3 1·4	10·3 3·3	16·3 5·3
44	4 56·0	4 56·8	4 42·5	4·4 1·4	10·4 3·4	16·4 5·3
45	4 56·3	4 57·1	4 42·8	4·5 1·5	10·5 3·4	16·5 5·4
46	4 56·5	4 57·3	4 43·0	4·6 1·5	10·6 3·4	16·6 5·4
47	4 56·8	4 57·6	4 43·2	4·7 1·5	10·7 3·5	16·7 5·4
48	4 57·0	4 57·8	4 43·5	4·8 1·6	10·8 3·5	16·8 5·5
49	4 57·3	4 58·1	4 43·7	4·9 1·6	10·9 3·5	16·9 5·5
50	4 57·5	4 58·3	4 43·9	5·0 1·6	11·0 3·6	17·0 5·5
51	4 57·8	4 58·6	4 44·2	5·1 1·7	11·1 3·6	17·1 5·6
52	4 58·0	4 58·8	4 44·4	5·2 1·7	11·2 3·6	17·2 5·6
53	4 58·3	4 59·1	4 44·7	5·3 1·7	11·3 3·7	17·3 5·6
54	4 58·5	4 59·3	4 44·9	5·4 1·8	11·4 3·7	17·4 5·7
55	4 58·8	4 59·6	4 45·1	5·5 1·8	11·5 3·7	17·5 5·7
56	4 59·0	4 59·8	4 45·4	5·6 1·8	11·6 3·8	17·6 5·7
57	4 59·3	5 00·1	4 45·6	5·7 1·9	11·7 3·8	17·7 5·8
58	4 59·5	5 00·3	4 45·9	5·8 1·9	11·8 3·8	17·8 5·8
59	4 59·8	5 00·6	4 46·1	5·9 1·9	11·9 3·9	17·9 5·8
60	5 00·0	5 00·8	4 46·3	6·0 2·0	12·0 3·9	18·0 5·9

Computing GHA of a star

On 6 April 1981 you sight **Aldebaran** at 20h 18m 44s GMT. Compute the total GHA and declination for this sight.

GHA is completed by entering the left hand daily page of the Nautical Almanac for the dates of 4, 5, and 6 April (**reproduced on page 8-6**) The entering arguments for this page are the date (6 April), the desired **GHA (Aries),** and the **GMT hour (20).** We extract the GHA of Aries for a GMT time of 20h is **135° 00.9'.** This data is entered in the work form.

The m/s correction is completed by entering the Increments and Corrections pages (reproduced above with the minutes and seconds of GMT time that were not accounted GHA (h) **(18m 44s).**

We must **make sure** that our correction is taken from the **Aries column** and **NOT the Sun/Planets column**, as we did in our previous solutions. A minutes and seconds correction of **4° 41.8'** is entered in our form.

The SHA column is completed by entering the sidereal hour angle (SHA) of the observed star **Aldebaran.** By looking in the far right-hand column of the left hand page of the Nautical Almanac, you will see the names of **57 selected stars**. To the **right of their names, the SHA and Dec.** for each star is listed. At this point, you should recall from our previous discussion that we stated that the GHA of a star was obtained by applying the SHA of a star to the GHA of Aries. We find the SHA of **Aldebaran** to be **291° 17.8'** and enter it in the work form below. The sum is the GHA of the star **Aldebaran.** 431° 00.5' or 071° 00.5'.

Almanac (Aldebaran)			
GHA Ɣ	135° 00.9'	**DEC**	N 16° 28.2'
M/S Ɣ	4° 41.8'	**d (+ 1.0)**	0.0'
GHA Ɣ	139° 42.7'	**DEC**	N 16° 28.2'
SHA/ v corr	291° 17.8'		
GHA *	431° 00.5'		

End of Chapter problems

1. 02175. On 13 November 1981, at 0438 ZT, morning stars were observed and the vessel's position was determined to be LAT 22° 14.0' S, LONG 79° 23.0' E. Your vessel is steaming at 13.0 knots on a course of 242° T. A sextant observation of the Sun's lower limb is made at 0822 ZT. The chronometer reads 03h 20m 16s. The chronometer error is 01m 47s slow. What is the GHA of the Sun?

2. 02176. On 9 November 1981, at 0426 ZT, morning stars were observed and your position was determined to be LAT 25° 17.0' S, LONG 154° 16.0' E. Your vessel is steaming at 14.0 knots on course 066° T. A sextant observation of the Sun's lower limb is made at 0837 ZT. The chronometer reads 10h 35m 21s, and the sextant altitude (hs) is 50° 26.9'. The chronometer error is 01m 48s slow. What is the GHA of the Sun?

3. 02177. On 21 November 1981, at 0430 ZT, morning stars were observed, and the vessel's position was LAT 22° 14.0 S, LONG 79° 23.0' E. Your vessel is steaming at 14.5 knots on a course of 246° T. A sextant observation of the Sun's lower limb is made at 0816 ZT. The chronometer reads 03h 14m 16s, and the sextant altitude (hs) is 44° 29.2'. The chronometer error is 01m 47s slow. What is the GHA of the Sun?

4. 02178. On 26 July 1981, your 1901 ZT position is LAT 28° 28' N, LONG 157° 16 E when you take an observation of **Jupiter**. The chronometer at the time of the sight reads 08h 54m 34s and is 06m 24s slow. What is the GHA of the **Jupiter**?

5. 02180. On 12 April 1981, at 0515 ZT, morning stars were observed, and the vessel's position was determined to be LAT 21° 05' S, LONG 16° 30' W. Your vessel is steaming at 19 knots on a course of 278° T. A sextant observation of the Sun's lower limb is made at 0930 ZT. The chronometer reads 10h 28m 25s. The chronometer error is 2m 15s slow. What is the GHA of the Sun?

Celestial Problems
Sight Reduction

Problem #1 (USCG) (2175)		Sun's Lower Limb			Chapter 11	

Date:	13 Nov	Time		04:38	LAT:	22° 14.0' S
					LONG	079° 23.0' E
	ZT	08:22	CT	03:20:16	S - 242°	
	ZD	- 5:00	CE	+ 01:47	C-13.0 Kts	
	GMT	03:22	CCT	03:22:03		
			GMT	03:22:03	DR	0822-0438
					Time	0822
					LAT	22° 36.7' S
					LONG	078° 36.0' E

Almanac						
	GHA	228° 56.1'	DEC	S 17° 54.9'	Hs	45° 49.7'
	M/S	+ 5° 30.8'	D (+ .7)	+ .3'	Ic	- 1.0'
	GHA	234° 26.9'	DEC	S 17° 55.2'	Dip (61)	- 7.6'
	±SHA/v				Sum	- 8.6'
	Sum	234° 26.9'			Ha	45° 41.1'
	a λ	+ 78° 33.1'			Alt	+ 15.3'
	LHA	313° 00.0'			Ho	45° 56.4'

Calculating GHA

Problem # 2 (USCG) (2176)		Sun's Lower Limb			Chapter 11	

Date:	9 Nov	Time		04:26	LAT:	25° 17.0' S
					LONG	154° 16.0' E
	ZT	08:37	CT	10:35:21	S - 066°	
	ZD	- 10:00	CE	+ 01:48	C-14.0 Kts	
	GMT	22:37	CCT	10:37:09		
8 Nov			GMT	22:37:09	DR	0837-0426
					Time	0837
					LAT	24° 52.0' S
					LONG	155° 18.0' E

Almanac						
	GHA	154° 02.8'	DEC	S 16° 44.8'	Hs	50° 26.9'
	M/S	+ 9° 17.3'	D(+ .7)	+ .4'	Ic	- 1.5'
	GHA	163° 20.1'	DEC	S 16° 45.2'	Dip (56)	- 7.3'
	±SHA/v				Sum	- 8.8'
	Sum	163° 20.1'			Ha	50° 18.1'
	a λ	+ 155° 39.9'			Alt	+ 15.4'
	LHA	319° 00.0'			Ho	50° 33.5'

Calculating GHA

Problem # 3 (USCG) (2177)		Sun's Lower Limb		Chapter 11-1	
Date:	**21 Nov 1981**	Time	0430	**LAT:**	22° 14.0' S
				LONG	079° 23.0' E
	ZT	08:16	CT	03:14:16	**C-246°**
	ZD	-5:00	CE	+0:01:47	**S-14.5 Kts**
	GMT	03:16	CCT	03:16:03	
			GMT	03:16:03	**DR**	08:16 – 04:30
					Time	08:16
					LAT	22° 26.3' S
					LONG	078° 30.0' E

Almanac

GHA	228° 32.9'	DEC	S 19° 52.4'	Hs	44° 29.2'
M/S	+ 4° 00.8'	D (+.5)	+0.1'	Ic	-1.0'
GHA	232° 33.7'	DEC	S 19° 52.5	Dip (61)	-7.6'
±SHA/v				Sum	-8.6'
Sum	232° 33.7'			Ha	44°-20.6'
a λ	+ 78° 26.3'			Alt	+15.3'
LHA	311° 00.0'			Ho	44°35.9'

Calculating GHA

Problem # 4 (USCG) (2178)		Jupiter Limb		Chapter 11-2	
Date:	26 July	Time	1901	**LAT:**	28° 28.0' N
				LONG	157° 16.0' E
	ZT	19:01	CT	08:54:34	**C-**
	ZD	-10:00	CE	+0:06:24	**S-**
	GMT	09:01	CCT	09:00:58	
			GMT	09:00:58	**DR**	
					Time	
					LAT	
					LONG	

Almanac

GHA	253° 39.9'	DEC	S 0° 58.5'	Hs	33° 51.5'
M/S	+ 0° 14.5'	d (+0.2)		Ic	+2.8'
GHA	253° 54.4'	DEC	S 0° 58.5'	Dip (48)	-6.7'
±SHA/v				Sum	-3.9'
Sum	253° 54.4'			Ha	33° 47.6'
a λ	+ 157° 05.6'			Alt	-1.4'
LHA	51° 00.0'			Ho	33° 46.2'

Calculating GHA

Problem # 5 (USCG) (2180)		Sun's Lower Limb			Chapter 11 - 3	

Date:	12 Apr	Time		05:15	**LAT:**	21° 05.0' S
					LONG	016° 30.0' W
	ZT	09:30	**CT**	10:28:25	**C**-278°	
	ZD	+1:00	**CE**	+ 2:15	**S**-19 KTS	
	GMT	10:30	**CCT**	10:30:40		
			GMT	10:30:40	**DR**	09:30 – 05:15
					Time	09:30
					LAT	21° 53.0' s
					LONG	017° 56.0' W

Almanac

GHA	329° 47.9'	**DEC**	N 8° 43.3'	**Hs**	40° 15.9'		
M/S	+ 7° 40.0'	**d(+0.9)**	+ 0.5'	**Ic**	+2.5'		
GHA	337° 27.9'	**DEC**	N 8° - 43.8'	**Dip (57)**	-7.3'		
±SHA/v				**Sum**	-4.8'		
Sum	337° 27.9'			**Ha**	40° 11.1'		
a λ	+ 17° 27.9'			**Alt**	+14.9'		
LHA	320° 00.0'			**Ho**	40° 26.0'		

Additional USCG problems worked-out for this chapter can be found in **Celestial Navigation Calculations (Upon Oceans Endorsement) Worked-Out for Master 500 GT through 2nd Mate Unlimited, Volume 3, part 2, Chapter 6, Determining Position by Sight Reduction.**

LOCAL HOUR ANGLE (LHA)
Chapter 9

Local hour angle is the name given to the angle of arc (expressed in degrees, minutes, and tenths of minutes) of the celestial equator between the celestial meridian of a place and the hour circle of a heavenly body. It is **always measured westward** from the local meridian **through 360 degrees**.

Computing LHA

Note: This step is computed the same for all sights (sun, planets and stars). Now that we know how to determine total GHA, it is possible to compute LHA. Assume Longitude should be within 30' of the DR Longitude.

Now that the accurate GHA of the Sun (from previous problem on page 8-5) for **09h 15m 38s on 31 March** is known, it is possible to compute the LHA. By remembering the formula, **LHA = GHA - W longitude or LHA = GHA + E longitude**, you will realize that for our problem **LHA = 317° 52.2' (GHA) - 18° 10.0' (west longitude)**.The total is **299° 42.2'**. Looking ahead, we must realize that **only whole degrees of LHA** and latitude are used to enter the Sight reduction Tables, Pub 229, which is where we will get the information to complete the final portion of our form. You might recall that earlier in our discussion on deterring a line of position an **assumed position (AP)** was established. We also stated that this AP was selected according to certain requirements of convenience in calculating. Like any position, an **AP must have a latitude and longitude**. To meet the requirements of entering Pub 229 (described later), we must have a LHA and latitude that is stated in terms of **whole degrees**. Since our longitude is applied to GHA to determine LHA, this is where we "conveniently" obtain our whole degrees of LHA. **To do this, we must subtract an assumed longitude from GHA (when in west longitude)** that is closest to our DR longitude that will yield whole degrees. **In east longitude, we would add an assumed longitude to GHA** that is closest to our DR longitude and yield whole degrees. For our problem, we would **subtract** an assumed longitude of **17° 52.2'** since this would be closest to our DR longitude, and when subtracted would yield a **LHA of 300 degrees**. If we had been in **east longitude**, we would have **added** an **assumed longitude of 18° 07.8'**, which would yield a LHA of **336 degrees**.

In our work form (reproduced below) we enter our **GHA 317° 52.2'**

Almanac (Sun)			
GHA	313° 57.7'	**DEC**	N 4° 17.3'
M/S	3° 54.5'	**d (+ 1.0)**	+ 0.3'
GHA	317° 52.2'	**DEC**	N 4° 17.6'
a ʎ (- W)	17° 52.2'		
	300° 00.0'		

Almanac (Sun)			
GHA	313° 57.7'	DEC	N 4° 17.3'
M/S	3° 54.5'	d (+ 1.0)	+ 0.3'
GHA	317° 52.2'	DEC	N 4° 17.6'
a ⋏ (+ E)	18° 07.8'		
	336° 00.0'		

Since it is impossible to have an angular measurement **greater than 360°** (a whole circle), you must **subtract 360 degrees from any arc greater than 360 degrees**. There are times when you work with **west longitude** (which must be subtracted from GHA to obtain LHA) **that GHA will be smaller than the longitude**. When this is the case, **borrow 360° and add it to the GHA before subtracting west longitude.**

End of Chapter Questions

	GHA	Longitude	
1.	253° 17.2′	012° 15.7′ E	_____
2.	017° 55.9′	122° 54.6′ W	_____
3.	224° 11.0′	090° 34.1′ E	_____
4.	000° 00.1′	003° 22.3′ W	_____
5.	311° 32.5′	131° 34.2′ E	_____

ANSWERS

1. 266
2. 255
3. 315
4. 357
5. 083

Answers to LHA Problems:

LHA Calculation # 1.	
GHA	253° 17.2'
a ʎ (+ E)	012° 42.8'
LHA	**266° 00.0'**

LHA Calculation # 2	
GHA	017° 55.9'
+	360° 00.0'
	377° 55.0'
a ʎ (- W)	122° 55.0'
LHA	**255° 00.0'**

LHA Calculation # 3	
GHA	224° 11.0'
a ʎ (+ E)	090° 49.0'
LHA	**315° 00.0'**

LHA Calculation # 4	
GHA	000° 00.1'
(+)	360° 00.0'
	360° 00.1'
a ʎ (- W)	003° 00.1'
LHA	**357°00.0'**

LHA Calculation # 5	
GHA	311° 32.5'
a ʎ (+ E)	131° 27.5'
LHA	443° 00.0'
-	360° 00.0'
LHA	**083° 00.0'**

USING PUBLICATION 229
THE SIGHT REDUCTION TABLES
Chapter 10

The entering arguments for Pub 229 are **whole degrees of latitude and LHA**. The figure below shows a part of a page from Pub 229. We have determined that our **latitude is 27° N** and our **LHA is 335°**. By inspecting our page from Pub 229 we can see that **latitude** is listed **across the top of the page** and that whole degrees of **declination (Dec.)** are listed **down each side** of the page since, our true declination (True Dec.) is **N 4° l7.6'**, it should be apparent that we must **interpolate** between the **4° and 5°** Dec. entries under the 27° latitude column. In the column under 27° latitude, you can see three sub-columns that are (1) tabulated altitude (Hc), (2) altitude difference (d), and (3) azimuth angle (Z). The d sub-column is the rate of change for the Ha between the whole degree entries of Dec.

25°, 335° L.H.A.　　　LATITUDE SAME NAME AS DEC

Dec.	23° Hc	d	Z	24° Hc	d	Z	25° Hc	d	Z	26° Hc	d	Z	27° Hc	d	Z
°	° ′	′	°	° ′	′	°	° ′	′	°	° ′	′	°	° ′	′	°
0	56 32.3	+42.2	130.0	55 53.3	+43.2	131.1	55 13.5	+44.1	132.2	54 32.8	+45.0	133.2	53 51.3	+45.9	134.2
1	57 14.5	+41.2	128.7	56 36.5	+42.3	129.8	55 57.6	+43.4	131.0	55 17.8	+44.3	132.1	54 37.2	+45.2	133.1
2	57 55.7	+40.4	127.3	57 18.8	+41.6	128.5	56 41.0	+42.6	129.7	56 02.1	+43.7	130.9	55 22.4	+44.6	132.0
3	58 36.1	+39.4	125.9	58 00.4	+40.6	127.2	57 23.6	+41.8	128.4	56 45.8	+42.8	129.6	56 07.0	+43.9	130.8
4	59 15.5	+38.4	124.4	58 41.0	+39.7	125.8	58 05.4	+40.9	127.1	57 28.6	+42.1	128.4	56 50.9	+43.1	129.6
5	59 53.9	+37.3	122.9	59 20.7	+38.7	124.3	58 46.3	+39.9	125.7	58 10.7	+41.2	127.0	57 34.0	+42.3	128.3
6	60 31.2	+36.2	121.3	59 59.4	+37.6	122.8	59 26.2	+39.0	124.3	58 51.9	+40.2	125.6	58 16.3	+41.5	126.9
7	61 07.4	+34.9	119.7	60 37.0	+36.4	121.3	60 05.2	+37.8	122.7	59 32.1	+39.2	124.2	58 57.8	+40.5	125.6
8	61 42.3	+33.6	118.0	61 13.4	+35.2	119.6	60 43.0	+36.8	121.2	60 11.3	+38.2	122.7	59 38.3	+39.5	124.1
9	62 15.9	+32.2	116.2	61 48.6	+33.9	117.9	61 19.8	+35.5	119.5	60 49.5	+37.0	121.1	60 17.8	+38.5	122.6
10	62 48.1	+30.8	114.4	62 22.5	+32.5	116.2	61 55.3	+34.2	117.8	61 26.5	+35.8	119.5	60 56.3	+37.3	121.0
11	63 18.9	+29.2	112.5	62 55.0	+31.1	114.3	62 29.5	+32.8	116.1	62 02.3	+34.5	117.8	61 33.6	+36.1	119.4
12	63 48.1	+27.5	110.6	63 26.1	+29.5	112.4	63 02.3	+31.4	114.3	62 36.8	+33.2	116.0	62 09.7	+34.8	117.7
13	64 15.6	+25.8	108.5	63 55.6	+27.8	110.5	63 33.7	+29.8	112.4	63 10.0	+31.6	114.2	62 44.5	+33.5	116.0
14	64 41.4	+23.9	106.4	64 23.4	+26.1	108.4	64 03.5	+28.1	110.4	63 41.6	+30.1	112.3	63 18.0	+32.0	114.1
15	65 05.3	+22.1	104.3	64 49.5	+24.3	106.3	64 31.6	+26.4	108.4	64 11.7	+28.5	110.3	63 50.0	+30.4	112.2
16	65 27.4	+20.0 •	102.0	65 13.8	+22.3 •	104.2	64 58.0	+24.6	106.2	64 40.2	+26.7	108.3	64 20.4	+28.8	110.3
17	65 47.4	+17.9 •	99.8	65 36.1	+20.3 •	101.9	65 22.6	+22.6 •	104.1	65 06.9	+24.9	106.2	64 49.2	+27.0	108.2
18	66 05.3	+15.7 •	97.4	65 56.4	+18.2 •	99.6	65 45.2	+20.6 •	101.8	65 31.8	+23.0 •	104.0	65 16.2	+25.2	106.1
19	66 21.0	+13.5 •	95.0	66 14.6	+16.0 •	97.3	66 05.8	+18.5 •	99.5	65 54.8	+20.9 •	101.7	65 41.4	+23.3 •	103.9

The work form with the required data entered is shown to the below. **Space 3** is completed by entering the difference between the whole degree of declination that we will be using for our base (4 degrees in this case) and the actual value of our True Dec. This value is the increment of declination (Inc. Dec.) **17.6.** The d value that is listed below to our base Dec is placed in **Space 2,** you will notice that a positive (+) sign has been assigned because the positive (+) sign is listed in the d value sub-column. **(+43.1)** Our given Ho **is 57° 06.7'** and is entered in **Space 7.**

Publication 229							
	LHA 335°				**Dec N 4° 17.6'**		**Lat 27 N**
			(9)	**Z (4)**		129.6	**Z to ZN**
(1)	**Hc**	56° 50.6'	(10)	**Z (5)**		128.3	(14)
(2)	**d**	+ 43.1	(11)	**D**		- 1.3	
(3)	**Inc Dec (X)**	17.6'	(3)	**Inc Dec (X)**		17.6'	**ZN = Z**
(4)	**Inv (÷)**	60	(4)	**Inv (÷)**		60	**129.2**
(5)	**Correction**	+ 12.6	(12)	**Correction**		- .4	
(6)	**Hc**	57° 03.2'	(13)	**Z**		**129.2**	
(7)	**Ho**	57° 06.7'					
(8)	**a**	**3.5 T**					

Space 1 is completed by entering the tabulated altitude (Hc) from the Pub 229 page that we entered with our latitude and LHA. (56° 50.6')

Space 4 is completed by entering the interval (in minutes) between the next tabulated entries. In this case 60 minutes or 1 degree of declination.

Space 5 is completed by finding the product of spaces 2, 3 and 4. (**+ 12.6**)

Space 6 is completed by applying the correction in space 5 to the Hc in space 1. In this case, it will be added since the d value was positive. (**57° 06.7**)

Space 8 is completed by finding the difference between spaces 6 and 7. You will notice that our intercept is away (T) since the computed value is less than the observed value. (**3.5 T**)

Space 9 is completed by entering the azimuth angle (Z) from the Pub 229 page that we have entered with our LHA (335°), Declination (4°) and latitude (27°).

Space 10 is completed by entering the azimuth angle (Z) for the next higher value Dec (5°) on the Pub 229 page that we have entered with our latitude and LHA

Space 11 is completed by finding the product of spaces 11, 3 and 4. (**-.4**)

Space 13 is the algebraic sum of spaces 9 and 12. (**129.2**)

The final space (14) is completed by converting the azimuth angle. (Z) to azimuth (Zn). This procedure is very simple since the following set of rules is given at the **top of every left-hand page of pub 229 for <u>north</u> latitude** and the **bottom of every right-hand page for <u>south</u> latitude.** Since we are North latitude and our LHA greater than 180 degrees, the Zn = Z. (129.2)

North Latitudes		South latitudes	
LHA greater than 180 degrees	Zn = Z	LHA greater than 180 degrees	Zn = 180 deg.-Z
LHA less than 180 degrees	Zn = 360 deg.-Z	LHA less than 180 degrees	Zn = 180 deg. +Z

End of Chapter Questions

1. 02176. On 9 November 1981, at 0426 ZT, morning stars were observed and your position was determined to be LAT 25° 17.0' S, LONG 154° 16.0' E. Your vessel is steaming at 14.0 knots on course 066° T. A sextant observation of the Sun's lower limb is made at 0837 ZT. The chronometer reads 10h 35m 21s, and the sextant altitude (hs) is 50° 26.9'. The index error is 1.5' on the arc, and the chronometer error is 01m 48s slow. Your height of eye on the bridge is 56.0 feet. What is the observed altitude (Ho) and azimuth (Zn) of this sight using the assumed position?

A. 50° 18.1', 086.3° T
B. 50° 18.1', 093.7° T
C. 50° 33.5', 085.9° T
D. 50° 33.5', 093.7° T

2. 02177. On 21 November 1981, at 0430 ZT, morning stars were observed, and the vessel's position was LAT 22° 14.0 S, LONG 79° 23.0' E. Your vessel is steaming at 14.5 knots on a course of 246° T. A sextant observation of the Sun's lower limb is made at 0816 ZT. The chronometer reads 03h 14m 16s, and the sextant altitude (hs) is 44° 29.2'. The index error is 1.0' on the arc, and the chronometer error is 01m 47s slow. Your height of eye is 61.0 feet. What is the azimuth (Zn) and intercept (a) of this sight using the assumed position?

A. Zn 084.2°, a 6.6A
B. Zn 084.2°, a 6.6T
C. Zn 095.6°, a 6.6A
D. Zn 095.6°, a 6.6T

3. 02178. On 26 July 1981, your 1901 ZT position is LAT 28° 28' N, LONG 157° 16 E when you take an observation of Jupiter. The chronometer at the time of the sight reads 08h 54m 34s and is 06m 24s slow. The sextant altitude (hs) is 33° 51.5'. The index error is 2.8 off the arc, and the height of eye is 48 feet. What are the azimuth (Zn) and intercept (a) for this sight using the assumed position?

A. Zn 110.8°, a 32.0 T
B. Zn 249.2°, a 32.0 A
C. Zn 249.2°, a 34.2 T
D. Zn 290.8°, a 44.2 A

4. 02180. On 12 April 1981, at 0515 ZT, morning stars were observed, and the vessel's position was determined to be LAT 21° 05' S, LONG 16° 30' W. Your vessel is steaming at 19 knots on a course of 278° T. A sextant observation of the Sun's lower limb is made at 0930 ZT. The chronometer reads 10h 28m 25s, and the sextant altitude (hs) is 40° 15.9'. The index error is 2.5' off the arc, and the chronometer error is 2m 15s slow. Your height of eye is 57.0 feet. What are the intercept (a) and azimuth (Zn) from the assumed are the intercept (a) and azimuth (Zn) from the assumed position of this sight?

A. Zn 057.0°, a 15.4T
B. Zn 057.7°, a 17.7A
C. Zn 122.3°, a 17.7A
D. Zn 123.0°, a 22.7A

5. 02181. On 4 June 1981, at 0630 ZT, morning stars were observed, and the vessel's position was determined to be LAT 26° 15' S, LONG 121° 20' W. Your vessel is steaming at 13.0 knots on a course of 246° T. A sextant observation of the Sun's lower limb is made at 0915 ZT. The chronometer reads 05h 14m 27s, and the sextant altitude is 25° 57.8'. The index error is 2.1' off the arc, and the chronometer error is 0m 53s slow. Your height of eye is 39.0 feet. What is the intercept (a) and azimuth (Zn) of this sight using the assumed position and azimuth (Zn) of this sight using the assumed position method?

A. Zn 044.9°, a 1.7A
B. Zn 044.9°, a 2.5T
C. Zn 135.1°, a 1.7A
D. Zn 135.1°, a 2.5T

Answers

1. 02176 C
2. 02177 D
3. 02178 C
4. 02180 B
5. 02181 B

Celestial Problems
Sight Reduction

Problem # 1 (USCG) (2176)	Sun's Lower Limb	Chapter 11

Date:	9 Nov	Time	04:26	LAT:	25° 17.0' S
				LONG	154° 16.0' E
	ZT	08:37	CT	10:35:21	S - 066°
	ZD	- 10:00	CE	+ 01:48	C-14.0 Kts
	GMT	22:37	CCT	10:37:09	
8 Nov			GMT	22:37:09	DR	0837-0426
				Time	0837
				LAT	24° 52.0' S
				LONG	155° 18.0' E

Almanac

GHA	154° 02.8'	DEC	S 16° 44.8'	Hs	50° 26.9'
M/S	+ 9° 17.3'	D(+ .7)	+ .4'	Ic	- 1.5'
GHA	163° 20.1'	DEC	S 16° 45.2'	Dip (56)	- 7.3'
±SHA/v				Sum	- 8.8'
Sum	163° 20.1'			Ha	50° 18.1'
a λ	155° 39.9'			Alt	+ 15.4'
LHA	319° 00.0'			Ho	50° 33.5'

LHA	319°	DEC	S 16° 45.2'	LAT	25° S	SAME

Publication 229

			Z (16)	095.1	Z to ZN
Hc	50° 42.8'	Z (17)	093.7	
d	+ 20.1	d	- 1.4	ZN=180-Z
Inc Dec (X)	45.2'	Inc Dec (X)	45.2'	180 - 094.0 = 086.0
Inv (÷)	60	Inv (÷)	60	**086.0**
Correction	+ 15.1	Correction	- 1.1	
Hc	50° 57.9''	Z	**094.0**	
Ho	50° 33.5'			
a	**24.4 A**			

Notes:

ANSWER   C

Celestial Problems
Sight Reduction

Problem # 2 (USCG) (2177)		Sun's Lower Limb		Chapter 10

Date:	21 Nov 1981		Time	0430	LAT:	22° 14.0' S
					LONG	079° 23.0' E
	ZT	08:16	CT	03:14:16	C-246°	
	ZD	-5:00	CE	+0:01:47	S-14.5 Kts	
	GMT	03:16	CCT	03:16:03		
			GMT	03:16:03	DR	08:16 – 04:30
					Time	08:16
					LAT	22° 36.3' S
					LONG	078° 30.0' E

		DEC	S 19° 52.4'	Hs	44° 29.2'
GHA	228° 32.9'	D (+.5)	+0.1'	Ic	-1.0'
M/S	+ 4° 00.8'	DEC	S 19° 52.5	Dip (61)	-7.6'
GHA	232° 33.7'			Sum	-8.6'
±SHA/v				Ha	44° 20.6'
Sum	232° 33.7'			Alt	+15.3'
a λ	+78° 26.3'			Ho	44° 35.9'
LHA	311° 00.0'				

LHA	311°	DEC	S 19° 52.5'	LAT	23 S	SAME

			Z (19)	085.4	Z to ZN
Hc	44° 17.0'	Z (20)	084.0	
d	+14.0	d	-1.4	ZN=180-Z
Inc Dec (X)	52.5	Inc Dec (X)	52.5	
Inv (÷)	60	Inv (÷)	60	180-84.2=
Correction	+12.3	Correction	-1.2	**095.8**
Hc	44° 29.3'	Z	**084.2**	
Ho	44° 35.9'			
a	**6.6 T**			

Notes:

ANSWER   D

Celestial Problems
Sight Reduction

Problem # 3   (USCG)   (2178)   JUPITER   Chapter 10

Date:	26 July	Time		1901	LAT:		28° 28.0' N	
					LONG		157° 16.0' E	
	ZT	19:01	CT	08:54:34		C-		
	ZD	-10:00	CE	+0:06:24		S-		
	GMT	09:01	CCT	09:00:58				
			GMT	09:00:58	DR			
					Time			
					LAT			
					LONG			

Almanac

GHA	253° 39.9'	DEC	S 0° 58.5'	Hs		33° 51.5'	
M/S	+ 0° 14.5'	d (+0.2)		Ic		+2.8'	
GHA	253° 54.4'	DEC	S 0° 58.5'	Dip (48)		-6.7'	
±SHA/v				Sum		-3.9'	
Sum	253° 54.4'			Ha		33° 47.6'	
a λ	157° 05.6'			Alt		-1.4'	
LHA	51° 00.0'			Ho		33° 46.2'	

LHA	51°	DEC	S 0° 58.5'	LAT	28 N	CONTRARY

Publication 229

					Z to ZN
			Z (0)	110.8	
Hc	33° 45.4'	Z (1)	111.8		
d	-34.2	d	+ 1.0		ZN=180-Z
Inc Dec (X)	58.5	Inc Dec (X)	58.5		360 - 111.8 =
Inv (÷)	60	Inv (÷)	60		**248.2**
Correction	-33.3	Correction	+ 1.0		
Hc	33° 12.1'	Z	**111.8**		
Ho	33° 46.2'				
a	**34.1 T**				

Notes:

ANSWER   C

Celestial Problems
Sight Reduction

Problem # 4 (USCG) (2180)	Sun's Lower Limb	Chapter 10

Date:	**12 Apr**	Time	05:15	LAT:	21° 05.0' S
				LONG	016° 30.0' W
	ZT	09:30	**CT** 10:28:25	**C**-278°	
	ZD	+1:00	**CE** + 2:15	**S**-19 KTS	
	GMT	10:30	**CCT** 10:30:40		
			GMT 10:30:40	**DR**	09:30 – 05:15
				Time	09:30
				LAT	20° 53.0' s
				LONG	017° 56.0' W

Almanac

GHA	329° 47.9'	**DEC**	N 8° 43.3'	**Hs**	40° 15.9'
M/S	+ 7° 40.0'	**d(+0.9)**	+ 0.5'	**Ic**	+2.5'
GHA	337° 27.9'	**DEC**	N 8° 43.8'	**Dip (57)**	-7.3'
±SHA/v				**Sum**	-4.8'
Sum	337° 27.9'			**Ha**	40° 11.1'
a λ	+17° 27.9'			**Alt**	+14.9'
LHA	320° 00.0'			**Ho**	40° 26.0'

LHA	320°	**DEC**	N 8° 43.8'	**LAT**	21 S	CONTRARY

Publication 229

					Z to ZN
		Z (8)	122.3		
Hc	41° 10.4'	**Z (9)**	123.3		
d	-36.6	**d**	+1.0		ZN = 180 - Z
Inc Dec (X)	43.8	**Inc Dec (X)**	43.8		180 – 123.0 = 057.0
Inv (÷)	60	**Inv (÷)**	60		**057.0**
Correction	-26.7	**Correction**	+0.7		
Hc	40° 43.7'	**Z**	**123.0**		
Ho	40° 26.0'				
a	**17.7A**				

Notes:

In USCG used closest Z

ANSWER   B

Celestial Problems
Sight Reduction

Problem # 5 (USCG) (2181)		Sun's Lower Limb			Chapter 10	

Date:	4 June		Time	06:30	LAT:	26° 15.0' S
					LONG	121° 20.0' W
	ZT	09:15	CT	05:14:27	C-246°	
	ZD	+8:00	CE	+0:53:	S-13 KTS	
	GMT	17:15	CCT	05:15:20		
			GMT	17:15:20	DR	09:15 – 06:30
					Time	09:15
					LAT	26° 29.5' S
					LONG	121° 55.0' W

Almanac

GHA	75° 26.1'	DEC	N 22° 28.6'	Hs		25° 57.8'
M/S	+ 3° 50.0'	d(+0.3)	+0.1'	Ic		+2.1'
GHA	79° 16.1'	DEC	N 22° 28.7'	Dip (39)		-6.1'
±SHA/v				Sum		-4.0'
Sum	79° 16.1'			Ha		25° 53.8'
a λ	- 122° 16.1'			Alt		+14.0'
LHA	317° 00.0'			Ho		26° 07.8'

LHA	317°	DEC	N 22° 28.7'	LAT	26 S	CONTRARY

Publication 229

			Z (22)	135.1	Z to ZN
Hc	26° 26.4'		Z (23)	135.8	
d	-43.9		d	+0.7	ZN = 180 - Z
Inc Dec (X)	28.7		Inc Dec (X)	28.7	180 – 135.4 = 044.6
Inv (÷)	60		Inv (÷)	60	**044.6**
Correction	-21.0		Correction	+0.3	
Hc	26° 05.4'		Z	135.4	
Ho	26° 07.8'				
a	**2.4 T**				

Notes:

In USCG used closest Z

ANSWER   B

Additional USCG problems worked-out for this chapter can be found in **Celestial Navigation Calculations (Upon Oceans Endorsement) Worked-Out for Master 500 GT through 2nd Mate Unlimited, Volume 3, part 2, Chapter 6, Determining Position By Sight Reduction.**

THE UNIVERSAL PLOTTING SHEET
Chapter 11

Universal plotting sheets are printed by DMAHTC. They are a **standard size**; part of the sheet is printed in advance. It has a **central compass rose, mid-parallel**; and **the central meridian is graduated in minutes of latitude**. In using the sheet it is necessary only to label the meridians and draw an oblique line and from it determine the interval and draw in and label additional parallels.

This sheet uses a constant relationship of latitude to longitude over the .entire sheet and fails to allow for the ellipticity of the earth. For our purposes and the small area involved this is not an important consideration. If we reduce our sights and plot them correctly we will achieve good results.

SETTING UP THE UNIVERSAL PLOTTING SHEET:

Given the DR position of latitude 32° 42.0' N, longitude 119° 35.0' W.

Step One:

Labeling Latitudes

Determine the mid-latitude that you will need to use. Using the DR given we would label the mid-latitude as 33 N, labeling the next above 34 and below as 32 N. **Remember: if we were in the southern latitudes this would be reversed.**

Step Two:

Plotting Longitudes

Using the numbering on the outside right of the compass rose; we find 33 north and south. Drawing a line with a straight edge through these two points you now have a longitude line of the appropriate dimension. Using our dividers we duplicate and label the longitudes as many times as necessary. Label the longitude line 120 W, the next to the right 119° W, and 121° W to the left. **Once again the longitudes would be reversed, if we were in eastern longitudes.**

Step Three:

Using the longitude distance measured along the mid-latitude line to determine the mid-latitude on the longitude scale in the lower right-hand side of the Universal Plotting Sheet. By doing it in this way you ensure that two scales match.

Your plotting sheet is now set up for our problem, using the DR given Lat 32° 42.0' N   Long 19° 35.0' W mid-latitude as 33 N.

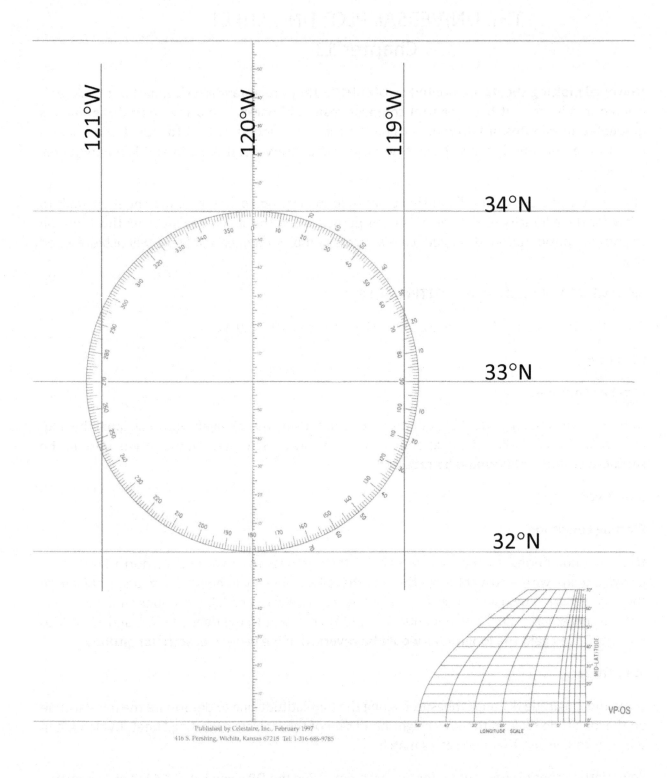

121°W

120°W

119°W

34°N

33°N

32°N

Published by Celestaire, Inc., February 1997
416 S. Pershing, Wichita, Kansas 67218 Tel: 1-316-686-9785

MID-LATITUDE

VP-OS

50'   40'   30'   20'   10'   0'   10'
LONGITUDE   SCALE

Example of using the plotting sheet Longitude scale

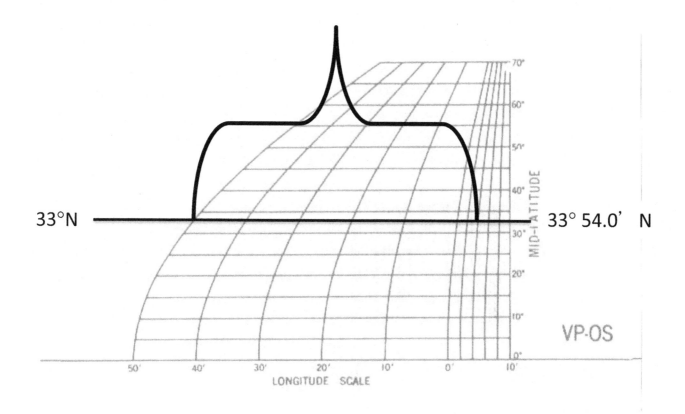

33°N   33° 54.0' N

VP-OS

MID-LATITUDE

70°
60°
50°
40°
30°
20°
10°
0°

50'   40'   30'   20'   10'   0'   10'
LONGITUDE   SCALE

Local Apparent Noon (LAN)
Chapter 12

Local apparent noon (LAN) is a sight taken of **the sun the instant it transits an observer's meridian**. At that time the sun is at its highest altitude. The LAN lines of position coincide with the ship's latitude.

OBSERVING LAN

Under most circumstances, there is a period in which the change of-altitude, as the sun approaches or recedes from the meridian, is too slight to be perceptible. **With altitudes up to about 50 degrees, the sun may appear to "hang" for several minutes**. With altitudes above 80 degrees, the change is much more perceptible.

The meridian altitude of the sun is observed in a number of ways. Two of these methods are discussed in the following text.

Following to Maximum Altitude

The oldest method of determining meridian altitude of the sun, and the one used most commonly is known as following to maximum altitude. It is recommended because of its adaptability to various conditions, and because its use develops an insight into how the altitude varies near the time of apparent noon.

At approximately 10 minutes before watch time of LAN, the observer contacts the sun's lower limb with the horizon in the sextant. He then swings the sextant from side to side and adjusts it until the sun, seen moving in an arc, just touches the horizon at the lowest part of the arc. This procedure is known as swinging the arc, which was described earlier in this chapter.

As the sun continues rising, a widening space appears between its lower limb and the horizon. By adjusting the tangent screw, the observer keeps this space closed and maintains the sun in contact with the horizon. The change in altitude becomes slower and slower, until the sun "hangs." While it is hanging, the observer swings the sextant to make certain of accurate contact with the horizon. He continues the observations until the sun dips, which is a signal that the sun is beginning to lose altitude. The sextant then shows the maximum altitude attached.

Numerous Sights

The method of taking numerous sights is a modification of the maximum altitude method. It is useful under conditions where heavy seas, clouds, and the like may make steady observation impossible. Well before watch time of LAN, the observer begins taking a series of altitudes. Their number depends on the difficulties of the situation and the possible error in computed time of transit. He reads off the altitudes to a recording assistant, turning the tangent screw slightly after each observation to ensure that the next altitude is an independent sight. Observations are discontinued when the altitude definitely shows signs of decreasing.

Under favorable conditions, a series of skillfully taken observations may show an occasional erratic deviation from the normal gradual rise and fall. After sights showing a radical difference from the preceding or succeeding series are discarded, however, the hang should become evident, and it should be possible to judge the maximum altitude. The figure selected will probably be less than the altitude shown in one observation and more than that next below it. **The result should give latitude with an error no more than 1 minute of arc**. This reading is considerably more accurate than could be obtained by a single sight under the conditions described.

1984 MARCH 28, 29, 30 (WED., THURS., FRI.)

G.M.T.	SUN G.H.A.	SUN Dec.	MOON G.H.A.	MOON v	MOON Dec.	MOON d	MOON H.P.	Lat.	Twilight Naut.	Twilight Civil	Sunrise	Moonrise 28	Moonrise 29	Moonrise 30	Moonrise 31
30 00	178 51.5 N 3 45.3		202 09.8 15.7		S11 42.5 11.6		54.0	N 40	18 21	18 49	19 21	14 31	15 31	16 30	17 29
01	193 51.7	46.3	216 44.5 15.8		11 30.9 11.7		54.0	35	18 19	18 44	19 14	14 42	15 39	16 35	17 31
02	208 51.9	47.3	231 19.3 15.8		11 19.2 11.6		54.0	30	18 17	18 41	19 09	14 51	15 46	16 39	17 32
03	223 52.0 ··	48.2	245 54.1 15.8		11 07.6 11.8		54.0	20	18 14	18 36	19 01	15 08	15 58	16 47	17 35
04	238 52.2	49.2	260 28.9 15.9		10 55.8 11.7		54.0	N 10	18 11	18 32	18 56	15 22	16 08	16 53	17 38
05	253 52.4	50.2	275 03.8 15.8		10 44.1 11.8		54.0	0	18 08	18 29	18 53	15 35	16 18	16 59	17 40
06	268 52.6 N 3 51.1		289 38.6 16.0		S10 32.3 11.9		54.0	S 10	18 05	18 26	18 51	15 48	16 28	17 05	17 42
07	283 52.8	52.1	304 13.6 15.9		10 20.4 11.9		54.0	20	18 03	18 25	18 50	16 02	16 38	17 12	17 44
08	298 53.0	53.1	318 48.5 16.0		10 08.5 11.9		54.0	30	18 00	18 24	18 52	16 18	16 50	17 19	17 47
F 09	313 53.2 ··	54.1	333 23.5 16.0		9 56.6 12.0		54.0	35	17 58	18 24	18 53	16 27	16 56	17 23	17 49
R 10	328 53.4	55.0	347 58.5 16.0		9 44.6 12.0		54.0	40	17 57	18 24	18 55	16 37	17 04	17 28	17 50
I 11	343 53.5	56.0	2 33.5 16.1		9 32.6 12.0		54.0	45	17 55	18 24	18 58	16 49	17 13	17 33	17 52
D 12	358 53.7 N 3 57.0		17 08.6 16.1		S 9 20.6 12.1		54.0	S 50	17 52	18 25	19 02	17 04	17 23	17 40	17 55
A 13	13 53.9	57.9	31 43.7 16.1		9 08.5 12.1		54.0	52	17 51	18 25	19 04	17 11	17 28	17 43	17 56
Y 14	28 54.1	58.9	46 18.8 16.2		8 56.4 12.2		54.0	54	17 50	18 25	19 06	17 18	17 33	17 46	17 57
15	43 54.3 3 59.9		60 54.0 16.1		8 44.2 12.2		54.0	56	17 49	18 26	19 09	17 27	17 39	17 50	17 58
16	58 54.5 4 00.8		75 29.1 16.2		8 32.0 12.2		54.0	58	17 48	18 26	19 12	17 36	17 46	17 53	18 00
17	73 54.7	01.8	90 04.3 16.2		8 19.8 12.3		54.0	S 60	17 46	18 27	19 16	17 47	17 53	17 58	18 01
18	88 54.9 N 4 02.8		104 39.5 16.3		S 8 07.5 12.3		54.0								
19	103 55.0	03.8	119 14.8 16.2		7 55.2 12.3		54.0								
20	118 55.2	04.7	133 50.0 16.3		7 42.9 12.4		54.0								
21	133 55.4 ··	05.7	148 25.3 16.3		7 30.5 12.4		54.0								
22	148 55.6	06.7	163 00.6 16.3		7 18.1 12.4		54.0								
23	163 55.8	07.6	177 35.9 16.3		7 05.7 12.5		54.1								

	SUN	MOON			
Day	Eqn. of Time 00° / 12°	Mer. Pass.	Mer. Pass. Upper / Lower	Age	Phase
	m s / m s	h m	h m / h m	d	
28	05 11 / 05 02	12 05	09 24 / 21 46	26	
29	04 52 / 04 43	12 05	10 08 / 22 29	27	
30	04 34 / 04 25	12 04	10 49 / 23 10	28	◑

S.D. 16.0 d 1.0   S.D. 14.7 14.7 14.7

Latitude by LAN

Our observed time of LAN was 12 hours 21minutes and 00 seconds local. The sextant reading at that time was 57° 16.4'. Below we show spaces 14 through 19 of the work form with the required data entered.

ZT LAN (OBS)	(14)	12 21 00
ZD	(15)	+1
GMT	(16)	13 21 00
Tab Dec.	(17)	N 3 57.9
d# / d Corr	(18)	(+1.0) +.4
True Dec.	(19)	N 3 58.3

The information for space 14 is given **(12-21-00)**

Space 15 is completed by entering the zone description of our stan9ard meridian (+1)

Space 16 is completed by applying the zone description in space 15 to the zone time in space 14. **(13-21-00)**

The next part of the work form is completed by using the Nautical Almanac. Notice that for each day there are hourly entries for the GHA and the declination (Dec.) of the sun.

The entry of 13 hours on 30 March is found on page 12-2 and information is entered on the work form as follows:

The Dec. for 13 hours **(N3° 57.9')** is entered in space 17.

Remain on this page and move down the Sun Dec. column to the bottom of the page. Determine as you move down this column whether the Dec. increases or decreases toward the bottom of the page. In a box at the bottom of the column is a small (italicized) letter d followed by 1.0; this is called the d# and is entered as follows:

The value of d **(+ 1.0)** is entered on the left side of space 18, leaving room to enter the d correction (corr) later. The d value IS NOT the correction itself but will be used later to locate the correction in the increment and correction pages. The d value is as signed a positive (+) or a **negative (-)** sign according to whether the Dec. increases (+) or decreases (-) as you move toward the bottom of the page dec. values on page 12-2 increase so a (+) has been assigned to d#

Remember Dec. in space 17 has been entered for the even hour of 1300, but GMT has 21m 00s remaining. An increment of arc for d corr is necessary to account for the remaining minutes and seconds of time. The increments and corrections page showing 21 minutes is shown below.

20ᵐ INCREMENTS AND CORRECTIONS 21ᵐ

20	SUN PLANETS	ARIES	MOON	v or d	Corrⁿ	v or d	Corrⁿ	v or d	Corrⁿ	21	SUN PLANETS	ARIES	MOON	v or d	Corrⁿ	v or d	Corrⁿ	v or d	Corrⁿ
00	5 00·0	5 00·8	4 46·3	0·0	0·0	6·0	2·1	12·0	4·1	00	5 15·0	5 15·9	5 00·7	0·0	0·0	6·0	2·2	12·0	4·3
01	5 00·3	5 01·1	4 46·6	0·1	0·0	6·1	2·1	12·1	4·1	01	5 15·3	5 16·1	5 00·9	0·1	0·0	6·1	2·2	12·1	4·3
02	5 00·5	5 01·3	4 46·8	0·2	0·1	6·2	2·1	12·2	4·2	02	5 15·5	5 16·4	5 01·1	0·2	0·1	6·2	2·2	12·2	4·4
03	5 00·8	5 01·6	4 47·0	0·3	0·1	6·3	2·2	12·3	4·2	03	5 15·8	5 16·6	5 01·4	0·3	0·1	6·3	2·3	12·3	4·4
04	5 01·0	5 01·8	4 47·3	0·4	0·1	6·4	2·2	12·4	4·2	04	5 16·0	5 16·9	5 01·6	0·4	0·1	6·4	2·3	12·4	4·4
05	5 01·3	5 02·1	4 47·5	0·5	0·2	6·5	2·2	12·5	4·3	05	5 16·3	5 17·1	5 01·8	0·5	0·2	6·5	2·3	12·5	4·5
06	5 01·5	5 02·3	4 47·8	0·6	0·2	6·6	2·3	12·6	4·3	06	5 16·5	5 17·4	5 02·1	0·6	0·2	6·6	2·4	12·6	4·5
07	5 01·8	5 02·6	4 48·0	0·7	0·2	6·7	2·3	12·7	4·3	07	5 16·8	5 17·6	5 02·3	0·7	0·3	6·7	2·4	12·7	4·6
08	5 02·0	5 02·8	4 48·2	0·8	0·3	6·8	2·3	12·8	4·4	08	5 17·0	5 17·9	5 02·6	0·8	0·3	6·8	2·4	12·8	4·6
09	5 02·3	5 03·1	4 48·5	0·9	0·3	6·9	2·4	12·9	4·4	09	5 17·3	5 18·1	5 02·8	0·9	0·3	6·9	2·5	12·9	4·6
10	5 02·5	5 03·3	4 48·7	1·0	0·3	7·0	2·4	13·0	4·4	10	5 17·5	5 18·4	5 03·0	1·0	0·4	7·0	2·5	13·0	4·7
11	5 02·8	5 03·6	4 49·0	1·1	0·4	7·1	2·4	13·1	4·5	11	5 17·8	5 18·6	5 03·3	1·1	0·4	7·1	2·5	13·1	4·7
12	5 03·0	5 03·8	4 49·2	1·2	0·4	7·2	2·5	13·2	4·5	12	5 18·0	5 18·9	5 03·5	1·2	0·4	7·2	2·6	13·2	4·7
13	5 03·3	5 04·1	4 49·4	1·3	0·4	7·3	2·5	13·3	4·5	13	5 18·3	5 19·1	5 03·8	1·3	0·5	7·3	2·6	13·3	4·8
14	5 03·5	5 04·3	4 49·7	1·4	0·5	7·4	2·5	13·4	4·6	14	5 18·5	5 19·4	5 04·0	1·4	0·5	7·4	2·7	13·4	4·8

Notice that the page also contains increments and corrections for 20 minutes.

Using the 21minute table, look at the three columns labeled v or d corr. Each of these columns has two sub-columns. The left sub-column (using smaller print) contains d #'s. The right sub-column (using larger print) contains d corrections. The d# in our problem is + 1.0. Look down the d# sub-column to 1.0 and you will find a corresponding d correction of 0.4. The d correction, 0.4 will have a positive (+) sign because the d# is positive.

The d correction (+ 0.4) is entered on the right side of space 18.

Space 19 is completed by applying the d correction in space 18 (adding) to the tabulated declination in space 17.

In the next series of steps, we will be correcting our sextant height **(hs) of 57°16.4'**. The index correction (IC) has been observed as **(+) 1.2.** Your ship's bridge height is 49.9 feet (15.2 meters). **NOTE: On the Coast Guard exam it is normal to be given Ho and not Hs.** Our work form shows spaces 20 through 26 with the required data entered.

A2 ALTITUDE CORRECTION TABLES 10°-90°—SUN, STARS, PLANETS

OCT.—MAR. SUN APR.—SEPT.						STARS AND PLANETS			DIP			
App. Alt.	Lower Limb	Upper Limb	App. Alt.	Lower Limb	Upper Limb	App. Alt.	Corrⁿ	App. Alt.	Additional Corrⁿ	Ht. of Eye	Corrⁿ	Ht. of Eye Corrⁿ / Ht. of Eye Corrⁿ

App. Alt. = Apparent altitude = Sextant altitude corrected for index error and dip.

12-4

The information for space 20 is given. **(+ 1.2)** Space 21 is completed by taking the height of your ship's bridge (height of eye) and entering the altitude correction tables of the Nautical Almanac. These tables are located inside the front cover. Page 17-4 illustrates the portion of the table that we will be using. The dip correction for space 21 is **(-) 6.9**.

IC	(20)	(+)1.2
D	(21)	(-)6.9
Sum	(22)	(-)5.7
hs	(23)	57 - 16.4
ha	(24)	57 - 10.7
Alt Corr	(25)	(+) 15.6
Ho	(26)	57 - 26.3

Space 22 is completed by finding the sum of the values in spaces 20 and 21. The information for space 23 is given. **(57° 16.4')**

Space 24 is completed by applying the value in space 22 to the hs (space 23). The result is the apparent altitude **(ha) 57° 10.7'**.

Space 25 is completed by entering the altitude correction tables (page 12-4) with the Ha. Since LAN is observed with the lower limb on the horizon, we will enter the column · for the lower limb. The apparent altitude (App. Alt) correction is **(+) 15.6**. The apparent altitude corrections for the sun in the tables include the effects of Semidiameter, parallax, and mean refraction.

Space 26 is completed by applying the apparent altitude correction (space 25 to the Ha space 24). The result is the corrected sextant (Ho).

Before we can finish the final steps of the LAN work form, we must give you some formulas.

1. Latitude and declination of different names: **L = z-d**

2. Latitude and declination of the same names with L less than d: **L = d-z**

3. Latitude and declination of the same name with L greater than d: **L=z+d**

The final work form with the required data entered is shown below.

Space 27 is completed by entering **89 degrees 60' (90 degrees)**. This arc is the arc from the horizon to the zenith.

89° 60'	(27)	89°60'
HO (-)	(28)	57° 26.3'
Z Dist	(29)	32° 33.7'
True Dec .	(30)	N 3° 58.3'
LAT	(31)	36°31.0'
Time	(32)	12 21 00

The information (Ho) for space 28 is given in space 26 of our previous work form. Space 29 is completed by subtracting the value in space 28 from the value in space 27.

The zenith distance (Z Dist) is shown as (z) on the work form.

The information (True Dec.) for space 30 is given in space 19 of our previous work form on page 12-2.

By using the formulas, we established earlier and the information given (latitude and declination the same name and latitude greater than declination). **(At the same time, we can also see that the only way to arrive at Latitude near our DR Latitude would be to add. You will find that in most cases this will be the simplest way to determine if you should add or subtract the true Dec.)** We know that space 31 will be completed by adding the values in spaces 29 and 30. **(36° 31.0')** Space 32 is completed by entering the time of observation. **(12-21-00)**

Once again please, **NOTE: On the Coast Guard exams it is normal to be given Ho and not Hs.**

End of Chapter USCG Questions

1. 00806. On 15 November 1981, your 0913 zone time fix gives you a position of LAT 22° 30.0' N, LONG 68° 28.0' W. Your vessel is on course 164° T, and your speed is 13.5 knots. Local apparent noon (LAN) occurs at 1218 zone time at which time a meridian altitude of the Sun's lower limb is observed. The observed altitude (Ho) for this sight is 49° 46.0'. What is the calculated latitude at local apparent noon (LAN)?

A. LAT 21° 36.0' N
B. LAT 21° 38.6' N
C. LAT 21° 40.0' N
D. LAT 21° 42.5' N

2. 00807. On 12 February 1981, your 0542 zone time fix gives you a position of LAT 26° 42.0' N, LONG 60° 18.0' W. Your vessel is on course 300° T, and your speed is 9.8 knots. Local apparent noon (LAN) occurs at 1220 zone time at which time a meridian altitude of the Sun's lower limb is observed. The observed altitude (Ho) for this sight is 49° 10.0'. What is the calculated latitude at local apparent noon (LAN)?

A. LAT 27° 13.5' N
B. LAT 27° 16.3' N
C. LAT 27° 17.6' N
D. LAT 27° 19.2' N

3. 00808. On 28 July 1981, your 0800 zone time fix gives you a position of LAT 25° 16.0' N, LONG 71° 19.0' W. Your vessel is on course 026° T, and your speed is 17.5 knots. Local apparent noon (LAN) occurs at 1149 zone time, at which time a meridian altitude of the Sun's lower limb is observed. The observed altitude (Ho) for this sight is 82° 28.7'. What is the calculated latitude at local apparent noon (LAN)?

A. LAT 26° 21.9' N
B. LAT 26° 23.4' N
C. LAT 26° 25.0' N
D. LAT 26° 27.7' N

4. 00809. On 7 November 1981, your 0830 zone time fix gives you a position of LAT 27° 36.0' N, LONG 163° 19.0' W. Your vessel is on course 289° T, and your speed is 19.0 knots. Local apparent noon (LAN) occurs at 1138 zone time, at which time a meridian altitude of the Sun's lower limb is observed. The observed altitude (Ho) for this sight is 45° 35.0'. What is the calculated latitude at local apparent noon (LAN)?

A. LAT 27° 52.3' N
B. LAT 27° 53.4' N
C. LAT 27° 55.1' N
D. LAT 27° 57.2' N

5. 00810. On 13 October 1981, your 0515 zone time fix gives you a position of LAT 26° 53.0' N, LONG 90° 05.0' W. Your vessel is on course 068° T, and your speed is 7.8 knots. Local apparent noon (LAN) occurs at 1145 zone time, at which time a meridian altitude of the Sun's lower limb is observed. The observed altitude (Ho) for this sight is 54° 51.5'. What is the calculated latitude at local apparent noon (LAN)?

A. LAT 27° 12.6' N
B. LAT 27° 14.1' N
C. LAT 27° 15.7' N
D. LAT 27° 16.2' N

Answers

1. 00806 B
2. 00807 B
3. 00808 C
4. 00809 D
5. 00810 A

Problems worked-out

1. LAN	
USCG #	806
Date	15 Nov
Lat:	22°-30 N
Long:	068° 28 W
ZT	1218
ZD	+5
GMT	1718
DEC	S 18° 35.2'
D (+.6)	+.2
DEC	S 18° 35.4''
	89° 60.0'
- Ho	49° 46.0'
Z Dist	40° 14.0'
± Dec	18° 35.4'
LAT	21° 38.6'

2. LAN	
USCG#	807
Date	12 Feb
Lat:	26° 42 N
Long:	060° 18.0 W
ZT	1220
ZD	+4
GMT	1620
DEC	S 13° 34.0'
D (-.8)	-.3'
DEC	S 13° 33.7'
	89° 60.0'
- Ho	49° 10.0'
Z Dist	40° 50.0'
± Dec	13° 33.7'
LAT	27° 16.3'

3. LAN	
USCG#	808
Date	28 Jul
Lat:	25° 16 N
Long:	071° 19 W
ZT	1149
ZD	+5
GMT	1649
DEC	N 18° 54.2'
D (-.6)	-.5'
DEC	N 18° 53.7'
	89° 60.0'
- Ho	82° 28.7'
Z Dist	7° 31.3'
± Dec	18° 53.7'
LAT	26° 25.0'

4. LAN	
USCG#	809
Date	7 Nov
Lat:	27° 36 N
Long:	163° 19 W
ZT	1138
ZD	+11
GMT	2238
DEC	S 16° 27.4'
D (+.7)	+.4'
DEC	S 16° 27.8'
	89° 60.0'
- Ho	45° 35.0'
Z Dist	44° 25.0'
± Dec	16° 27.8'
LAT	27° 57.2'

5. LAN	
USCG#	810
Date	13 Oct
Lat:	26° 53 N
Long:	090° 05 W
ZT	1145
ZD	+6
GMT	1745
DEC	S 7° 55.2'
D (+.9)	+.7'
DEC	7° 55.9 '
	89°60.0'
- Ho	54° 51.5'
Z Dist	35° 08.5'
± Dec	7° 55.9'
LAT	27° 12.6'

RUNNING FIXES
Chapter 13

LINE OF POSITION (LOP) FROM CELESTIAL OBSERVATIONS

You have seen how lines of position, obtained through bearings on terrestrial objects, are used to fix a ship's position in piloting. You know that a line of position is a locus of possible positions of the ship. In other words, the ship's position must be somewhere along that line. **A FIX**, by definition, is a **relatively accurate determination of latitude and longitude**. In practice, this position is **the intersection of two or more lines of position**; but often it is not the ship's exact position because you can always assume some errors in observation, plotting, and the like.

In celestial navigation you must establish lines of position by applying the results of observations of heavenly bodies. A line of position obtained at one time may be used at a later time. All you need to do is move the line paralleled to itself, a distance equal to the run of the ship in the interim, and in the same direction as the run. Such a line of position cannot be as accurate as a new line because the amount and direction of its movement can be determined only by the usual DR methods. **If two new lines cannot be obtained, however, an old line, advanced and intersected, with a new one, may be the only possible way of establishing a fix**. This is called a **running fix**. Naturally, the distance an old line may be advanced without a substantial loss of accuracy depends on how closely the run can be reckoned.

In celestial navigation, as in piloting, you essentially are trying to establish the intersection of two or more lines of position. **A single observation is insufficient to obtain a fix.**

CIRCLES OF EQUAL ALTITUDE

Observation of two bodies at the same time gives the navigator two circles of equal altitude.

The circles intersect each other at two points, and, because the ship is somewhere on each one of them, it must be at one or the other points of intersection. In the figure to the right, circles of equal altitude have been determined by observations of the stars **Alphard and Rigel**. In this example, the navigator of the ship knows that the ship cannot be at the southern point of intersection; consequently, **the northern point, illustrated, must be the fix**.

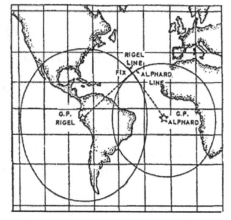

LINE OF POSITION (LOP}

Under normal conditions it is neither practical nor necessary to plot the whole of the circle of equal altitude. The position is always known within 30 miles at the most probably it is considered less than that distance, if you maintain an appropriate DR. Inside these limits, the curve of the arc of a circle of equal altitude is hardly perceptible, and the arc is plotted and regarded as a straight line.

Such a line, comprising enough of the arc of a circle of equal altitude to cover the probable limits of a position is called a Sumner line of position or just a line of position.

Although a single line of position cannot establish a fix, it is (as mentioned earlier) a locus of possible positions of the ship. In modern celestial navigation, a line of position is determined by first locating an assumed position (AP) on the chart, drawing from it a line along the azimuth of the observed body, and intersecting that line with the LOP. The LOP is always perpendicular to the line of the azimuth. But that LOP is a single line of position, and you must still plot another one intersecting it to obtain a true fix.

Because the LOP is always at right angles to the line of the azimuth, it follows that when an observed body bears due east or west, the line of position coincides with a meridian of longitude. When the body bears due north or south, the line coincides with a parallel of latitude. That is why the sun is always observed at local apparent noon, when it is on the meridian, to determine the ship's latitude. **It follows, too, that by observing a celestial body bearing dead ahead or dead astern, the navigator can establish a single line of position that will tell whether the ship has overrun the DR position.** Taking observations on an object abeam, you can discover whether the ship is right or left of the course line.

INTERSECTING LINES

The preferable method of establishing two lines of position is by observing two different bodies, although two lines may be obtained from the same body by observations taken at different times. *As* mentioned previously, the nearer the two lines approach a right angle to each other, the more accurate is the fix.

When two lines are determined by observing the same body, the first line established is brought forward the distance run on the course steered. For example, if a ship steams 27 miles on course 315 degrees between the first and second observations, it is obvious that the ship's position is on a line parallel with the first one established, but drawn 27 miles away (to scale) on the course line 315 degrees, Intersection of the line established by the second observation with the advanced line of the first observation is a fix. The fix progressively decreases in accuracy, depending on how far the first line is advanced.

It is not considered good practice to advance such a line for more than 5 hours of run.

DETERMINING LINE OF POSITION

You might be entitled to complain that much has been said concerning what a line of position tells you, but very little has been told about how you determine it in the first place. We are coming that to that part now.

You probably have grasped the idea already that what you .want to find out is which circle of equal altitude you are on, and what this altitude is. But you have seen that to draw such a circle you would need a chart covering an extensive area, unless the heavenly body's altitude approached 90 degrees. Consequently, you do not determine the entire circle but merely a portion of its arc, which is so small that it is plotted and regarded as a straight line.

Alexander F. Hickethier MBA © 1988-2019

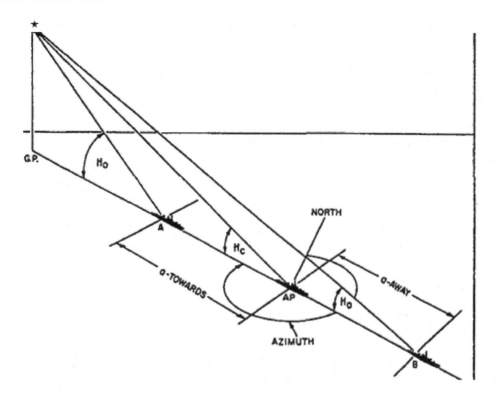

The figure above illustrates, the method used in establishing a single line of position by observing a star. An assumed position (AP) is selected according to certain requirements of convenience in calculating (described later). Observation of a star provides sextant altitude (hs). Sextant altitude is then corrected to obtain observed altitude (Ho). The star's altitude from the assumed position, called the computed altitude (Hc) and its azimuth angle are determined from tables by a procedure you will soon learn. The azimuth angle is then converted to azimuth.

After selecting an AP, draw the azimuth through the AP. Along the azimuth, measure off the altitude intercept (difference between the observed altitude and the computed attitude). At the end of this measurement, draw a perpendicular line which is the LOP.

You must know whether altitude intercept (a) should be measured from AP toward the star **(HoMoTo for Ho More Toward)** or measured from AP away from the star. The initials for Coast Guard Academy (CGA) are found to be helpful. If the computed altitude is greater than the observed altitude, altitude intercept is (a) is measured away from the star. In other words, applying the CGA memory aid you have **computed, greater, away or CGA**

Actual plotting of the line of position is as follows:

1. Plot the AP (you already have taken your sight) and obtain the azimuth from tables.

2. Lay off the azimuth line from the AP toward or away from the body, depending on whether the observed altitude is greater or less than the computed altitude.

3. Measure in the proper direction, along the azimuth line, the difference between the observed and the computed altitude in miles and tenths of miles.

4. Draw a line at the extremity of altitude intercept (a), perpendicular to the azimuth line. At the time of observation, this perpendicular line is a line of position.

5. Label the line of position with the time of observation and the name of the observed body.

ADVANCING THE LOP

Several methods may be used to advance a line of position. The most frequent method consists simply of advancing the AP in the direction of and for the distance of the run, as shown in the figure and drawing the new LOP.

In **figure 1**, note that the plots are made from three separate APs, using the same assumed latitude but different assumed longitudes. We will use this method in this course.

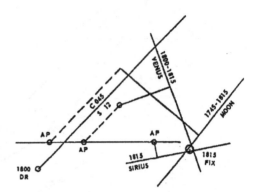

Figure 1

The manner of advancing lines of position from sights of the Moon, Venus, and Sirius to obtain an 1815 fix is seen in the **figure 2** to the right.

Three lines of position by observation, like those obtained in piloting, do not always intersect exactly. Quite often a triangle is formed. If one or more of the LOPs must be advanced, the triangle is likely to be larger. Frequently, the center of the triangle is assumed to be the fix. If, however, one or more lines have been advanced, more weight may be given to a line that has not been advanced, or to a line that you have more confidence in; for example, favoring a first magnitude star over a third magnitude star.

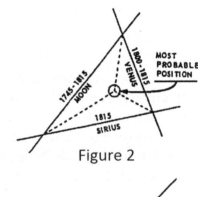

Figure 2

The **figure 3** illustrates a situation where the AP was advanced paralleled to the course line for the distance run, and a new LOP was plotted from its new position. The new LOP was necessary because the same P would have produced an **LOP** that would have intersected the course line beyond the limits of the chart. In this illustrative case, it is unnecessary to draw the first dashed construction on the chart.

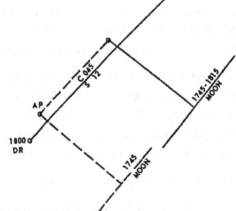

Figure 3

13-4

End of Chapter USCG Questions

1. 00983. On 17 January 1981, your 0730 zone time position was LAT 22° 26.0' N, LONG 152° 17.0' E. Your vessel was steaming on course 136° T at a speed of 17.0 knots. An observation of the Sun's lower limb was made at 1015 ZT. The chronometer read 00h 13m 23s and was slow 01m 49s. The observed altitude (Ho) was 40° 25.7'. LAN occurred at 1222 zone time. The observed altitude (Ho) was 47° 48.1'. What was the longitude of your 1200 zone time running fix?

A. LONG 153° 04.2' E
B. LONG 153° 08.3' E
C. LONG 153° 13.1' E
D. LONG 153° 18.6' E

2. 00984. On 28 July 1981, your 0800 zone time fix gives you a position of LAT 25° 16.0' N, LONG 71° 19.0' W. Your vessel is steaming a course of 026° T at a speed of 17.5 knots. An observation of the Sun's upper limb is made 0905 zone time, and the observed altitude (Ho) is 51° 06.8'. The chronometer reads 02h 07m 10s, and the chronometer error is 02m 24s fast. Local apparent noon occurs at 1149 zone time, and a meridian altitude of the Sun's lower limb is made. The observed altitude (Ho) for this sight is 82° 28.7'. Determine the vessel's 1200 zone time position.

A. LAT 26° 21.9' N,   LONG 70° 46.1' W
B. LAT 26° 25.0' N,   LONG 70° 46.0' W
C. LAT 26° 25.0' N,   LONG 70° 48.1' W
D. LAT 26° 27.9' N,   LONG 70° 45.5' W

3. 00987. On 17 January 1981, your 0730 zone time fix gives you a position of LAT 22° 26.0' S, LONG 152° 17.0' E. Your vessel is steaming on a course of 116° T at a speed of 17 knots. An observation of the Sun's lower limb is made at 1015 zone time. The chronometer reads 00h 13m 23s, and the chronometer error is 01m 49s slow. The observed altitude (Ho) is 66° 02.1'. LAN occurs at 1152 zone time and a meridian altitude of the Sun's lower limb is made. The observed altitude (Ho) is 87° 54.2'. Determine the vessel's 1200 zone time position.

A. LAT 22° 53.8' S,   LONG 153° 25.6' E
B. LAT 22° 53.8' S,   LONG 153° 28.8' E
C. LAT 22° 56.3' S,   LONG 153° 25.6' E
D. LAT 22° 56.3' S,   LONG 153° 28.8' E

4. 00988. On 29 June 1981, your 0800 zone time fix gives you a position of LAT 26° 16.0' S, LONG 61° 04.0' E. Your vessel is steaming a course of 079° T at a speed of 15.5 knots. An observation of the Sun's upper limb is made at 0905 zone time, and the observed altitude (Ho) is 25° 20.1. The chronometer reads 05h 08m 12s, and the chronometer error is 02m 27s fast. Local apparent noon occurs at 1154 zone time, and a meridian altitude of the Sun's lower limb is made. The observed altitude (Ho) for this sight is 40° 44.2'. Determine the vessel's 1200 zone time position.

A. LAT 26° 01.7' S,   LONG 62° 03.1' E
B. LAT 26° 02.0' S,   LONG 62° 23.2' E
C. LAT 26° 05.1' S,   LONG 62° 06.3' E
D. LAT 25° 56.0' S,   LONG 62° 03.0' E

5. 00989. On 2 April 1981, your 0830 zone time fix gives you a position of LAT 20° 16.0' S, LONG 4° 12.0' E. Your vessel is steaming a course of 143° T at a speed of 18.0 knots. An observation of the Sun's upper limb is made at 0903 zone time, and the observed altitude (Ho) is 42° 39.6'. The chronometer reads 09h 05m 40s, and the chronometer error is 02m 15s fast. Local apparent noon occurs at 1145 zone time, and a meridian altitude of the Sun's lower limb is made. The observed altitude (Ho) for this sight is 63° 46.2'. Determine the vessel's 1200 zone time position.

A. LAT 21° 10.1' S,   LONG 004° 53.9' E
B. LAT 21° 14.0' S,   LONG 004° 55.0' E
C. LAT 21° 18.0' S,   LONG 005° 00.5' E
D. LAT 22° 42.0' S,   LONG 004° 57.0' E

Answers

1. 00983 C
2. 00984 D
3. 00987 A
4. 00988 A
5. 00989 C

Problems worked-out

<table>
<tr><td colspan="6" align="center">Celestial Problems
Sight Reduction – LAN Running Fix</td></tr>
<tr><td colspan="3">Problem # 1 (USCG) (00983)</td><td colspan="3" align="center">Chapter 13</td></tr>
<tr>
<td>Date: 17 Jan.</td><td align="right">Time</td><td align="right">0730</td><td>LAT:</td><td colspan="2">22° 26.0' N</td>
</tr>
<tr>
<td></td><td></td><td></td><td>LONG</td><td colspan="2">152° 17.0' E</td>
</tr>
<tr>
<td>ZT</td><td align="right">10:15</td><td>CT 00:13:23</td><td>C-136°</td><td></td><td></td>
</tr>
<tr>
<td>ZD</td><td align="right">- 10:00</td><td>CE + 01:49</td><td>S -17.0 kts</td><td></td><td></td>
</tr>
<tr>
<td>GMT</td><td align="right">00:15</td><td>CCT 00:15:12</td><td></td><td></td><td></td>
</tr>
<tr>
<td></td><td></td><td>GMT 00:15:12</td><td>DR</td><td colspan="2">0730-1015</td>
</tr>
<tr>
<td></td><td></td><td></td><td>Time</td><td colspan="2">1015</td>
</tr>
<tr>
<td></td><td></td><td></td><td>LAT</td><td colspan="2">21° 52.0' N</td>
</tr>
<tr>
<td></td><td></td><td></td><td>LONG</td><td colspan="2">152° 52.3' E</td>
</tr>
<tr><td colspan="6" align="center">Almanac</td></tr>
<tr>
<td>GHA</td><td align="right">177° 29.8'</td><td>DEC S 20° 47.9'</td><td colspan="3" align="center">LAN</td>
</tr>
<tr>
<td>M/S</td><td align="right">3° 48.0'</td><td>d (-0.5) - .1'</td><td>ZT</td><td colspan="2" align="right">12:22</td>
</tr>
<tr>
<td>GHA</td><td align="right">181° 17.8'</td><td>DEC S 20° 47.8'</td><td>ZD</td><td colspan="2" align="right">- 10:00</td>
</tr>
<tr>
<td>a λ</td><td align="right">+ 152° 42.2'</td><td></td><td>GMT</td><td colspan="2" align="right">02:22</td>
</tr>
<tr>
<td>LHA</td><td align="right">334° 00.0'</td><td></td><td>DEC</td><td colspan="2" align="right">S 20° 46.9'</td>
</tr>
<tr>
<td></td><td></td><td></td><td>d (-0.5)</td><td colspan="2" align="right">- .2'</td>
</tr>
<tr>
<td></td><td></td><td></td><td>DEC</td><td colspan="2" align="right">S 20° 46.7'</td>
</tr>
<tr>
<td></td><td></td><td></td><td></td><td colspan="2" align="right">89°-60.0'</td>
</tr>
<tr>
<td></td><td></td><td></td><td>- Ho</td><td colspan="2" align="right">47° 48.1'</td>
</tr>
<tr>
<td></td><td></td><td></td><td>Z Dist</td><td colspan="2" align="right">42° 11.9'</td>
</tr>
<tr>
<td></td><td></td><td></td><td>± Dec</td><td colspan="2" align="right">20° 46.7'</td>
</tr>
<tr>
<td></td><td></td><td></td><td>LAT</td><td colspan="2" align="right">21° 25.2'</td>
</tr>
</table>

LHA	334°	**DEC**	S 20° 47.8'	**LAT**	22 N	CONTRARY

<table>
<tr><td colspan="5" align="center">Publication 229</td></tr>
<tr>
<td></td><td></td><td>Z (20)</td><td>147.0</td><td align="center">Z to ZN</td>
</tr>
<tr>
<td>Hc</td><td>40° 55.0'</td><td>Z (21)</td><td>147.7</td><td></td>
</tr>
<tr>
<td>d</td><td>- 50.7'</td><td>d</td><td>+ .7</td><td align="center">ZN=Z</td>
</tr>
<tr>
<td>Inc Dec (X)</td><td>47.8'</td><td>Inc Dec (X)</td><td>47.8</td><td></td>
</tr>
<tr>
<td>Inv (÷)</td><td>60.0'</td><td>Inv (÷)</td><td>60.0</td><td align="center">147.6</td>
</tr>
<tr>
<td>Correction</td><td>- 40.4'</td><td>Correction</td><td>+ .6</td><td></td>
</tr>
<tr>
<td>Hc</td><td>40° 14.6'</td><td>Z</td><td>147.6</td><td></td>
</tr>
<tr>
<td>Ho</td><td>40° 25.7'</td><td></td><td></td><td></td>
</tr>
<tr>
<td>A</td><td>11.1 T</td><td></td><td></td><td></td>
</tr>
</table>

Notes:

Required Fix at 1200

DR   1200 – 1015 = 105" x 17.0 / 60 =29.75

DR   1222 – 1200 = 22" x 17.0 / 60 = 6.2

Dlat =6.2 x cos 136° = 4.5

ANSWER   C

Celestial Problems
Sight Reduction – LAN Running Fix

Problem # 2 (USCG) (00984)	Chapter 13 - 1

Date:	28 July 1981		Time	0800	**LAT:**	25° 16.0 N
					LONG	071° 19.0 W
	ZT	09:05	**CT**	02:07:10	**C-** 026°	
	ZD	+5:00	**CE**	-0:02:24	**S-**17.5 kts	
	GMT	14:05	**CCT**	02:04:10		
			GMT	14:04:46	**DR**	
					Time	08:00 - 0905
					LAT	25° 33.0′ N
					LONG	71° 10.0′ W

GHA	28°-23.9′	**DEC**	N 18°-55.4′		**LAN**	
M/S	+ 1° 11.5′	**d (-.6)**	.0	**ZT**	11:49	
GHA	29° 35.4′	**DEC**	N 18°-55.4′	**ZD**	+5:00	
a λ	- 71° 35.4′			**GMT**	16:49	
LHA	318° 00.0′			**DEC**	N 18° 54.2′	
				D (-.6)	-.5′	
				DEC	N 18° 54.7′	
					89° 60.0′	
				- Ho	- 82° 28.7′	
				Z Dist	7° 31.3′	
				± Dec	+ 18° 53.7′	
				LAT	26° 25.0′	

LHA	318°	**DEC**	N 18° 55.4′	**LAT**	26 N	SAME

			Z (18)	092.9	**Z to ZN**
Hc	50° 25.0′	**Z (19)**	091.9	
d	+19.3	**d**	-1.5	**ZN=Z**
Inc Dec (X)	55.4	**Inc Dec (X)**	55.4	
Inv (÷)	60	**Inv (÷)**	60	**091.5**
Correction	+17.8	**Correction**	-1.4	
Hc	50° 42.8′	**Z**	091.5	
Ho	51° 06.8′			
a	**24.0 T**			

Notes:

Required fix at 1200
DR 09:05 to 12:00 175 x 17.5 / 60 = 51.0 nm
DR 11:49 to 12:00 11 x 17.5 / 60 = 3.2 nm
Dlat = 3.2 x cos 026 = 2.79
ANSWER   D

Celestial Problems
Sight Reduction – LAN Running Fix

Problem # 3 (USCG) (00987)				Chapter 13 - 2	

Date:	17 Jan		Time	0730	**LAT:**	22° 26.0' S
					LONG	152° 17.0' E
	ZT	10:15	**CT**	00:13:23	**C**-116°	
	ZD	-10:00	**CE**	+1:49	**S**-17 kts	
	GMT	00:15	**CCT**	00:15:12		
			GMT	00:15:12	**DR**	
					Time	0730 - 1015
					LAT	22° 45.0' S
					LONG	153° 03.0' E

Almanac

						LAN	
GHA	177° 29.8'		**DEC**	S 20° 47.9'			
M/S	+ 3° 48.0'		**d (-0.5)**	- 0.1'	**ZT**	11:52	
GHA	181° 17.8'		**DEC**	S 20° 47.8'	**ZD**	-10:00	
a λ	+ 152° 42.2'				**GMT**	01:52	
LHA	334° 00.0'				**DEC**	S 20° 47.4'	
					d	-0.4'	
					DEC	S 20° 47.0'	
						89° 60.0'	
					- Ho	- 87° 54.2'	
					Z Dist	2° 05.8'	
					± Dec	+ 20° 47.0'	
					LAT	22° 52.8'	

LHA	334°	**DEC**	S 20° 47.8'	**LAT**	23° S	SAME

Publication 229

				Z (20)	092.1	**Z to ZN**	
	Hc	65° 39.4		**Z (21)**	089.7		
	d	+11.1		**d**	- 2.4	ZN=180 - Z	
	Inc Dec (X)	47.8		**Inc Dec (X)**	47.8	180 – 090.2 = 089.8	
	Inv (÷)	60		**Inv (÷)**	60	**089.8**	
	Correction	+8.0		**Correction**	-1.9		
	Hc	65° 48.2'		**Z**	**090.2**		
	Ho	66° 02.1'					
	a	**13.9T**					

Notes:

Required Fix at

DR

DR

Dlat =

ANSWER   A

Celestial Problems
Sight Reduction – LAN Running Fix

Problem # 4 (USCG) (0988)				Chapter 13 -3	

Date:	29 June		Time	0800	**LAT:**	26° 16.0' S
					LONG	061° 04.0' E
	ZT	09:05	**CT**	05:08:12	**C**-079°	
	ZD	-4:00	**CE**	- 0:02:27	**S**-15.5 Kts	
	GMT	05:05	**CCT**	05:05:45		
			GMT		**DR**	
					Time	08:00 - 0905
					LAT	26° 12.0' S
					LONG	61° 22.0' E

Almanac

	GHA	254° 10.5'	**DEC**	N 23° 14.1'		**LAN**	
	M/S	+ 1° 26.3'	**d (-0.1)**	0'	**ZT**	11:54	
	GHA	255° 36.8'	**DEC**	N 23° 14.1'	**ZD**	-4:00	
	a λ	+ 61° 23.2'			**GMT**	07:54	
	LHA	317° 00.0'			**DEC**	N 23° 13.9'	
					D(-0.1)	-0.1	
					DEC	N 23° 13.8'	
						89° 60.0'	
					- Ho	- 40° 44.2'	
					Z Dist	49° 15.8'	
					± Dec	-23° 13.8'	
					LAT	26° 02.0'	

LHA	317°	**DEC**	N 23° 14.1'	**LAT**	26 S	CONTRARY

Publication 229

			Z (23)	135.8	**Z to ZN**
			Z (24)	136.6	
Hc	25°-42.5		**d**	+ 0.8	ZN=180-Z
d	- 44.1		**Inc Dec (X)**	14.1	180-136.0 = 044.0
Inc Dec (X)	14.1		**Inv (÷)**	60	44.0
Inv (÷)	60		**Correction**	+0.2	
Correction	-10.4		**Z -**	**136.0**	
Hc	25° 32.1				
Ho	25° 20.1				
a	**12.0A**				

Notes:

Required Fix at 1200
DR   175 x 15.5 / 60 = 45.2 nm
DR   6 X 15.5 /60 = 0.3 nm
Dlat =D x cos C = 1.6 x cos 079 = .73
ANSWER   A

Celestial Problems
Sight Reduction – LAN Running Fix

Problem # 5 (USCG) (00989)				Chapter 13-4	

Date:	2 April		Time	0830	**LAT:**	20° 16.0' S
					LONG	004° 12.0' E
	ZT	09:03	**CT**	09:05:40	**C**-143°	
	ZD	00:00	**CE**	-0:02:15	**S** -18.0 kts	
	GMT	09:03	**CCT**	09:03:25		
			GMT	09:03:25	**DR**	
					Time	08:30 - 0903
					LAT	20° 23.0' S
					LONG	004° 18.0' E

Almanac

						LAN	
GHA	314° 05.7'	**DEC**	N 4° 57.1'				
M/S	+ 0° 51.3'	**D (+1.0)**	+ 0.1'	**ZT**		11:45	
GHA	314° 57.0'	**DEC**	N 4° 57.2'	**ZD**		0	
a λ	+ 4° 03.0'			**GMT**		11:45	
LHA	319° 00.0'			**DEC**		N4° 59.0'	
				D (+1.0)		+ 0.8'	
				DEC		N 4° 59.8'	
						89° 60.0'	
				- Ho		- 63° 46.2'	
				Z Dist		26° 13.8'	
				± Dec		- 4° 59.8'	
				LAT		21° 14.0'	

LHA	319°	**DEC**	N 4° 57.2'	**LAT**	20 S	CONTRARY

Publication 229

			-	**Z (4)**	116.3	**Z to ZN**
Hc	43° 07.6			**Z (5)**	117.4	
d	- 32.5			**d**	+1.1	ZN=180-Z
Inc Dec (X)	57.2			**Inc Dec (X)**	57.2	180-117.3 =
Inv (÷)	60			**Inv (÷)**	60	**062.7**
Correction	-31.0			**Correction**	117.3	
Hc	42° 36.6			**Z**		
Ho	42° 39.6					
a	**3.0T**					

Notes:

Required Fix at 1200
DR   177 X 18 / 60 = 53.1
DR   15 X 18 / 60 = 4.5
Dlat =4.5 x cos 143 = 3.6
ANSWER   C

Additional USCG problems worked-out for this chapter can be found in **Celestial Navigation Calculations (Upon Oceans Endorsement) Worked-Out for Master 500 GT through 2nd Mate Unlimited, Volume 3, part 2, Chapter 6, Determining Position by Sight Reduction.**

THREE LINE RUNNING FIXES
Chapter 14

In the problems to follow the U.S. Coast Guard is evaluating the Mariner's ability to enter Publication 229, calculate **intercept (a)** and true bearing of the object **(ZN)** and your plotting accuracy of the resulting LOP'S. You **will not** be required to calculate **GHA, Altitude (Ho) and Declination**. Prior to completing the required calculations you should review Chapters **11, 12 and 13** (Using Publication 229, The Universal Plotting Sheet and Running Fixes) and the work form below. Once you reduced the sights and set-up the Universal Plotting for a Mid-latitude of 24N and longitudes 136 through 138W we can plot our LOP.

Example 1

10.
1085. On 20 February, your vessel is enroute from Honolulu, HI to San Francisco, CA, steering course 033° T and making a speed of 18 knots. Your 0530 zone time DR is LAT 24° 15.0' N, LONG 137° 33.0' W. Three stars are observed, and the following information is determined:

BODY'S STAR	ZT	GHA	BODY'S DECLINATION	OBSERVED ALTITUDE (Ho)
Regulus	0540	218° 35.9'	N 12° 03.5'	13° 02.2'
Antares	0552	126° 23.5'	S 26° 23.3'	38° 04.1'
Vega	0600	096° 23.2'	N 38° 45.8'	52° 33.5'

What is the position of your vessel at 0600?

A. LAT 24° 24.3' N,   LONG 137° 35.5' W
B. LAT 24° 26.0' N,   LONG 137° 25.8' W
C. LAT 24° 27.5' N,   LONG 137° 31.8' W
D. LAT 24° 30.1' N,   LONG 137° 24.5' W

We plot our assumed longitude 137° 35.9' W on latitude 24° N. Then advance 0540 AP along our course for the distance traveled in 20 min at 18 Kts. (20 x 18 / 60 = 6 NM). Label 0600 AP. Next we plot the True Bearing (ZN) of Regulus·277.5 from the 0600 AP.

Last, we draw a line perpendicular to the ZN 3.0 NM Towards (intercept) our ZN (277.5) from the advanced AP (AP'). This is our LOP of **Regulus** advanced to 0600.

10.		20 February	
USCG # 1085	Latitude	24° 15.0' N	
0530	Longitude	137° 33.0' W	
		C -033	S – 18.0
Object Name	**Regulus**	**Antares**	**Vega**
ZT Sight	0540	0552	0600
Fix Time	0600	0600	0600
D	40	8	0
Speed x Time	18 x 40	18 x 8	18 x 0
Divided by 60	60	60	60
= Advance	12.0	2.4	0

We then repeat this process for the LOP's for **Antares** and **Antares.**

When taking the USCG Upon Oceans Examination you **WILL** be given Local Time of the sight, GHA of the object (Sun, Moon, Star or Planet. The Coast Guards intent is to test your ability to use the sight reduction tables (pub. 229) and plot your results to obtain a 3 LOP fix. You will be required to calculate distance run to advance or retard your LOP's, LHA of the object and reduce the sight using the Sight reduction tables (Pub 229).

Convert GHA to LHA			
GHA	218° 35.9'	126° 23.5	96° 23.2'
± Longitude	- 137° 35.9'	- 137° 23.5'	- 137° 23.2'
LHA	081° 0.0'	349° 00.0'	319° 00.0'

Declination			
Declination	N 12° 03.5'	S 26° 23.3'	N 38° 45.8'
	SAME	CONTRARY	SAME

Pub 229 Work			
Intercept Computed			
Hc	12° 57.9'	38° 52.8'	52° 33.0
d	+ 22.5	-58.5	- 10.9
Dec inc (x)	03.5'	23.3'	45.8'
60 (\)	60	60	60
Correction	+ 1.3	- 22.7	- 8.3
HC Corrected	12° 59.2	38° 35.8'	52° 24.7'
Ho	13° 02.2'	38° 04.1'	52° 33.5'
a: (intercept)	**3.0 T**	**31.7 A**	**8.8 T**

Direction Computer			
Z	082.5	167.3	058.2
Z	081.5	167.6	056.6
d	- 1.0	+ .3	-1.6
Dec inc (x)	03.5'	23.3'	45.8'
60 (\)	60	60	60
Correction	- .1	+ .1	- 1.2
Corrected Z	082.4	167.4	057.0
± 180, 360	360-	0	0
Convert Z to Zn	**277.6**	**167.4**	**057.0**

End of Chapter USCG Problems

1. 1076. On 25 March, your 0500 ZT DR position is LAT 28° 14.0' S, LONG 93° 17.0' E. You are on course 291° T at a speed of 16.0 knots. The following bodies are observed and information determined:

BODY	ZONE TIME	GHA	OBSERVED ALTITUDE (Ho)	DECLINATION
Peacock	0520	226° 18.5'	49° 42.9'	S 56° 47.6'
Altair	0535	238° 38.2'	43° 53.1'	N 8° 48.9'
Spica	0550	338° 48.5'	21° 11.7'	S 11° 03.8'

What are the latitude and longitude of your 0550 zone time running fix?

A. LAT 28° 15.9' S,   LONG 92° 56.9' E
B. LAT 28° 19.3' S,   LONG 92° 59.0' E
C. LAT 28° 06.4' S,   LONG 93° 02.5' E
D. LAT 27° 53.2' S,   LONG 93° 17.6' E

2. 1077. On 15 July, your 1845 ZT DR position is LAT 27° 42.0' N, LONG 167° 02.0' E. You are on course 243° T at a speed of 16.0 knots. The following bodies are observed and information determined:

BODY	ZONE TIME	GHA	OBSERVED ALTITUDE (Ho)	DECLINATION
Deneb	1905	104° 08.0'	19° 52.4'	N 45° 12.8'
Antares	1924	172° 02.1'	32° 22.1'	S 26° 23.5'
Denebola	1945	247° 20.6'	38° 22.3'	N 14° 40.7'

What are the latitude and longitude of your 1945 zone time running fix?

A. LAT 27° 31.1' N,   LONG 166° 43.0' E
B. LAT 27° 38.5' N,   LONG 166° 45.1' E
C. LAT 27° 45.3' N,   LONG 166° 32.2' E
D. LAT 27° 46.9' N,   LONG 166° 39.8' E

3. 1078. On 6 April, your 1830 ZT DR position is LAT 26° 33.0' N, LONG 64° 31.0' W. You are on course 082° T at a speed of 16 knots. The following bodies are observed and information determined:

BODY	ZONE TIME	GHA	OBSERVED ALTITUDE (Ho)	DECLINATION
Sirius	1836	73° 02.7'	46° 00.5'	S 16° 41.7'
Regulus	1842	23° 46.9'	49° 07.2'	N 12° 03.5'
Mirfak	1900	129° 24.3'	35° 51.6'	N 49° 47.7'

What are the latitude and longitude of your 1900 zone time running fix?

A. LAT 26° 49.5' N,   LONG 64° 06.5' W
B. LAT 26° 32.5' N,   LONG 64° 27.1' W
C. LAT 26° 28.7' N,   LONG 64° 32.1' W
D. LAT 26° 31.2' N,   LONG 64° 32.1' W

4. 1079. On 12 December, your 1830 ZT DR position in LAT 24° 16.0' S, LONG 41° 18.0' W. You are on course 235° T at a speed of 16.0 knots. The following bodies are observed and information determined:

BODY	ZONE TIME	GHA	OBSERVED ALTITUDE (Ho)	DECLINATION
Rigel	1845	329° 19.7'	19° 54.7'	S 08° 13.4'
Peacock	1910	107° 58.4'	32° 43.9'	S 56° 47.8'
Markab	1930	73° 04.1'	39° 53.1'	N 15° 06.5'

What are the latitude and longitude of your 1930 zone time running fix?

A. LAT 24° 12.5' S,   LONG 41° 10.9' W
B. LAT 24° 16.9' S,   LONG 41° 18.2' W
C. LAT 24° 25.2' S,   LONG 41° 39.9' W
D. LAT 27° 46.9' S,   LONG 41° 31.2' W

5. 1080. On 20 February, your 0530 ZT DR position is LAT 24° 15.0' N, LONG 137° 33.0' W. You are on course 033° T at a speed of 18 knots. The following bodies are observed and information determined:

BODY	ZONE TIME	GHA	OBSERVED ALTITUDE (Ho)	DECLINATION
Regulus	0540	218° 35.9'	13° 02.2'	N 12° 03.5'
Antares	0552	126° 23.5'	38° 04.1'	S 26° 23.3'
Vega	0600	96° 23.2'	52° 33.5'	N 38° 45.8'

What are the latitude and longitude of your 0600 zone time running fix?

A. LAT 24° 23.3' N,   LONG 137° 35.5' W
B. LAT 24° 26.0' N,   LONG 137° 25.8' W
C. LAT 24° 27.5' N,   LONG 137° 31.8' W
D. LAT 24° 30.1' N,   LONG 137° 24.5' W

3 LOP FIXES
(STARS, SUN, MOON AND PLANES)

1. 01076 A
2. 01077 A
3. 01078 B
4. 01079 B
5. 01080 C

USCG Problems worked-out

3 LOP FIXES (STARS, SUN, MOON AND PLANES)

1.		**25 March**	
USCG # 1076	Latitude		28° 14.0' S
0500	Longitude		093° 17.0' E
		C- 291	S- 16.0
Object Name	**Peacock**	**Antares**	**Spica**
ZT Sight	0520	0535	0550
Fix Time	0550	0550	0550
D	30	15	0
Speed x Time	16 x 30	16 x 15	16 x 0
Divided by 60	60	60	60
= Advance	8.0	4.0	0

Convert GHA to LHA			
GHA	226° 18.5'	238° 38.2'	338° 48.5'
± Longitude	+ 93° 41.5'	+ 93° 21.8'	+ 93° 11.5
LHA	319° 00.0'	332° 00.0'	72° 00.0'

Declination			
Declination	S 56° 47.6'	N 8° 48.9'	S 11° 03.8'
	SAME	CONTRARY	SAME

Pub 229 Work			
Intercept Computed			
Hc	50° 07.4	44° 57.9'	20° 56.5
d	- 28.3	- 48.8	+ 26.1
Dec inc (x)	47.6'	48.9'	03.8'
60 (\)	60	60	60
Correction	- 22.5	- 39.7	+ 1.7
HC Corrected	49° 44.9'	44° 18.2	20° 58.2'
Ho	49° 42.9'	43° 53.1'	21° 11.7'
a: (intercept)	**2.0 A**	**25.1 A**	**13.5 T**

Direction Computer			
Z	034.1	138.9	088.4
Z	032.7	139.7	087.4
d	- 1.4	+ .8	- 1.0
Dec inc (x)	47.6'	48.9'	03.8'
60 (\)	60	60	60
Correction	- 1.1	+ .8	- .1
Corrected Z	033.0	138.5	088.3
± 180, 360	180 -	180 -	180 -
Convert Z to Zn	**147.0**	**041.5**	**268.3**

Notes:
ANSWER A

2.		**15 July**	
USCG # 1077	Latitude		27° 42.0' N
1845	Longitude		167° 02.0' E
		C -243	S - 16
Object Name	**Deneb**	**Antares**	**Denebola**
ZT Sight	1905	1924	1945
Fix Time	1945	1945	1945
D	40	21	0
Speed x Time	16 x 40	16 x 40	16 x 0
Divided by 60	60	60	60
= Advance	10.7	5.5	0

Convert GHA to LHA			
GHA	104° 08.0'	172° 02.1'	247° 20.6'
± Longitude	+ 166° 52.0'	+ 166° 57.9'	+ 166° 39.4'
LHA	271° 00.0'	339° 00.0'	054° 00.0'

Declination			
Declination	N 45° 12.8'	S 26° 23.5'	N 14° 40.7'
	SAME	CONTRARY	SAME

Pub 229 Work			
Intercept Computed			
Hc	20° 03.1'	32° 20.9'	38° 06.5'
d	+ 20.3	- 55.6	+ 24.8
Dec inc (x)	12.8'	23.5	40.7'
60 (\)	60	60	60
Correction	+ 4.3	- 21.7	+ 16.8
HC Corrected	20° 07.4'	31° 59.2'	38° 23.3'
Ho	19° 52.4'	32° 22.1'	38° 22.3'
a: (intercept)	**15.0 A**	**22.9 T**	**1.0 A**

Direction Computer			
Z	048.8	157.6	093.9
Z	047.8	158.0	092.8
d	- 1.0	+ .4	- 1.1
Dec inc (x)	12.8'	23.5'	40.7'
60 (\)	60	60	60
Correction	- .2	+ .2	- .7
Corrected Z	048.6	157.8	093.2
± 180, 360			180 -
Convert Z to Zn	**048.6**	**157.8**	**266.8**

Notes:
ANSWER A

3.		**6 April**	
USCG # 1078	Latitude		26° 33.0' N
1830	Longitude		064° 31.0' W
		C- 082	S- 16.0
Object Name	**Sirius**	**Regulus**	**Mirfak**
ZT Sight	1836	1842	1900
Fix Time	1900	1900	1900
D	24	18	0
Speed x Time	16 x 24	16 x 18	16 x 15
Divided by 60	60	60	60
= Advance	6.4	4.8	0
Convert GHA to LHA			
GHA	73° 02.7'	23° 46.9'	129° 24.3'
± Longitude	64° 02.7'	64° 46.9'	064°24.3'
LHA	009° 00.0'	319° 00.0'	065° 00.0'
Declination			
Declination	S 16° 41.7'	N 12° 03.5'	N 49° 47.7'
	CONTRARY	SAME	SAME
Pub 229 Work			
Intercept Computed			
Hc	46° 07.3'	48° 46.6'	36° 08.0'
d	- 58.8	+ 27.2	+ .7
Dec inc (x)	41.8'	03.5'	47.7'
60 (\)	60	60	60
Correction	- 40.9	+ 1.6	+ .6
HC Corrected	45° 26.4'	48° 48.2'	36° 08.6'
Ho	46° 00.5'	49° 07.2'	35° 51.6'
a: (intercept)	**34.1 T**	**19.0 T**	**17.0 A**
Direction Computer			
Z (16)	167.5	103.1	047.4
Z (17)	167.7	101.8	046.2
d	+ .3	- 1.3	- 1.2
Dec inc (x)	41.8'	03.5'	47.7'
60 (\)	60	60	60
Correction	+ .2	- .1	-1.0
Corrected Z	167.7	103.0	46.2
± 180, 360	360 -		360
Convert Z to Zn	**192.3**	**103.0**	**313.8**

Notes:
ANSWER   B

4.		**12 December**	
USCG # 1079	Latitude		24° 16.0' S
1830	Longitude		41° 18.0' W
		C - 235°	S ~ 16.0
Object Name	**Rigel**	**Peacock**	**Markab**
ZT Sight	1845	1910	1930
Fix Time	1930	1930	1930
D	45	20	0
Speed x Time	16 x 30	16 x 20	16 x 0
Divided by 60	60	60	60
= Advance	12.0	5.3	0
Convert GHA to LHA			
GHA	329° 19.7'	107° 58.4'	073° 04.1'
± Longitude	- 41° 19.7'	-41° 58.5'	- 41° 04.1'
LHA	288° 00.0'	066° 00.0'	032° 00.0'
Declination			
Declination	S 8° 13.4'	S 56° 47.8'	N 15° 06.5'
	SAME	SAME	CONTRARY
Pub 229 Work			
Intercept Computed			
Hc	19° 38.6	33° 01.4	40° 01.2'
d	- 23.0	- 6.1	- 46.6'
Dec inc (x)	13.4'	47.8'	06.5'
60 (\)	60	60	60
Correction	+ 5.1	- 4.9	- 5.0
HC Corrected	19° 43.7'	32° 56.5'	39v 56.2'
Ho	19° 54.7'	32° 43.9'	39° 53.1'
a: (intercept)	**11.0 T**	**12.6 A**	**3.1 A**
Direction Computer			
Z	089.8	037.5	138.1
Z	088.9	036.4	138.9
d	- .9	- 1.1	+ .8
Dec inc (x)	13.4'	47.8'	06.5'
60 (\)	60	60	60
Correction	- .2	- 0.9	+ .1
Corrected Z	089.6	036.6	138.2
± 180, 360	180 -	180 +	180 +
Convert Z to Zn	**090.4**	**216.6**	**318.2**

Notes:
ANSWER   B

5.		20 February	
USCG # 1080	Latitude		24° 15.0' N
0530	Longitude		137° 33.0' W
		C- 033	S- 18.0
Object Name	**Regulus**	**Antares**	**Vega**
ZT Sight	0540	0552	0600
Fix Time	0600	0600	0600
D	20	8	0
Speed x Time	18 x 20	18 x 8	18 x 0
Divided by 60	60	60	60
= Advance	6.0	2.4	0

Convert GHA to LHA			
GHA	218° 35.9'	126° 23.5'	96° 23.2'
± Longitude	- 137° 35.9'	- 137° 23.5'	- 137° 23.2'
LHA	81° 00.0'	349° 00.0'	319° 00.0'

Declination			
Declination	N 12° 03.5'	S 26° 23.3'	N 38° 45.8'
	SAME	CONTRARY	SAME

Pub 229 Work
Intercept Computed

Hc	12° 57.9'	38° 52.8'	52° 32.0'
d	+ 22.5	- 58.5	- 10.9
Dec inc (x)	03.5'	23.3	45.8'
60 (\)	60	60	60
Correction	+ 1.3	- 22.7	- 8.3
HC Corrected	12° 59.2'	38° 30.1'	52° 23.7
Ho	13° 02.2'	38° 04.1'	52° 33.5'
a: (intercept)	**3.0 T**	**26.0 A**	**9.8 T**

Direction Computer

Z	082.5	167.3	058.2
Z	081.5	167.6	056.6
d	- 1.0	+ .3	- 1.6
Dec inc (x)	03.5'	23.3'	45.8'
60 (\)	60	60	60
Correction	- .1	+ 1	- 1.2
Corrected Z	082.4	167.4	057.0
± 180, 360	360 -		
Convert Z to Zn	**277.6**	**167.4**	**057.0**

Notes:
ANSWER   C

Additional USCG problems worked-out for this chapter can be found in **Celestial Navigation Calculations (Upon Oceans Endorsement) Worked-Out for Master 500 GT through 2nd Mate Unlimited, Volume 3, part 2, Chapter 6, Determining Position by Sight Reduction.**

Star Identification and Selection
Chapter 15

Various devices have been invented to help an observer find individual stars. The most widely used is the **Star Finder and Identifier**, formerly published by the U.S. Navy Hydrographic Office as *No. 2102D*, but it is still available commercially. Currently available navigation calculator or computer programs are much quicker, more accurate, and less tedious. They are **NOT** allowed in the testing room, thus we will discuss the use of the Star Finder and Identifier below.

The data required by the calculator or program consists of the DR position, the sextant altitude of the body, the time, and the azimuth of the body. The name of the body is not necessary because there will be only one possible body meeting those conditions, which the computer will identify. Computer sight reduction programs can also automatically predict twilight on a moving vessel and create a plot of the sky at the vessel's twilight location (or any location, at any time). This plot will be free of the distortion inherent in the mechanical star finders and will show all bodies, even planets, Sun, and Moon, in their correct relative orientation centered on the observer's zenith. It will also indicate which stars provide the best geometry for a fix.

Computer sight reduction programs or celestial navigation calculators are especially useful when the sky is only briefly visible thorough broken cloud cover. The navigator can quickly shoot any visible body without having to identify it by name, and let the computer do the rest.

Using the Rude Star Finder and Identifier

The unit consists of a base plate (northern hemisphere on one side, southern on the other) plus a set of latitude plates. Use the **nautical almanac** to look up the Greenwich Hour Angle of Aries for the time of interest (usually Civil Twilight - also obtained from the nautical almanac), then set the closest latitude disk on the base plate. Rotate the arrow on the latitude disk to the **Local Hour Angle of Aries** on the graduated edge of the base-plate, and you have in your hand a picture of the sky around you, showing the stars visible at twilight. From the disk you can read the azimuths (bearings), and altitudes (angular height above the horizon) of the stars.

Plotting the planets, sun and moon

The planets, sun and moon can be marked in pencil onto the base-plate number for a specific date and their approximate positions in the sky obtained at the same time as the starts, template number 10, **the red disk with the open slot.** We plot **planets, sun and moon** using Right Ascension (RA) and Declination. (360 – SHA = RA). The SHA's for the planets are found at the bottom right of the planets daily prediction page of the almanac.

STAR IDENTIFICATION - MAJOR

1. 01851. On 23 September 1981, while taking stars for an evening fix, an unidentified star is observed bearing 261° T at an observed altitude of 61° 35'. Your 1836 zone time DR position is LAT 25° 18' S, LONG 162° 36' E. The chronometer reads 07h 34m 12s, and the chronometer error is 01m 54s slow. Your vessel is steaming on a course of 230° T at a speed of 18 knots. Which star did you observe?

A. Antares
B. Canopus
C. Achernar
D. Sirius

2. 01852. On 26 November 1981, at 0535 ZT while taking sights for a morning fix, you observe an unidentified planet bearing 074° T at an observed altitude (Ho) of 38° 29.8'. Your DR position is LAT 27° 18.9' S, LONG 30° 18.4' E. The chronometer time of the sight is 03h 33m 16s, and the chronometer is 01m 48s slow. Which planet did you observe?

A. Saturn
B. Jupiter
C. Mars
D. Venus

3. 01853. On 8 April 1981, while taking observations for an evening fix, you observe an unidentified star bearing 250.7° T at an observed altitude of 51° 44.8'. Your DR position at the time of the sight was LAT 22° 16.0' N, LONG 157° 58.3' W. The chronometer reads 05h 09m 57s and is 01m 23s slow. Which star did you observe?

A. Betelgeuse
B. Aldebaran
C. Alnilam
D. Bellatrix

4. 01854. On 22 July 1981, your 1759 ZT DR position is LAT 24° 50.2 S, LONG 005° 16.0' E. You observe an unidentified star bearing 231° T at an observed altitude (Ho) of 26° 10.0'. The chronometer reads 06h 01m 31s and is 02m 15s fast. What star did you observe?

A. Acamar
B. Capella
C. Miaplacidus
D. Suhail

5. 01855. On 22 July 1981, your 0442 ZT DR position is LAT 26° 35.6' N, LONG 22° 16.7' W. You observe an unidentified star bearing 112° T at an observed altitude (Ho) of 44° 16.0'. The chronometer reads 05h 39m 03s and is 03m 14s slow. What star did you observe?

A. Hamal
B. Rigel
C. Menkar
D. Acamar

Answers to Star Identification

1. 01851 A
2. 01852 A
3. 01853 D
4. 01854 D
5. 01855 C

15-2

Celestial Problems
Unknown Star

Problem # 1 (USCG) (1851)				Chapter 15	

Date:	23 Sept		Time		**LAT:**	25° 18' S
					LONG	162° 36' E
	ZT	1836	**CT**	07:34:12	**C-230°**	
	ZD	- 11	**CE**	+ 1:54	**S- 18 kts**	
	GMT	0736	**CCT**	07:36:06		
			GMT	07:36:06	**Unknown Star**	
					Ho	61° 35'
					Bearing	261°

Almanac		Star Finder (Notes)
GHA Aries	107° 02.4'	
M/S	+ 9° 03.0'	
GHA Aries	116° 05.4'	
±SHA/v		
Sum	116° 05.4'	
Long	+ 162° 36.0'	
LHA Aries	278° 41.4'	

Celestial Problems
Unknown Planet

Problem # 2 (USCG) (1852)				Chapter 15	

Date:	26 Nov		Time		**LAT:**	27° 18.9' S
					LONG	030° 18.4' E
	ZT	0535	**CT**	03:33:16	**C-**	
	ZD	- 2	**CE**	+ 01:48	**S-**	
	GMT	0335	**CCT**	03:35:04		
			GMT	03:35:04	**Unknown Star**	
					Ho	38° 29.8'
					Bearing	074°

Almanac		Star Finder (Notes)				
GHA Aries	109° 57.5'					
M/S	+ 8° 47.4'	Name	360 - SHA	=	RA	Dec
GHA Aries	118° 44.9'					
±SHA/v		Venus	360 - 69°		291°	S 25° 07.9'
Sum	118° 44.9'	Mars	360 - 189°		171°	N 05° 38.8'
Long	+ 30° 18.4'	Jupiter	360 - 152°		208°	S 11° 22.1'
LHA Aries	149° 03.3'	Saturn	360 - 162°		198°	S 05° 11.8'

Celestial Problems
Unknown Star

Problem # 3 (USCG) (1853)   Chapter 15

Date:	8 April	Time			LAT:	22° 16.0' N
					LONG	157° 58.3' W
	ZT	1800	CT	05:09:57	C-	
	ZD	+ 11	CE	+ 01:23	S-	
	GMT	2900	CCT	05:11:20		
9 April 05:00			GMT	05:11:20	**Unknown Star**	
					Ho	51° 44.8'
					Bearing	250.7°

Almanac | **Star Finder (Notes)**

GHA Aries	271° 22.2'
M/S	+ 2° 50.5'
GHA Aries	274° 12.7'
±SHA/v	
Sum	274° 12.7'
Long	- 157° 58.3'
LHA Aries	117° 14.4'

Celestial Problems
Unknown Star

Problem # 4 (USCG) (1854)   Chapter 15

Date:	22 July	Time1759			LAT:	24° 50.2' S
					LONG	005° 16.0' E
	ZT	17:59	CT	06:01:31	C-	
	ZD	0	CE	- 02:15	S-	
	GMT	1759	CCT	05:59:16		
			GMT	17:59:16	**Unknown Star**	
					Ho	26° 10.0'
					Bearing	231°

Almanac | **Star Finder (Notes)**

GHA Aries	195° 21.3'
M/S	+ 14° 51.4'
GHA Aries	210° 12.7'
±SHA/v	
Sum	210° 12.7'
Long	+ 5° 16.0'
LHA Aries	215° 28.7'

Celestial Problems
Unknown Star

Problem # 5 (USCG) (1855)	Chapter 15

Date:	22 July	Time	0442	**LAT:**	26° 35.6' N
				LONG	022° 16.7' W
	ZT	0442	**CT**	05:39:03	**C-**
	ZD	+ 1	**CE**	+ 03:14	**S-**
	GMT	0542	**CCT**	05:42:17	
			GMT	05:42:17	**Unknown Star**
				Ho	44° 16.0'
				Bearing	112°

Almanac		Star Finder (Notes)
GHA Aries	014° 51.8'	
M/S	+ 010° 36.0'	
GHA Aries	025° 27.8'	
±SHA/v		
Sum	025° 27.8	
Long	- 22° 16.7'	
LHA Aries	003° 11.1'	

STARS SELECTION
Chapter 15 Celestial for Master/Mate limited Upon Oceans

1. 02001. On 3 February 1981, your 0451 zone time DR position is LAT 24° 15.0' S, LONG 124° 24.0' W. Considering their magnitude, azimuth, and altitude, which of the following groups includes the three bodies best suited for a fix at star time?

A. Alphard, Denebola, Acrux
B. Spica, Venus, Procyon
C. Jupiter, Dubhe, Antares
D. Mars, Arcturus, Spica

2. 02002. On 16 July 1981, your 1810 zone time DR position is LAT 24° 16.5' S, LONG 162° 52.0' E. Considering their magnitude, azimuth, and altitude, which of the following groups includes the three bodies best suited for a fix at star time?

A. Arcturus, Spica, Antares
B. Jupiter, Acrux, Alphecca
C. Pollux, Mars, Deneb
D. Vega, Hadar, Venus

3. 02003. On 20 June 1981, your 1742 zone time DR position is LAT 24° 55.0' S, LONG 8° 19.6' E. Considering their magnitude, azimuth, and altitude, which of the following groups includes the three stars best suited for a fix at star time?

A. Regulus, Canopus, Antares
B. Spica, Arcturus, Alioth
C. Arcturus, Achernar, Pollux
D. Avior, Sabik, Fomalhaut

4. 02004. On 28 February 1981, your 1850 zone time DR position is LAT 27° 49.0' N, LONG 159° 24.0' W. Considering their magnitude, azimuth, and altitude, which of the following groups includes the three stars best suited for a fix at star time?

A. Rigel, Schedar, Regulus
B. Sirius, Mirfak, Elnath
C. Hamal, Alkaid, Canopus
D. Bellatrix, Vega, Regulus

5. 02005. On 17 July 1981, your 1951 zone time DR position is LAT 24° 26.0' N, LONG 51° 16.0' W. Considering their magnitude, azimuth, and altitude, which of the following groups includes the three bodies best suited for a fix at star time?

A. Hadar, Deneb, Alphard
B. Regulus, Venus, Antares
C. Mars, Vega, Dubhe
D. Kochab, Jupiter, Rasalhague

Answers to Star Selection

1. 02001 A
2. 02002 B
3. 02003 A
4. 02004 A
5. 02005 D

Celestial Problems
Star Selection

Problem # 1 (USCG) (2001) — Chapter 15

Date:	3 Feb	Time			LAT:	24° 15.0′ S
					LONG	124° 24.0′ W
	ZT	0451	CT		C-	
	ZD	+ 8	CE		S-	
	GMT	1251	CCT			
			GMT		Star Selection	
					Ho	
					Bearing	

Almanac			Star Finder (Notes)				
GHA	313° 34.6′		Plotting the Planets				
M/S	+ 12° 47.1′		360 -	SHA	=	RA	DEC
GHA	326° 21.7′	Venus	360	058°	=	302°	S 21
±SHA/v		Mars	360	030°	=	330°	S 13
Sum	326° 21.7′	Jupiter	360	170°	=	190°	S 3
Long	- 124° 24.0′						
LHA	201° 57.7′						

Celestial Problems
Star Selection

Problem # 2 (USCG) (2002) — Chapter 15

Date:	16 Jul	Time	1810		LAT:	24° 16.5′ S
					LONG	162° 52.0′ E
	ZT	1810	CT		C-	
	ZD	- 11	CE		S-	
	GMT	0710	CCT			
			GMT		Star Selection	
					Ho	
					Bearing	

Almanac			Star Finder (Notes)				
GHA	39° 01.9′		Plotting the Planets				
M/S	+ 2° 30.4′		360 -	SHA	=	RA	DEC
GHA	41° 32.3′	Venus	360	217°	=	143°	N 16
±SHA/v		Mars	360	271°	=	089°	N 23
Sum	41° 32.3′	Jupiter	360	176°	=	184°	S 0
Long	+ 162° 52.0′						
LHA	204° 24.3′						

Celestial Problems
Star Selection

Problem # 3 (USCG) (2003)   Chapter 15

Date:	20 June	Time	1742	LAT:	24° 55.0' S

LONG   008° 19.6' E

ZT	1742	CT		C-	
ZD	- 1	CE		S-	
GMT	1642	CCT			
		GMT			

Star Selection

Ho

Bearing

Almanac

GHA	148° 46.4'
M/S	10° 31.7'
GHA	159° 18.1'
±SHA/v	
Sum	159° 18.1'
Long	+ 008° 19.6'
LHA	167° 37.7'

Star Finder (Notes)

Celestial Problems
Star Selection

Problem # 4 (USCG) (2004)   Chapter 15

Date:	28 Feb	Time	1850	LAT:	27° 49.0' N

LONG   159° 24.0' W

ZT	1850	CT		C-	
ZD	+ 11	CE		S-	
Mar 1 GMT	0550	CCT			
		GMT			

Star Selection

Ho

Bearing

Almanac

GHA	233° 54.9'
M/S	12° 32.1'
GHA	246° 27.0'
±SHA/v	
Sum	246° 27.0'
Long	- 159° 24.0'
LHA	87° 03.0'

Star Finder (Notes)

Celestial Problems				
Star Selection				
Problem # 5 (USCG) (2005)				Chapter 15
Date: 17 July	Time		1951	**LAT:** 24° 26.0' N
				LONG 051° 16.0' W
ZT	1951	CT		**C-**
ZD	+ 3	CE		**S-**
GMT	2251	CCT		
		GMT		**Star Selection**
				Ho
				Bearing

Almanac				Star Finder (Notes)			
GHA	265° 38.0'		Plotting the Planets				
M/S	12° 47.1'		**360 -**	**SHA**	**=**	**RA**	**DEC**
GHA	278° 25.1'	Venus	360	217°	=	143°	N 16
±SHA/v		Mars	360	271°	=	089°	N 23
Sum	278° 25.1'	Jupiter	360	176°	=	184°	S 0
Long	-51° 16.0'						
LHA	227° 09.1'						

LATITUDE BY POLARIS
Chapter 16

Since **Polaris, the Northern Pole Star** is located at the approximate pole, we can calculate our Latitude similar to LAN of the Sun by making mathematical adjustment to our Ho. Except in this case we correct Ho for the difference in the pole stars position related to the true pole vice using corrections of Declination.

The method taught here will require the use of the Nautical Almanac page reproduced on pages **16-3.** We will only calculate the items that are new to you and will not repeat the steps for calculating GMT, GHA, LHA of Aries or Ho.

Example

00737. On 29 July 1981, your 1930 zone time DR position is LONG 164° 26.0' E. At that time you observe Polaris with a sextant altitude (hs) of 23° 46.8'. The chronometer time of the sight is 08h 32m 18s, and the chronometer error is 02m 26s fast. The index error is 2.7' on the arc, and the height of eye is 56.0 feet. What is your latitude by Polaris?

Entering the data from the information given above and the calculations of GMT, Ho and GHA of Aries **(refer to Chapters 7, 8, and 9 respectively)** are entered in the appropriate spaces of our work form on **page 16-2.**

We are now ready to calculate the required corrections (a_0, a_1 and a_2) to Ho. We will be required to calculate a_0 by interpolations of the Nautical Almanac, but a_1 and a_2 will require only inspection of these tables.

Taking our LHA of Aries, Latitude **(Ho, if latitude is not given),** and month of the year from our work form we enter the Almanac Polaris correction below.

Enter the Pole star tables in the back of the Nautical Almanac for the LHA of Aries at the top of the page. Follow down the column until across from the single degree of LHA as tabulated in the left hand margin. The exact value for a_0 is found for the minutes of LHA by interpolation. **Pay attention to the entire value. It is sometimes 0 degrees and sometimes it is 1 degree.**

The last two corrections to Ho are now found by inspection of the Polaris tables in same way as we did to find base a_0, remaining in the same column as was used for LHA, go to the next table below the a_0 table. Find the tabulated latitude nearest to your DR latitude on the left hand column or Ho if latitude is not given in the problem, **Do not interpolate**, we find a_1 is **0.6**. Next, to determine a_2 we continue down the same column to the month of the year **(July)** in the left hand column and find a correction of **1.0'**. We sum the three corrections for an answer of **1° 44.9'**

Adding these corrections to Ho we have **25° 19.5'** which is exactly one degree more than our latitude.

Lastly, we subtract 1° from **25° 19.5'** to get our corrected Latitude of **24° 19.5'** and compare this to the answers given by the U.S. Coast Guard. We **will always subtract 1°** from our corrected **Ho.**

Celestial Problems Latitude By Polaris					
Problem # (USCG) (0737)				Chapter 16	

Date:	29 **July**	Time			LAT:	**No latitude Given**
			CT	08:32:18	LONG	164° 26.0' E
	ZT	1930	CE	- 02:26	S-	
	ZD	- 11	CCT	08:29:52	C-	
	GMT	0830	GMT	08:29:52		

Almanac						
GHA	65° 54.0'	LHA a0	1° 43.3'	Hs	23° 46.8'	
M/S	+ 7° 292	LAT a1	.6'	Ic	- 2.7'	
GHA	74° 232'	DATE a2	1.0'	Dip (56.0)	- 7.3'	
±SHA/v		Total a	1° 44.9'	Sum	-10.0'	
Sum	74° 23.2'			Ha	23° 36.8'	
a λ	+ 164° 26.0'			Alt	- 2.2'	
LHA	**237° 49.2'**			Ho	**23° 34.6'**	
Notes:				+ a	1° 45.3'	
				Sum	25° 19.9'	
				- 1°	- 1	
				Lat	**24° 19.9'**	

POLARIS (POLE STAR) TABLES, 1981
FOR DETERMINING LATITUDE FROM SEXTANT ALTITUDE AND FOR AZIMUTH

275

L.H.A. ARIES	120°– 129°	130°– 139°	140°– 149°	150°– 159°	160°– 169°	170°– 179°	180°– 189°	190°– 199°	200°– 209°	210°– 219°	220°– 229°	230°– 239°
	a_0	a_0	a_0	a_0	a_0	a_0	a_0	a_0	a_0	a_0	a_0	a_0
°	° ′	° ′	° ′	° ′	° ′	° ′	° ′	° ′	° ′	° ′	° ′	° ′
0	0 56·4	1 05·0	1 13·3	1 21·2	1 28·5	1 34·8	1 40·0	1 44·1	1 46·7	1 47·9	1 47·7	1 46·0
1	57·2	05·8	14·1	22·0	29·1	35·4	40·5	44·4	46·9	48·0	47·6	45·7
2	58·1	06·7	15·0	22·7	29·8	35·9	41·0	44·7	47·1	48·0	47·4	45·4
3	59·0	07·5	15·8	23·5	30·5	36·5	41·4	45·0	47·2	48·0	47·3	45·2
4	0 59·8	08·3	16·6	24·2	31·1	37·0	41·8	45·3	47·4	48·0	47·2	44·9
5	1 00·7	1 09·2	1 17·4	1 25·0	1 31·8	1 37·6	1 42·2	1 45·6	1 47·5	1 48·0	1 47·0	1 44·6
6	01·5	10·0	18·1	25·7	32·4	38·1	42·6	45·8	47·6	47·9	46·8	44·3
7	02·4	10·8	18·9	26·4	33·0	38·6	43·0	46·1	47·7	47·9	46·6	43·9
8	03·2	11·7	19·7	27·1	33·6	39·1	43·4	46·3	47·8	47·8	46·4	43·6
9	04·1	12·5	20·5	27·8	34·2	39·6	43·7	46·5	47·9	47·8	46·2	43·2
10	1 05·0	1 13·3	1 21·2	1 28·5	1 34·8	1 40·0	1 44·1	1 46·7	1 47·9	1 47·7	1 46·0	1 42·8

Lat.	a_1	a_1	a_1	a_1	a_1	a_1	a_1	a_1	a_1	a_1	a_1	a_1
°	′	′	′	′	′	′	′	′	′	′	′	′
0	0·2	0·2	0·2	0·3	0·4	0·4	0·5	0·6	0·6	0·6	0·6	0·5
10	·2	·3	·3	·3	·4	·5	·5	·6	·6	·6	·6	·6
20	·3	·3	·3	·4	·4	·5	·5	·6	·6	·6	·6	·6
30	·4	·4	·4	·4	·5	·5	·6	·6	·6	·6	·6	·6
40	0·5	0·5	0·5	0·5	0·5	0·6	0·6	0·6	0·6	0·6	0·6	0·6
45	·5	·5	·5	·6	·6	·6	·6	·6	·6	·6	·6	·6
50	·6	·6	·6	·6	·6	·6	·6	·6	·6	·6	·6	·6
55	·7	·7	·7	·7	·6	·6	·6	·6	·6	·6	·6	·6
60	·8	·8	·8	·7	·7	·7	·6	·6	·6	·6	·6	·6
62	0·8	0·8	0·8	0·8	0·7	0·7	0·7	0·6	0·6	0·6	0·6	0·6
64	0·9	0·9	0·9	·8	·8	·7	·7	·6	·6	·6	·6	·6
66	1·0	1·0	0·9	·9	·8	·7	·7	·6	·6	·6	·6	·7
68	1·1	1·0	1·0	0·9	0·9	0·8	0·7	0·6	0·6	0·6	0·6	0·7

Month	a_2	a_2	a_2	a_2	a_2	a_2	a_2	a_2	a_2	a_2	a_2	a_2
	′	′	′	′	′	′	′	′	′	′	′	′
Jan.	0·6	0·6	0·6	0·6	0·5	0·5	0·5	0·5	0·5	0·5	0·5	0·5
Feb.	·8	·7	·7	·7	·7	·6	·6	·6	·5	·5	·5	·5
Mar.	·9	0·9	0·9	0·8	·8	·8	·7	·7	·6	·6	·5	·5
Apr.	0·9	1·0	1·0	1·0	0·9	0·9	0·9	0·8	0·8	0·7	0·7	0·6
May	·9	1·0	1·0	1·0	1·0	1·0	1·0	1·0	0·9	0·9	·8	·7
June	·8	0·9	0·9	1·0	1·0	1·0	1·0	1·0	1·0	1·0	0·9	0·9
July	0·7	0·7	0·8	0·9	0·9	0·9	1·0	1·0	1·0	1·0	1·0	1·0
Aug.	·5	·6	·6	·7	·7	·8	0·9	0·9	0·9	1·0	1·0	1·0
Sept.	·4	·4	·5	·5	·6	·6	·7	·7	·8	0·8	0·9	0·9
Oct.	0·3	0·3	0·3	0·3	0·4	0·4	0·5	0·6	0·6	0·7	0·7	0·8
Nov.	·2	·2	·2	·2	·3	·3	·3	·4	·4	·5	·6	·6
Dec.	0·3	0·3	0·2	0·2	0·2	0·2	0·2	0·2	0·3	0·3	0·4	0·4

Lat.						AZIMUTH						
°	°	°	°	°	°	°	°	°	°	°	°	°
0	359·2	359·2	359·2	359·3	359·4	359·5	359·6	359·7	359·9	0·0	0·2	0·3
20	359·1	359·1	359·2	359·3	359·4	359·5	359·6	359·7	359·9	0·0	0·2	0·3
40	358·9	359·0	359·0	359·1	359·2	359·3	359·5	359·7	359·8	0·0	0·2	0·4
50	358·7	358·8	358·8	358·9	359·1	359·2	359·4	359·6	359·8	0·0	0·3	0·5
55	358·6	358·6	358·7	358·8	358·9	359·1	359·3	359·6	359·8	0·0	0·3	0·5
60	358·4	358·4	358·5	358·6	358·8	359·0	359·2	359·5	359·8	0·0	0·3	0·6
65	358·1	358·1	358·2	358·4	358·6	358·8	359·1	359·4	359·7	0·1	0·4	0·7

ILLUSTRATION

On 1981 April 21 at G.M.T. 23ʰ 18ᵐ 56ˢ in longitude W. 37° 14′ the apparent altitude (corrected for refraction), Ho, of Polaris was 49° 31′·6.

From the daily pages:	° ′
G.H.A. Aries (23ʰ)	194 55·4
Increment (18ᵐ 56ˢ)	4 44·8
Longitude (west)	–37 14
L.H.A. Aries	162 26

	° ′
Ho	49 31·6
a_0 (argument 162° 26′)	1 30·1
a_1 (lat. 50° approx.)	0·6
a_2 (April)	0·9
Sum – 1° = Lat. =	50 03·2

16-3

End of Chapter Problems

1. 00726. On 16 December 1981, your 1810 zone time DR position is LONG 129° 46.5' W. At that time you observe Polaris with a sextant altitude (hs) of 23° 56.8'. The chronometer time of the sight is 03h 12m 31s, and the chronometer error is 02m 16s fast. The index error is 2.5' off the arc, and the height of eye is 52.6 feet. What is your latitude by Polaris?

A. 23° 07.8' N
B. 23° 12.3' N
C. 24° 11.9' N
D. 24° 18.6' N

2. 00727. On 11 February 1981, your 1832 zone time DR position is LONG 110° 52.6' W. At that time you observe Polaris with a sextant altitude (hs) of 26° 19.8'. The chronometer time of the sight is 01h 34m 56s, and the chronometer error is 02m 16s fast. The index error is 2.7' off the arc, and the height of eye is 60.2 feet. What is your latitude by Polaris?

A. 25° 27.2' N
B. 25° 34.2' N
C. 26° 27.2' N
D. 26° 34.2' N

3. 00728. On 2 January 1981, your 1759 zone time DR position is LONG 45° 17.6' W. At that time you observe Polaris with a sextant altitude (hs) of 24° 16.5'. The chronometer time of the sight is 08h 57m 10s, and the chronometer error is 02m 16s slow. The index error is 3.5 on the arc, and the height of eye is 42.5 feet. What is your latitude by Polaris?

A. 22° 50.2' N
B. 23° 18.8' N
C. 23° 30.2' N
D. 24° 07.3' N

4. 00729. On 24 September 1981, your 1841 zone time DR position is LONG 129° 34.5' E. At that time you observe Polaris with a sextant altitude (hs) of 25° 20.8'. The chronometer time of the sight is 09h 38m 12s, and the chronometer error is 03m 12s slow. The index error is 4.3' off the arc, and the height of eye is 52 feet. What is your latitude by Polaris?

A. 24° 28.1' N
B. 25° 16.0' N
C. 25° 37.6' N
D. 25° 42.3' N

5. 00730. On 18 November 1981, your 1750 zone time DR position is LONG 110° 16.0' W. At that time you observe Polaris with a sextant altitude (hs) of 21° 29.8'. The chronometer time of the sight is 00h 52m 43s, and the chronometer error is 02m 18s fast. The index error is 3.2' on the arc, and the height of eye is 49.5 feet. What is your latitude by Polaris?

A. 21° 03.4' N
B. 21° 13.4' N
C. 21° 28.1' N
D. 21° 35.1' N

Answers to Latitude by of Polaris:

1. A
2. A
3. B
4. C
5. A

Latitude by of Polaris worked-out

Celestial Problems				
Latitude By Polaris				

Problem # 1 (USCG) (0726)			Chapter 16	

Date:	16 Dec.	Time		LAT:		
			CT	03:12:31	LONG	129° 46.5' W
	ZT	18:10	CE	-2:16	S-	
	ZD	+ 9	CCT	03:10:15	C-	
17 Dec	GMT	03:10	GMT	03:10:15		

Almanac						
GHA	130° 39.4'	LHA a0	0° 16.2'	Hs	23°56.8'
M/S	+ 2° 34.2'	LAT a1	.5'	IC	+2.5'
GHA	133° 13.6'	DATE a2	1.0'	Dip (52.6)	- 7.0'
±SHA/v		Total a	0° 17.7'	Sum	-4.5'
Sum	133° 13.6'			Ha	23° 52.3'
a λ	- 129° 46.5'			Alt	- 2.2'
LHA	3° 27.1'			Ho	23°50.1'
Notes:				+ a	0° 17.7'
ANSWER A				Sum	24° 07.8'
				- 1°	- 1°
				Lat	23° 07.8'

Celestial Problems
Latitude By Polaris

Problem # 2 (USCG) (0727)   Chapter 16

Date:	11 Feb	Time			LAT:	
			CT	01:34:56	LONG	110° 52.6'
	ZT	18:32	CE	- 02:16	S-	
	ZD	+ 7	CCT	01:32:40	C-	
12 Feb	GMT	01:32	GMT	01:32:40		

Almanac

GHA	156° 59.7'	LHA a0	0° 12.9'	Hs	26° 19.8'
M/S	+ 8° 11.3'	LAT a1	.6'	IC	+ 2.7'
GHA	165° 11.0'	DATE a2	.7'	Dip (60.2)	- 7.5'
±SHA/v		Total a	0° 14.2'	Sum	- 4.8'
Sum	165° 11.0'			Ha	26° 15.0'
a λ	- 110° 52.6'			Alt	- 2.0'
LHA	54° 18.4'			Ho	26° 13.0'

Notes:

ANSWER   A

+ a	0° 14.2'
Sum	26° 27.2'
- 1°	-1°
Lat	25° 27.2'

Celestial Problems
Latitude By Polaris

Problem # 3 (USCG) (0728)   Chapter 16

Date:	02 Jan	Time			LAT:	
			CT	08:57:10	LONG	45° 17.6' W
	ZT	17:59	CE	+ 02:16	S-	
	ZD	+9	CCT	20:59:26	C-	
	GMT	20:59	GMT	20:59:26		

Almanac

GHA	42° 21.9'	LHA a0	0° 13.0'	Hs	24° 16.5'
M/S	+ 14° 53.9'	LAT a1	.6'	IC	- 3.5'
GHA	57° 15.8'	DATE a2	.7'	Dip (42.5)	- 6.3'
±SHA/v		Total a	0° 14.3'	Sum	- 9.8'
Sum	57° 15.8'			Ha	24° 06.7'
a λ	-45° 17.6'			Alt	- 2.2'
LHA	11° 58.2'			Ho	24° 04.5'

Notes:

ANSWER   B

+ a	0° 14.3'
Sum	24° 18.8'
- 1°	- 1°
Lat	23° 18.8'

Celestial Problems
Latitude By Polaris

Problem # 4 (USCG) (0729)			Chapter 16	

Date:	24 Sep	Time		**LAT:**	
		CT	09:38:12	**LONG**	129° 34.5' E
ZT	18:41	**CE**	+ 03:12	**S-**	
ZD	- 9	**CCT**	09:41:24	**C-**	
GMT	09:41	**GMT**	09:41:24		

Almanac

GHA	138° 06.5'	**LHA a0**	1° 20.2'	**Hs**	25°20.8'
M/S	+ 10° 22.7'	**LAT a1**	.4'	**IC**	+ 4.3'
GHA	148° 29.2'	**DATE a2**	.9'	**Dip (52)**	- 7.0'
±SHA/v		**Total a**	1° 21.5'	**Sum**	- 2.7
Sum	148° 29.2'			**Ha**	25° 18.1'
a λ	-129° 34.5'			**Alt**	- 2.0'
LHA	278° 03.7'			**Ho**	25° 16.1'
Notes:				**+ a**	1° 21.5'
ANSWER C				**Sum**	26° 37.6'
				- 1°	- 1°
				Lat	25° 37.6'

Celestial Problems
Latitude By Polaris

Problem # 5 (USCG) (0730)			Chapter 16	

Date:	18 Nov	Time		**LAT:**	
		CT	00:52:43	**LONG**	110° 16.0' W
ZT	17:50	**CE**	- 02:18	**S-**	
ZD	+ 7	**CCT**	00:50:25	**C-**	
GMT 19 Nov	00:50	**GMT**	00:50:25		

Almanac

GHA	57° 56.1'	**LHA a0**	0° 44.8'	**Hs**	21°29.8'
M/S	+ 12° 38.3'	**LAT a1**	.3'	**IC**	- 3.2'
GHA	70° 34.4'	**DATE a2**	1.0'	**Dip (49.5)**	- 6.8'
±SHA/v		**Total a**	0° 46.1'	**Sum**	- 10.0'
Sum	70° 34.4'			**Ha**	21° 19.8'
a λ	- 110° 16.0'			**Alt**	- 2.5'
LHA	320° 18.4'			**Ho**	21° 17.3'
Notes:				**+ a**	+ 0° 46.1'
ANSWER A				**Sum**	22° 03.4'
				- 1°	- 1°
				Lat	21° 03.4'

Additional USCG problems worked-out for this chapter can be found in **Celestial Navigation Calculations (Upon Oceans Endorsement) Worked-Out for Master 500 GT through 2nd Mate Unlimited, Volume 3, part 2, Chapter 5, Determining Latitude**

WATCH TIME OF MERIDIAN PASSAGE
WATCH TIME OF LAN
Chapter 17

The purpose of determining watch time of LAN is merely to enable you to arrive on the bridge within a few minutes of the time you should take your sight.   Normally ten minutes prior to LAN. Since watch time of LAN is founded upon your dead reckoning (DR) longitude, it seldom coincides with the exact instant of the transit of the sun when it is at its meridian altitude.

The work form for computing Watch Time of LAN is shown on page 17-2.

Example:

01183. On 25 June 1981, your 0900 zone time DR position is LAT 24° 10.0' S, LONG 148° 30.0' W. Your vessel is on course 230° T at a speed of 18.0 knots. What is the zone time of local apparent noon (LAN)?

A. 1154
B. 1156
C. 1200
D. 1204

TIME OF MERIDIAN PASSAGE is entered by finding the appropriate date in the Nautical Almanac. In this case, the date is 35 June. At the bottom of the right-hand daily page, the time of meridian passage (Mer. Pass.) of the sun is listed as 1203. This time is given for the meridian of Greenwich, but the rate of change is so slight that it can be used at any longitude without significant error.

DR AT PREDICTED TIME OF LAN, if your ship is moving (and it probably will be), it sufficiently accurate to DR from our 0900 to the predicted time of LAN 1203. A new DR position can be plotted and the watch time of LAN can be computed; and is the one used for LAN observations.

LONGITUDE CORRECTION is completed by applying the time difference from the Dlo 0° 43.0' time 4 or approximately **3 minutes** from the Standard Meridian 150° to the time west of the standard meridian, the time difference is added. If you are east of the standard meridian, it will be subtracted.

Celestial Problems			
Watch Time of LAN			
Problem # (USCG) (1183)		Chapter 17	

Date: 25 Jun		FIX TIME	09:00
Required		LAT	24° 10.0' S
Watch Time of LAN		LONG	148° 30.0' W
		C- 230°	
		S- 18.0	

LONGITUDE CORRECTION		**Time of Meridian Passage**		**DR AT PREDICTED TIME OF LAN**	
		Base Time of	12:03	TIME	12:03
STD MER	150° 00.0'	Mer. Pass.		LAT	24° 45.0' S
LONG	149° 17.0'	Correction	- 3	LONG	149° 17.0' W
Dlo	0° 43.0'	Mer. Pass.	12:00		
dtime (E)	- 3.0				

NOTE:

End of Chapter USCG Problems

1. 01175. On 12 February 1981, your 0900 zone time DR position is LAT 16° 43.0' N, LONG 51° 42.0' W. Your vessel is on course 093° T at a speed of 18.5 knots. What is the zone time of local apparent noon (LAN)?

A. 1237
B. 1233
C. 1230
D. 1226

2. 01176. On 24 January 1981, your 0700 zone time DR position is LAT 22° 25.0' N, LONG 46° 10.0' W. Your vessel is on course 110° T at a speed of 12.0 knots. What is the zone time of local apparent noon (LAN)?

A. 1203
B. 1208
C. 1212
D. 1215

3. 01177. On 2 April 1981, your 0900 zone time DR position is LAT 28° 04.0' S, LONG 94° 14.0' E. Your vessel is on course 316° T at a speed of 18.5 knots. What is the zone time of local apparent noon (LAN)?

A. 1138
B. 1143
C. 1146
D. 1149

4. 01178. On 27 August 1981, your 0900 zone time DR position is LAT 24° 25.0' N, LONG 94° 20.0' W. Your vessel is on course 071° T at a speed of 20.0 knots. What is the zone time of local apparent noon (LAN)?

A. 1214
B. 1208
C. 1206
D. 1158

5. 01179. On 26 September 1981, your 0830 zone time DR position is LAT 26° 04.0' N, LONG 129° 16.0' W. Your vessel is on course 119° T at a speed of 20.0 knots. What is the zone time of local apparent noon (LAN)?

A. 1124
B. 1127
C. 1130
D. 1133

Answers

1. 01175 A
2. 01176 C
3. 01177 D
4. 01178 A
5. 01179 A

USCG Problems worked-out

Celestial Problems - Watch Time of LAN

Problem # 1 (USCG) (1175)		Chapter 17		
Date: 12 Feb		**FIX TIME**		09:00
Required		**LAT**		16° 43.0' N
Watch Time of LAN		**LONG**		016° 43.0' W
		C- 093°		
		S- 18.5		

LONGITUDE CORRECTION		Time of Meridian Passage		DR AT PREDICTED TIME OF LAN	
		Base Time of	12:14	**TIME**	12:14
STD MER	45° 00.0'	**Mer. Pass.**		**LAT**	16° 40.0' N
LONG	50° 38.0'	**Correction**	+ 23	**LONG**	050° 38.0' W
Dlo	5° 38.0'	**Mer. Pass.**	12:37		
dtime (W)	+ 22.5				

NOTE:

Celestial Problems - Watch Time of LAN

Problem # 2 (USCG) (1176)		Chapter 17		
Date: 24 Jan		**FIX TIME**		07:00
Required		**LAT**		22° 25.0' N
Watch Time of LAN		**LONG**		046° 0.0' W
		C- 110°		
		S- 12.0		

LONGITUDE CORRECTION		Time of Meridian Passage		DR AT PREDICTED TIME OF LAN	
		Base Time of	12:12	**TIME**	12:12
STD MER	45° 00.0'	**Mer. Pass.**		**LAT**	22° 04.0' N
LONG	45° 02.0'	**Correction**	0	**LONG**	045° 02.0' W
Dlo	02.0'	**Mer. Pass.**	12:12		
dtime (W)	0				

NOTE:

Celestial Problems - Watch Time of LAN

Problem # 3 (USCG) (1177)		Chapter 17	

Date:	2 Apr	FIX TIME	09:00
	Required	LAT	28° 04.0' S
	Watch Time of LAN	LONG	094° 14.0' E
		C- 316°	
		S- 18.5	

LONGITUDE CORRECTION		Time of Meridian Passage		DR AT PREDICTED TIME OF LAN	
STD MER	90° 00.0'	Base Time of Mer. Pass.	12:04	TIME	12:04
				LAT	27° 23.0' S
LONG	93° 27.0'	Correction	- 14	LONG	093° 27.0' E
Dlo	3° 27'	Mer. Pass.	11:50		
dtime (E)	- 13.8				

NOTE:

Celestial Problems - Watch Time of LAN

Problem # 4 (USCG) (1178)		Chapter 17	

Date:	27 Aug	FIX TIME	09:00
	Required	LAT	24° 25.0' N
	Watch Time of LAN	LONG	094° 20.0' W
		C- 071°	
		S- 20.0	

LONGITUDE CORRECTION		Time of Meridian Passage		DR AT PREDICTED TIME OF LAN	
STD MER	090° 00.0'	Base Time of Mer. Pass.	12:01	TIME	12:01
				LAT	24° 45.0' N
LONG	093° 15.0'	Correction	+ 13	LONG	093° 15.0' W
Dlo	3° 15.0'	Mer. Pass.	12:14		
dtime (E)	+ 13.0				

NOTE:

Celestial Problems - Watch Time of LAN

Problem # 5 (USCG) (1179)		Chapter 17	

Date: 26 Sep		**FIX TIME**	08:30
Required		**LAT**	26° 04.0' N
Watch Time of LAN		**LONG**	129° 16.0" W
		C- 119°	
		S- 20.0	

LONGITUDE CORRECTION		**Time of Meridian Passage**		**DR AT PREDICTED TIME OF LAN**	
		Base Time of	11:51	**TIME**	11:51
STD MER	135° 00.0'	**Mer. Pass.**		**LAT**	25° 32.0' N
LONG	128° 12.0'	**Correction**	- 27	**LONG**	128° 12.0' W
Dlo	6° 48.0'	**Mer. Pass.**	11:24		
dtime (E)	- 27.2				

NOTE:

Additional USCG problems worked-out for this chapter can be found in **Celestial Navigation Calculations (Upon Oceans Endorsement) Worked-Out for Master 500 GT through 2nd Mate Unlimited, Volume 3, part 2, Chapter 4, Time and Time Zone Calculations.**

SUN AND MOON RISING, SETTING, AND TWILIGHT
Chapter 18

Rising, Setting, and Twilight

In both *Air and Nautical Almanacs*, the times of sunrise, sunset, moonrise, moonset, and twilight information, at various latitudes between 72° N and 60° S, is listed to the nearest whole minute. By definition, rising or setting occurs when the upper limb of the body is on the visible horizon, assuming standard refraction for zero height of eye. Because of variations in refraction and height of eye, computation to a greater precision than 1 minute of time is not justified.

In high latitudes, some of the phenomena **do not** occur during certain periods. Symbols are used in the almanacs to indicate:

1. Sun or Moon does not set, but remains continuously above the horizon, indicated by an open rectangle.

2. Sun or Moon does not rise, but remains continuously below the horizon, indicated by a solid rectangle.

3. Twilight lasts all night, indicated by 4 slashes (/////).

The *Nautical Almanac* makes no provision for finding the times of rising, setting, or twilight in Polar Regions. The *Air Almanac* has graphs for this purpose.

In the *Nautical Almanac,* **sunrise, sunset, and twilight tables are given only once for the middle of the three days** on each page opening. For navigational purposes this information can be used for all three days. **Both almanacs have moonrise and moonset tables for each day**.

Lat.	Twilight Naut.	Twilight Civil	Sunrise
°	h m	h m	h m
N 72	////	////	01 33
N 70	////	////	02 22
68	////	00 23	02 53
66	////	01 45	03 15
64	////	02 20	03 33
62	00 21	02 45	03 47
60	01 34	03 04	03 59
N 58	02 06	03 20	04 10
56	02 29	03 33	04 19
54	02 48	03 45	04 27
52	03 03	03 54	04 34
50	03 15	04 03	04 40
45	03 41	04 21	04 54
N 40	04 00	04 36	05 06
35	04 15	04 48	05 15
30	04 28	04 58	05 24
20	04 48	05 15	05 38
N 10	05 03	05 29	05 50
0	05 16	05 41	06 02
S 10	05 26	05 52	06 13
20	05 36	06 03	06 26
30	05 46	06 14	06 39
35	05 51	06 21	06 47
40	05 55	06 28	06 56
45	06 01	06 35	07 06
S 50	06 06	06 45	07 19
52	06 08	06 49	07 25
54	06 11	06 53	07 31
56	06 13	06 58	07 38
58	06 16	07 03	07 46
S 60	06 19	07 09	07 55

Lat.	Sunset	Twilight Civil	Naut.

The tabulations are in LMT. On the zone meridian, this is the zone time (ZT). For every 15' of longitude the observer's position differs from the zone meridian, the zone time of the phenomena differs by 1m, being later if the observer is west of the zone meridian, and earlier if east of the zone meridian. The LMT of the phenomena varies with latitude of the observer, declination of the body, and hour angle of the body relative to the mean Sun.

The UT of the phenomenon is found from LMT by the formula:

UT = LMT + W Longitude.

UT = LMT - E Longitude.

To use this formula, convert the longitude to time using the table on page i or by computation, and add or subtract as indicated. Apply the zone description (ZD) to find the zone time of the phenomena. Sunrise and sunset are also tabulated in the tide tables (from 76° N to 60° S).

Finding Times of Sunrise and Sunset

To find the time of sunrise or sunset in the *Nautical Almanac*, enter the table on the daily page, and extract the LMT for the latitude next smaller than your own (unless it is exactly the same). Apply a correction from **Table I** on almanac **page xxxii** to interpolate for altitude, determining the sign by inspection. Then convert LMT to ZT using the difference of longitude between the local and zone meridians.

For the *Air Almanac*, the procedure is the same as for the *Nautical Almanac*, except that the LMT is taken from the tables of sunrise and sunset instead of from the daily page, and the latitude correction is by linear interpolation. The tabulated times are for the Greenwich meridian. Except in high latitudes near the time of the equinoxes, the time of sunrise and sunset varies so little from day to day that no interpolation is needed for longitude. In high latitudes interpolation is not always possible. Between two tabulated entries, the Sun may in fact cease to set. In this case, the time of rising and setting is greatly influenced by small variations in refraction and changes in height of eye.

Twilight

Morning twilight ends at sunrise, and evening twilight begins at sunset. The time of the darker limit can be found from the almanacs. The time of the darker limits of both civil and nautical twilights (center of the Sun 6° and 12°, respectively, below the celestial horizon) is given in the *Nautical Almanac*.

The *Air Almanac* provides tabulations of civil twilight from 60° S to 72° N. The brightness of the sky at any given depression of the Sun below the horizon may vary considerably from day to day, depending upon the amount of cloudiness, haze, and other atmospheric conditions. In general, the most effective period for observing stars and planets occurs when the center of the Sun is between about 3° and 9° below the celestial horizon.

Hence, the darker limit of civil twilight occurs at about the mid-point of this period. At the darker limit of nautical twilight, the horizon is generally too dark for good

The Almanac Observations.

At the darker limit of astronomical twilight (center of the Sun 18° below the celestial horizon), full night has set in. The time of this twilight is given in the *Astronomical Almanac*. Its approximate value can be determined by extrapolation in the *Nautical Almanac*, noting that the duration of the different kinds of twilight is proportional to the number of degrees of depression for the center of the Sun. More precise determination of the time at which the center of the Sun is any given number of degrees below the celestial horizon can be determined by a large-scale diagram on the plane of the celestial meridian, or by computation. Duration of twilight in latitudes higher than 65° N is given in a graph in the *Air Almanac*.

In both **Nautical** and **Air Almanacs**, the method of finding the darker limit of twilight is the same as that for sunrise and sunset.

Sometimes in high latitudes the Sun does not rise but twilight occurs. This is indicated in the *Air Almanac* by a solid black rectangle symbol in the sunrise and sunset column. To find the time of beginning of morning twilight, subtract half the duration of twilight as obtained from the duration of twilight graph from the time of meridian transit of the Sun; and for the time of ending of evening twilight, add it to the time of meridian transit. The LMT of meridian transit never differs by more than 16.4m (approximately) from 1200. The actual time on any date can be determined from the almanac.

Rising, Setting, and Twilight on a Moving Craft

Instructions to this point relate to a fixed position on the Earth. Aboard a moving craft the problem is complicated somewhat by the fact that time of occurrence depends upon the position of the craft, which itself depends on the time. At ship speeds, it is generally sufficiently accurate to make an approximate mental solution and use the position of the vessel at this time to make a more accurate solution. If greater accuracy is required, the position at the time indicated in the second solution can be used for a third solution. If desired, this process can be repeated until the same answer is obtained from two consecutive solutions. However, it is generally sufficient to alter the first solution by 1m for each 15' of longitude that the position of the craft differs from that used in the solution, adding if west of the estimated position, and subtracting if east of it. In applying this rule, use both longitudes to the nearest 15'. The first solution is the **first estimate**; the second solution is the **second estimate.**

A navigation team keeping an appropriate DR needs only make one calculation for the approximate position at estimated Rising, Setting, and Twilight for that day.

Example

01251. On 16 August 1981, your 1600 ZT DR position is LAT 26° 17.0' N, LONG 165° 17.0' E. You are on course 301° T at a speed of 15 knots. What will be the zone time of sunset at your vessel?

Step 1 - Enter all data given in the example problem into the top portion of the work form, Date, Time, latitude, longitude, course and speed.

Step 2 - Enter the Nautical Almanac for 16 August 1981 for latitudes 20 N and 30 N. Enter the data in the work form **LATITUDE CORRECTION BOX.** For the next lower latitude **20 N** we find the sunset is **1829** and for next higher tabulated latitude **30 N** sunset is **1841.**

Step 3. Layout a universal plotting sheet (see Chapter 11) for mid-latitude 26 N and mid-longitude 165 E and plot you **1600** position. **LAT 26° 17.0' N, LONG 165° 17.0' E**

Step 4. Layout a DR to the approximate time of sunset 1635. We obtain **Lat. 26° 37' N   Long. 164° 41' E** and enter it in the **DR AT PREDICTED TIME OF SUNRISE OR SUNSET BOX** of our work form. Also enter the DR longitude into the **LONGITUDE CORRECTION BOX** of our work form.

Step 5. The latitude correction, comparing base sunset 1829 with 1841 Correction for latitude, we enter the difference 12 assigning a positive (+) since time of sunset is increasing relative to the base time.

Complete the calculations within the **LATITUDE CORRECTION BOX,** We calculate a ratio of the difference in the times of sunset between latitudes 20 N and 30 N, **+ 12'** x the increments of Latitude from our base of 20 N and 26° 37' in minutes of arc (**6° 37' x 60 = 397"**) divided by the interval between reading expressed in minutes of arc (**10° x 60 = 600**) or **+ 12 x 397 / 60 = + 7.9'** for the **Latitude correct or using a calculator that has the ° ' " function + 12 x 6° 37' / 10 = + 7.9.**

Step 6. The longitude correction, Now we must determine the time correction for the difference between our longitude **164° 41' E** and the closest

standard meridian 165° E; This is completed by entering the arc difference between the standard meridian Dlo 0° 19' and **multiplying the Dlo by 4**, or we can use the arc to time table of the nautical Almanac which equals **1.2".** If our longitude is the **east** of the Standard Meridian we **assign a (-)** to the value and **a (+)** if it is the **West** of the Standard Meridian. **It is important to note we are not saying east and west longitude, east or west of the Standard Meridian.**

Lat.	Sunset	Twilight Civil	Twilight Naut.
°	h m	h m	h m
N 72	21 40	////	////
N 70	21 09	23 35	////
68	20 47	22 20	////
66	20 30	21 44	////
64	20 15	21 19	23 39
62	20 04	21 00	22 32
60	19 53	20 45	22 00
N 58	19 45	20 31	21 37
56	19 37	20 20	21 18
54	19 30	20 11	21 03
52	19 24	20 02	20 51
50	19 19	19 54	20 40
45	19 07	19 39	20 18
N 40	18 57	19 26	20 01
35	18 49	19 15	19 47
30	18 41	19 06	19 36
20	18 29	18 52	19 19
N 10	18 18	18 40	19 05
0	18 08	18 29	18 54
S 10	17 58	18 19	18 44
20	17 47	18 10	18 36
30	17 35	18 00	18 28
35	17 29	17 55	18 25
40	17 21	17 49	18 21
45	17 12	17 42	18 17
S 50	17 01	17 35	18 13
52	16 56	17 32	18 11
54	16 51	17 28	18 10
56	16 45	17 24	18 08
58	16 38	17 20	18 06
S 60	16 30	17 15	18 04

Day	SUN Eqn. of Time 00ʰ	SUN Eqn. of Time 12ʰ	Mer. Pass.
	m s	m s	h m
14	04 42	04 37	12 05
15	04 31	04 25	12 04
16	04 19	04 13	12 04

Step 7. We sum the latitude and longitude corrections algebraically and apply them to our base in the lower right of our work form. **7.9 – 1.3 = 6.6** Rounded to the nearest minute **+7'** Base time **1829 + 7 = 1836. The time of Sun Set on 16 Aug. is 1836.**

Celestial Problems					
Sunrise and Sunset					
Problem # (USCG) (1251)			Chapter 18		
Date: 16 Aug			**FIX TIME**	16:00	
Required			LAT	26° 17' N	
Sunset			LONG	165° 17' E	
			C-	301°	
			S-	15	
LATITUDE CORRECTION		**LONGITUDE CORRECTION**		**DR AT PREDICTED TIME OF SUNRISE OR SUNSET**	
				TIME	18:35
LAT (20)	18:29	**STD MER**	165°	**LAT**	26° 37' N
LAT (30)	18:41	**LONG**	164° 41'	**LONG**	164° 41' E
d	+ 12	**Dlo**	0° 19'		
Inc LAT (x)	397 (6° 37')	**dtime (E)**	– 1.3	**Base Time**	18:29
Inv Lat (÷)	600 (10)			**tcorr**	+0:07
Correction	+ 7.9			**Time of S/R - S/S**	18:36
NOTE:					

End of Chapter USCG Problems

1. 01252. On 13 August 1981, your 0345 ZT DR position is LAT 21° 35.0' N, LONG 135° 26.0' W. You are on course 052° T at a speed of 14 knots. What will be the zone time of sunset at your vessel?

A. 0443
B. 0449
C. 0536
D. 0540

2. 01253. On 8 August 1981, your 0400 ZT DR position is LAT 23° 16.0' S, LONG 105° 33.0' W. You are on course 295° T at a speed of 25 knots. What will be the zone time of sunrise at your vessel?

A. 0623
B. 0629
C. 0636
D. 0654

3. 01254. On 19 July 1981, your 1500 ZT DR position is LAT 28° 15.0' N, LONG 120° 28.0' W. You are on course 233° at a speed of 10 knots. What will be the zone time of sunset at your vessel?

A. 1842
B. 1853
C. 1901
D. 1909

4. 01255. On 12 June 1981, your 0400 ZT DR position is LAT 22° 31.0' N, LONG 31° 45.0'' W. You are on course 240° T at a speed of 16.5 knots. What will be the zone time of sunrise at your vessel?

A. 0507
B. 0515
C. 0523
D. 0645

5. 01256. On 17 May 1981, your 0300 ZT DR position is LAT 27° 21.0' N, LONG 146° 14.0' E. You are on course 107° T at a speed of 18 knots. What will be the zone time of sunrise at your vessel?

A. 0457
B. 0511
C. 0519
D. 0522

Answers

1. 01252 C
2. 01253 C
3. 01254 C
4. 01255 C
5. 01256 D

USCG Problems worked-out

Celestial Problems Sunrise and Sunset		
Problem # 1 (USCG) (1252)		Chapter 18

Date: 13 Aug	FIX TIME	03:45
Required	LAT	21° 35' N
Sunrise	LONG	135° 26' W
	C-	052°
	S-	14

LATITUDE CORRECTION		LONGITUDE CORRECTION		DR AT PREDICTED TIME OF SUNRISE OR SUNSET	
				TIME	05:30
LAT (20)	05:39	STD MER	135° 00'	LAT	21° 50' N
LAT (30)	05:25	LONG	135° 05'	LONG	135° 05' W
d	- 14	Dlo	0° 05'		
Inc LAT (x)	110 (1° 50)	dtime (W)	+ 0	Base Time	05:39
Inv Lat (÷)	600 (10)			tcorr	- 0:03
Correction	- 2.6 (-3)			Time of S/R - S/S	05:36

NOTE: Problem States sunset vise sunrise
ANSWER   C

Celestial Problems Sunrise and Sunset		
Problem # 2 (USCG) (1253)		Chapter 18

Date: 8 Aug 81	FIX TIME	04:00
Required	LAT	23° 16' S
Sunrise	LONG	105° 33' W
	C-	295°
	S-	25

LATITUDE CORRECTION		LONGITUDE CORRECTION		DR AT PREDICTED TIME OF SUNRISE OR SUNSET	
				TIME	06:30
LAT (20)	06:26	STD MER	105° 00'	LAT	22° 50' S
LAT (30)	06:39	LONG	106° 35'	LONG	106° 35' W
d	+ 0:13	Dlo	1° 35'		
Inc LAT (x)	170 (2° 50)	dtime (W)	+ 6.3	Base Time	06:26
Inv Lat (÷)	600 (10)			tcorr	+0:10
Correction	+ 3.7			Time of S/R - S/S	06:36

NOTE:
ANSWER   C

Celestial Problems Sunrise and Sunset				
Problem # 3 (USCG) (1254)			Chapter 18	
Date: 19 July Required Sunset			**FIX TIME** LAT LONG C- S-	15:00 28° 01'5 N 120° 28' W 233° 10

LATITUDE CORRECTION		LONGITUDE CORRECTION		DR AT PREDICTED TIME OF SUNRISE OR SUNSET	
				TIME	19:00
LAT (20)	18:42	**STD MER**	120° 00'	**LAT**	27° 50' N
LAT (30)	19:01	**LONG**	121° 06'	**LONG**	121° 06' W
d	+ 19	**Dlo**	1° 06'		
Inc LAT (x)	470 (7° 50)	**Dtime (W)**	+ 4	**Base Time**	18:42
Inv Lat (÷)	600 (10)			**tcorr**	+ 19
Correction	14.9			**Time of S/R - S/S**	19:01
	+ 15				

NOTE:
ANSWER   C

Celestial Problems Sunrise and Sunset				
Problem # 4 (USCG) (1255)			Chapter 18	
Date: 12 June **Required** Sunrise			**FIX TIME** LAT LONG C- S-	04:00 22° 31' N 031° 45' W 240° 16.5

LATITUDE CORRECTION		LONGITUDE CORRECTION		DR AT PREDICTED TIME OF SUNRISE OR SUNSET	
				TIME	05:20
LAT (20)	05:20	**STD MER**	30° 00'	**LAT**	22° 20' N
LAT (30)	04:58	**LONG**	32° 06'	**LONG**	032° 06' W
d	- 22	**Dlo**	2° 06'		
Inc LAT (x)	140 (2° 20)	**dtime (W)**	+ 8.4	**Base Time**	05:20
Inv Lat (÷)	600 (10)			**tcorr**	+0:03
Correction	- 5.1			**Time of S/R - S/S**	05:23

NOTE:
ANSWER   C

Celestial Problems Sunrise and Sunset			
Problem # 5 (USCG) (1256)		Chapter 18	

Date:	17 May		FIX TIME	03:00
	Required		LAT	27° '21 N
	Sunrise		LONG	146° 14' E
			C-	107°
			S-	18

LATITUDE CORRECTION		LONGITUDE CORRECTION		DR AT PREDICTED TIME OF SUNRISE OR SUNSET	
				TIME	05:20
LAT (20)	05:23	**STD MER**	150° 00'	**LAT**	27° 10' N
LAT (30)	05:05	**LONG**	146° 54'	**LONG**	146° 54' E
d	- 18	**Dlo**	-3° 06'		
Inc LAT (x)	430 (7° 10)	**dtime (W)**	+ 12.4	**Base Time**	05:23
Inv Lat (÷)	600 (10)			**Tcorr**	- 0:01
Correction	- 12.9			**Time of S/R - S/S**	05:22

NOTE:
ANSWER   D

Additional USCG problems worked-out for this chapter can be found in **Celestial Navigation Calculations (Upon Oceans Endorsement) Worked-Out for Master 500 GT through 2nd Mate Unlimited, Volume 3, part 2, Chapter 4, Time and Time Zone Calculations.**

COMPASS ERROR BY AMPLITUDE
Chapter 19

To determine compass error, an azimuth observation of a celestial body at low altitude is desirable because it can be measured easiest and most accurately. Amplitude of the sun or other celestial body can also be used to determine gyro error. An **amplitude (A)** is the arc of the horizon between the prime vertical circle (the vertical circle through the east and west points of the horizon) and the observed body. The prime vertical circle may be true or magnetic, depending upon which east or west points are involved. If the body is observed when its center is on the celestial horizon, the amplitude can be taken directly from **table 27 of Bowditch, volume II** or **table 22 in the newer Bowditch.** <u>The USCG is using Bowditch, volume II in the examination room.</u> An alternative method is the use the formula for Amplitude:

$$\sin A = \frac{\sin Dec}{\cos Lat}$$

We will determine Amplitude by table and formula in our example.

The celestial horizon differs from the one seen (the visible horizon) because it runs through the center of the earth. There are a lot of computations that must be done to determine the celestial horizon of a body, but for now we will just say that it is the horizon that a navigator uses for all celestial computations. When the center of the sun is on the celestial horizon, its lower limb (lower edge) is about **two-thirds of the diameter** of the sun above the visible horizon **or 20 minutes of arc** above the visible horizon. When the center of the moon is on the celestial horizon, its upper limb (upper edge) is on the visible horizon. When planets and stars are on the celestial horizon, they are a little more than one sun diameter above the visible horizon.

The amplitude of a body is given the prefix **E (east)** if the body is **rising** and the prefix **W (west)** if the body is **setting**. Additionally, the amplitude of a body is given the suffix **N (north)** if the body has **northerly declination** and the suffix **S (south)** if it has **southerly declination**.

If the body is observed when its center is on the visible horizon, a correction from **table 28 of Bowditch, volume II,** or **table 23 of the newer Bowditch** is applied to the observed altitude.

Amplitude on the Celestial Horizon

As discussed above, the amplitude of a body can be taken directly from table 23/27 of Bowditch, volume II, if the body is observed when its center is on the celestial horizon. Since the sun is most commonly used for amplitudes, it will be the topic of our discussion. First of all, to observe the sun when it is on the celestial horizon, its lower limb should be about two-thirds of the diameter above the visible horizon. Next, if you know the Greenwich Mean Time (GMT) of your observation, you can use the right-hand daily pages of the Nautical Almanac to determine the sun's declination. For example, the DR latitude of your ship **51° 04.6' N** at a time when the declination of the setting sun was **19° 00.4 'N.**, your observed bearing (as observed by a telescopic alidade or azimuth circle) to the sun was **300°.**

From this known information, we can use **table 22/27** of Bowditch to determine the amplitude. The figure below shows an excerpt from table 27. By inspection of table 27 you can see that you must enter the left and column with your ship's DR latitude. You can also see that the sun's declination is listed across the top of the table. Since **latitude 51°** and **declination 19°** are close to our entering values, we determine that the amplitude of the sun when it is on the celestial horizon is **31.2°.** Now that we have the amplitude, what do we do with it? First of all, there are some basic rules that must be applied that relate to our previous discussion of the assigned prefix and suffix of an amplitude. Our amplitude was taken when the sun was setting, and its declination name is north. The amplitude would be labeled as follows:

W 31.2° N

	TABLE 27													
	Amplitudes													
	Declination													
Latitude	18°0	18°5	19°0	19°5	20°0	20°5	21°0	21°5	22°0	22°5	23°0	23°5	24°0	Latitude
0	18.0	18.5	19.0	19.5	20.0	20.5	21.0	21.5	22.0	22.5	23.0	23.5	24.0	0
10	18.3	18.8	19.3	19.8	20.3	20.8	21.3	21.8	22.4	22.9	23.4	23.9	24.4	10
15	18.7	19.2	19.7	20.2	20.7	21.3	21.8	22.3	22.8	23.3	23.9	24.4	24.9	15
20	19.2	19.7	20.3	20.8	21.3	21.9	22.4	23.0	23.5	24.0	24.6	25.1	25.6	20
25	19.9	20.5	21.1	21.6	22.2	22.7	23.3	23.9	24.4	25.0	25.5	26.1	26.7	25
30	20.9	21.5	22.1	22.7	23.3	23.9	24.4	25.0	25.6	26.2	26.8	27.4	28.0	30
32	21.4	22.0	22.6	23.2	23.8	24.4	25.0	25.6	26.2	26.8	27.4	28.0	28.7	32
34	21.9	22.5	23.1	23.7	24.4	25.0	25.6	26.2	26.9	27.5	28.1	28.7	29.4	34
36	22.5	23.1	23.7	24.4	25.0	25.7	26.3	26.9	27.6	28.2	28.9	29.5	30.2	36
38	23.1	23.7	24.4	25.1	25.7	26.4	27.1	27.7	28.4	29.1	29.7	30.4	31.1	38
40	23.8	24.5	25.2	25.8	26.5	27.2	27.9	28.6	29.3	30.0	30.7	31.4	32.1	40
41	24.2	24.9	25.6	26.3	26.9	27.6	28.3	29.1	29.8	30.5	31.2	31.9	32.6	41
42	24.6	25.3	26.0	26.7	27.4	28.1	28.8	29.5	30.3	31.0	31.7	32.5	33.2	42
43	25.0	25.7	26.4	27.2	27.9	28.6	29.3	30.1	30.8	31.6	32.3	33.0	33.8	43
44	25.4	26.2	26.9	27.6	28.4	29.1	29.9	30.6	31.4	32.1	32.9	33.7	34.4	44
45	25.9	26.7	27.4	28.2	28.9	29.7	30.5	31.2	32.0	32.8	33.5	34.3	35.1	45
46	26.4	27.2	27.9	28.7	29.5	30.3	31.1	31.8	32.6	33.4	34.2	35.0	35.8	46
47	26.9	27.7	28.5	29.3	30.1	30.9	31.7	32.5	33.3	34.1	35.0	35.8	36.6	47
48	27.5	28.3	29.1	29.9	30.7	31.6	32.4	33.2	34.0	34.9	35.7	36.6	37.4	48
49	28.1	28.9	29.8	30.6	31.4	32.3	33.1	34.0	34.8	35.7	36.6	37.4	38.3	49
50	28.7	29.6	30.4	31.3	32.1	33.0	33.9	34.8	35.6	36.5	37.4	38.3	39.3	50
51	29.4	30.3	31.2	32.0	32.9	33.8	34.7	35.6	36.5	37.5	38.4	39.3	40.3	51
52	30.1	31.0	31.9	32.8	33.7	34.7	35.6	36.5	37.5	38.4	39.4	40.4	41.3	52
53	30.9	31.8	32.8	33.7	34.6	35.6	36.5	37.5	38.5	39.5	40.5	41.5	42.5	53
54	31.7	32.7	33.6	34.6	35.6	36.6	37.6	38.6	39.6	40.6	41.7	42.7	43.8	54

By formula

$$\sin A = \frac{\sin Dec}{\cos Lat} = \frac{\sin 19° 00.4}{\cos 51° 04.6} = .518363647409 = \sin^{-1}.518363647409 = 31.22262543$$

W 31.2° N

With the amplitude properly labeled, we can now follow another set of rules to determine the azimuth. These rules are as follows:

1. Rising sun with north declination subtract the amplitude from 090°.

2. Rising sun with south declination add the amplitude to 090°

3. Setting sun with north declination add the amplitude to 270°

4. Setting sun with south declination subtract the amplitude from 270 °.

By following the rules above, our amplitude can now be converted to an azimuth as follows:

N31.2° W + 270°= 301.2°

Our observed bearing to the sun was **300.0° pgc** and **285.0° psc.** Gyro error or deviation can be determined as follows:

True	301.2	+ W⇩	True	301.2
Error	1.2 E	- E⇩	Variation	14.0 E
Gyro (pgc)	300.0		Magnetic	287.2
		+ E⇧	Deviation	2.2 E
		- W⇧	Compass	285.0

Amplitude on the visible horizon

When the center of the sun is on the visible horizon, its center is below the celestial horizon. Since table 27 of Bowditch is used when the sun's center is on the celestial horizon, it should be apparent that we must make additional corrections to an observation of the sun on the visible horizon. The corrections come from table 23/28 of Bowditch.

On the following page is an excerpt from table 23/28. The values needed to enter the table are latitude and declination. The correction obtained from this table is applied to the observed amplitude pgc or psc.

For an example, let us say that we took a bearing of the rising sun when its center was on the visible horizon. Our gyro bearing by telescopic alidade was **063°** pgc. The **latitude** of our ship at that time (GMT) was **44°30' N**, the sun's **declination** was **20°01' N**. The first thing we did was enter table 27 as we did before and find the amplitude of the sun, which, in our example, it is **E 28.4° N**.

We can now apply the set of rules that converts the amplitude to an azimuth. This step is shown below:

90° - 28.7° = 061.3°

We will use the same method of interpolation used throughout the text as shown below for table 28:

You will notice that the latitude in this table is listed in 1° increments, but our latitude falls halfway between two latitude entries (**44°**and **45°**).

The next thing we need to do is **enter table 28** and find the correction that will be applied to the observed amplitude. The correction in our example is **.8°**. You will notice that no interpolation is needed here because the correction is the same for an entry of **44°** and **46°**. Now that you have the correction, what do you do with it? Is it added or subtracted? The answer is that it depends on your latitude (north or south) and the age of the sun (rising or setting).

TABLE 28
Correction of Amplitude as Observed on the Visible Horizon

Latitude	0°	2°	4°	6°	8°	10°	12°	14°	16°	18°	20°	22°	24°	Latitude
0	0.0	0.0	0.0	0.0	0.0	0.0	0.0	0.0	0.0	0.0	0.0	0.0	0.0	0
10	0.1	0.1	0.1	0.1	0.1	0.1	0.1	0.1	0.1	0.1	0.1	0.1	0.1	10
15	0.2	0.2	0.2	0.2	0.2	0.2	0.2	0.2	0.2	0.2	0.2	0.2	0.2	15
20	0.3	0.3	0.3	0.3	0.3	0.3	0.3	0.3	0.3	0.3	0.3	0.3	0.3	20
25	0.3	0.3	0.3	0.3	0.3	0.4	0.3	0.3	0.3	0.3	0.3	0.3	0.3	25
30	0.4	0.4	0.4	0.4	0.5	0.4	0.4	0.4	0.4	0.4	0.4	0.5	0.5	30
32	0.4	0.4	0.4	0.4	0.5	0.4	0.4	0.4	0.4	0.4	0.5	0.5	0.5	32
34	0.5	0.5	0.5	0.5	0.5	0.5	0.5	0.5	0.5	0.5	0.5	0.5	0.5	34
36	0.5	0.5	0.5	0.5	0.5	0.5	0.5	0.5	0.6	0.5	0.6	0.6	0.6	36
38	0.6	0.6	0.6	0.6	0.6	0.6	0.6	0.6	0.6	0.6	0.6	0.6	0.6	38
40	0.6	0.6	0.6	0.6	0.6	0.6	0.6	0.6	0.6	0.6	0.7	0.7	0.7	40
42	0.6	0.6	0.6	0.6	0.7	0.7	0.7	0.7	0.7	0.7	0.7	0.7	0.7	42
44	0.7	0.7	0.7	0.6	0.6	0.7	0.7	0.7	0.8	0.8	0.8	0.8	0.9	44
46	0.7	0.7	0.7	0.7	0.7	0.8	0.8	0.8	0.8	0.8	0.8	0.9	0.9	46
48	0.8	0.8	0.8	0.8	0.8	0.8	0.8	0.8	0.9	0.9	1.0	1.0	1.0	48
50	0.8	0.8	0.8	0.8	0.9	0.9	0.9	0.9	0.9	1.0	1.0	1.1	1.0	50
51	0.8	0.8	0.8	0.8	0.9	0.9	0.9	0.9	0.9	1.0	1.1	1.1	1.1	51
52	0.9	0.9	0.9	0.9	0.9	0.9	1.0	1.0	1.0	1.1	1.1	1.1	1.3	52
53	0.9	0.9	0.9	0.9	0.9	0.9	1.0	1.0	1.0	1.1	1.2	1.2	1.3	53
54	1.0	1.0	1.0	1.0	1.0	1.0	1.1	1.1	1.1	1.2	1.2	1.3	1.3	54
75.0	2.6	2.7	2.8	2.9	3.2	3.7	4.7	9.3						75.0
75.5	2.7	2.8	2.8	3.0	3.3	3.9	5.3							75.5
76.0	2.8	2.8	2.9	3.2	3.5	4.2	5.6							76.0
76.5	2.9	3.0	3.1	3.3	3.7	4.5	7.3							76.5
77.0	3.0	3.1	3.2	3.5	4.0	5.1	10.2							77.0

For the sun, a planet, or a star, apply the correction to the observed amplitude in the direction away from the elevated pole. For the moon apply half the correction toward the elevated pole.

The following set of rules applies:

1. Rising sun, north latitude-add table 28 correction from our observation.

2. Setting sun, north latitude-subtract table 28 correction from our observation.

3. Rising sun, south latitude-subtract table 28 correction from our observation.

4. Setting sun, south latitude-add table 28 correction from our observation.

Following the above set of rules, the correction in our example is applied as follows:

Observed Amplitude.	063.0 pgc
Correction from table 28	+ .8°
Corrected observed amplitude	063.8 pgc

The final step in our example is to determine the gyro error. This step is shown below.

True	061.3°	(azimuth by amplitude)
Error	+ 2.5° W	(gyro error)
Gyro (pgc)	063.8°	(gyro bearing corrected)

End of Chapter USCG Problems

1. 01651. On 23 October 1981, in DR position LAT 21° 13.0' N, LONG 152° 18.0 E, you observe the amplitude of the Sun. The Sun's center is on the visible horizon and bears 259° psc. The chronometer reads 07h 21m 46s and is 01m 32s slow. Variation in the area is 5° E. What is the deviation of the magnetic compress?

A. 0.9° E
B. 1.5° W
C. 5.9° W
D. 6.5° E

2. 01652. On 22 October 1981, in DR position LAT 21° 51.0' S, LONG 76° 24.0 E, you observe the amplitude of the Sun. The Sun's center is on the visible horizon and bears 256° psc. The chronometer reads 01h 01m 25s and is 01m 15s fast. Variation for the area is 2° E. What is the deviation of the magnetic compass?

A. 0.3° E
B. 0.3° W
C. 2.0° E
D. 2.0° W

3. 01653. On 28 Sept., 1981, in DR position LAT 24° 12.0' S, LONG 85° 25.0' E, you observe the amplitude of the Sun. The Sun's center is on the visible horizon and bears 094° psc. The chronometer reads 11h 29m 42s and is 03m 30s slow. Variation in the area is 4° W. What is the deviation of the magnetic compass?

A. 1.5° W
B. 2.1° W
C. 2.4° E
D. 4.2° E

4. 01654. On 28 September 1981, in DR position LAT 27° 16.7' S, LONG 113° 27.2' W, you observe the amplitude of the Sun. The Sun's center is on the celestial horizon and bears 273° psc. The chronometer reads 01h 17m 26s and is 01m 49s slow. Variation in the area is 6° W. What is the deviation of the magnetic compass?

A. 0.2° W
B. 0.4° E
C. 0.8° E
D. 0.6° W

5. 01655. On 22 October 1981, in DR position LAT 21° 51.0' S, LONG 76° 24.0' E, you observe the amplitude of the Sun. The Sun's center is on the visible horizon and bears 256° psc. The chronometer reads 01h 01m 25s and is 01m 15s fast. Variation in the area is 2° E. What is the deviation of the magnetic compass?

A. 0.3° E
B. 0.3° W
C. 2.0° E
D. 2.3° W

Answers

1. 01651 C
2. 01652 B
3. 01653 C
4. 01654 B
5. 01655 B

USCG Problems worked-out
Celestial Problems
Sight Reduction Amplitude

Problem # 1 (USCG) (1651)					Chapter 19		

Date 23 Oct			Time				

	ZT	17	CT	07:21:46	**LAT 21° 13.0' N**		
	ZD	-10	CE	+1:32	**LONG 152° 18.0' E**		
	GMT	07	CCT	07:23:18	GYRO	COMPASS	

						T	257.8
DECLINATION			GMT	07:23:18	T	V	5.0 E
DEC		S 11° 23.8'			E	M	252.8
d (+0.9)		+0.4'			G	D	**5.9 W**
DEC		S 11° 24.2'				C	258.7

Calculating True Bearing	Table 28 or

$$\sin^{-1}\left(\frac{\sin Dec}{\cos Lat}\right) = Amplitude$$

$$\sin^{-1}\left(\frac{\sin 11°24.2'}{\cos 21°13.0'}\right) = 12.244$$

pcs/pgc	259
Correction (±)	-0.3
psc/pgc	258.7

Correcting Amplitude to TRUE	
270 / 090	270
± Amplitude	S 12.2 W
TRUE	**257.8**

```
        N
      - | +
270 ―――――――― 090
      + | -
        S
```

NOTE:

ANSWER C

```
      + | -
270 ―――――――― 090
      - | +
```

Celestial Problems
Sight Reduction Amplitude

Problem # 2 **(USCG)** (1652)		Chapter 19	

Date 22 October 1981   Time

					LAT 21° 51.0' S
	ZT	1800	CT	01:01:25	LONG 076° 24.0' E

	ZD	-5	CE	-1:15	GYRO		COMPASS	
	GMT	1300	CCT				T	258.0
DECLINATION			GMT	13:00:10	T		V	2.0E
DEC		S 11° 08.0'			E		M	256.0
d (+0.9)		0			G		D	0.3W
DEC		S 11° 08.0'					C	256.3

Calculating True Bearing	Table 28 or

$$\sin^{-1}\left(\frac{\sin Dec}{\cos Lat}\right) = Amplitude$$

	pcs/pgc	256.0
	Correction (±)	+0.3
	psc/pgc	256.3

$$\sin^{-1}\left(\frac{\sin 11° 08.0'}{\cos 21° 51.0'}\right) = 12.007$$

Correcting Amplitude to TRUE	
270 / 090	270
± Amplitude	S 12.0 W
TRUE	**258.0**

```
        N
      - | +
270 ------+------ 090
      + | -
        S
```

NOTE:

ANSWER B

```
      + | -
270 ------+------ 090
      - | +
```

Celestial Problems
Sight Reduction Amplitude

Problem # 3 (USCG) (1653)	Chapter 19

Date 28 Sep		Time					
				LAT 24° 12.0' S			
	ZT	0500	**CT**	11:28:42	**LONG 085° 25.0' E**		
	ZD	6	**CE**	+3:30	**GYRO**		**COMPASS**
	GMT	2300	**CCT**	11:32:12		**T**	092.1
	DECLINATION		**GMT**	23:32:12	**T**	**V**	4.0 W
DEC	S 1° 52.9'		27 SEP		**E**	**M**	096.1
d (+1.0)	+0.5'				**G**	**D**	2.4 E
DEC	S 1° 53.4'					**C**	093.7

Calculating True Bearing	**Table 28 or**

$$\sin^{-1}\left(\frac{\sin Dec}{\cos Lat}\right) = Amplitude$$

pcs/pgc	094
Correction (±)	-0.3
psc/pgc	093.7

$$\sin^{-1}\left(\frac{\sin 1°53.4'}{\cos 24°12.0'}\right) = 2.072$$

Correcting Amplitude to TRUE

270 / 090	90
± Amplitude	S 2.1 E
TRUE	**092.1**

```
        N
      -  +
270 ———+——— 090
      +  -
        S
```

```
      +  -
270 ———+——— 090
      -  +
```

NOTE:

ANSWER C

Celestial Problems
Sight Reduction Amplitude

Problem # 4 (USCG) (1654)			Chapter 19	

Date 28 Sep   **Time**

LAT   27° 16.7' S

LONG   113° 27.2' W

ZT	1700	CT	01:17:26	**GYRO**		**COMPASS**
ZD	+8	CE	+01:49		T	267.4
GMT	2500	CCT	01:19:15	T	V	6.0 W
DECLINATION		GMT	01:19:15	E	M	273.4
DEC	S 2° 18.2'	29 Sep		G	D	0.4 E
d (+ 1.0)	+.3'				C	273.0
DEC	S 2° 18.5'					

Calculating True Bearing	**Table 28 or**

$$\sin^{-1}\left(\frac{\sin Dec}{\cos Lat}\right) = Amplitude$$

pcs/pgc

Correction (±) _____

psc/pgc

$$\sin^{-1}\left(\frac{\sin 2°18.5'}{\cos 27°16.7'}\right) = 2.597$$

Correcting Amplitude to TRUE

270 / 090	270	
± Amplitude	S 2.6 W	
TRUE	**267.4**	

```
          +    -
270  ──────┼──────  090
          -    +
```

```
          -    +
270  ──────┼──────  090
          +    -
```
N   S

270   090

NOTE:

       ANSWER   B

Celestial Problems
Sight Reduction Amplitude

Problem # 5 (USCG) (1655)	Chapter 19

Date 22 Oct		Time			LAT 21° 51.0' S

					LONG 076-24.0' E
	ZT	1800	CT	01:01:25	
	ZD	-5	CE	-01:15	GYRO	COMPASS
	GMT	1300	CCT	01:00:10	T	258.0
	DECLINATION		GMT	13:00:10	T	V	2.0 E
DEC		S 11° 08.0'			E	M	256.0
d (+.9)		0			G	D	0.3 W
DEC		S 11° 08.0'				C	256.3

Calculating True Bearing	Table 28 or

$$\sin^{-1}\left(\frac{\sin Dec}{\cos Lat}\right) = Amplitude$$

$$\sin^{-1}\left(\frac{\sin 11°08.0'}{\cos\ 21°51.0'}\right) = 12.0$$

pcs/pgc			256.0
Correction (±)			+0.3
psc/pgc			256.3

Correcting Amplitude to TRUE	

270 / 090	270
± Amplitude	S 12.0 W
TRUE	**258.0**

```
        N
    -  |  +
270 ───────── 090
    +  |  -
        S
```

```
    +  |  -
270 ───────── 090
    -  |  +
```

NOTE:

ANSWER B

Additional USCG problems worked-out for this chapter can be found in **Celestial Navigation Calculations (Upon Oceans Endorsement) Worked-Out for Master 500 GT through 2nd Mate Unlimited, Volume 3, part 1, Chapter 3, Magnetic and Gyro Compass Error Calculations.**

COMPASS BY AZIMUTH
Chapter 20

Mariners may use Pub 229, Sight Reduction Tables for Marine Navigation to compute the Sun's azimuth. They compare the computed azimuth to the azimuth measured with the compass to determine compass error. In computing an azimuth, interpolate the tabular azimuth angle for the difference between the table arguments and the actual values of declination, latitude, and local hour angle. Do this triple interpolation of the azimuth angle as follows:

1. Enter the Sight Reduction Tables with the nearest integral values of declination, latitude, and local hour angle. For each of these arguments, extract a base azimuth angle.

2. Reenter the tables with the same latitude and LHA arguments but with the declination argument 1° greater or less than the base declination argument, depending upon whether the actual declination is greater or less than the base argument. Record the difference between the respondent azimuth angle and the base azimuth angle and label it as the azimuth angle difference (Z Diff.).

3. Reenter the tables with the base declination and LHA arguments, but with the latitude argument 1° greater or less than the base latitude argument, depending upon whether the actual (usually DR) latitude is greater or less than the base argument. Record the Z Diff. for the increment of latitude.

4. Reenter the tables with the base declination and latitude arguments, but with the LHA argument 1° greater or less than the base LHA argument, depending upon whether the actual LHA is greater or less than the base argument. Record the Z Diff. for the increment of LHA.

5. Correct the base azimuth angle for each increment.

Example:

In DR latitude **33° 24.0 ' N**, the azimuth of the Sun is **096.5° pgc**. At the time of the observation, the declination of the Sun is **20° 13.8' N**; the local hour angle of the Sun is **316° 41.2'**. Determine gyro compass error.

Example Worked-out

LHA	316° 41.2'	DEC	N 20° 13.8'	LAT	33°24.0' N

T	097.7
E	1.2 E
G	096.5°

LHA	316° 41.2'	DEC	N 20° 13.8'	LAT	33° 24.0' N
		Publication 229			
Z (316)	097.1°	Z (20)	097.1°	Z (33)	097.1°
Z (317)	097.8°	Z (21)	095.7°	Z (34)	098.2°
d	+ .7	d	−1.4°	d	+1.1°
Inc Dec (X)	41.2'	Inc Dec (X)	13.8'	Inc Dec (X)	24.0'
Inv	60	Inv	60	Inv	60
correction	+ .5	correction	− .3	correction	+ .4
Base Z	097.1°	Z to ZN	097.7		
tcorr	+ .6	ZN = Z			
Z	097.7				
Note: SAME					

Figure 1 Azimuth by Pub. No. 229

Solution:

See Figure 1 Enter the actual value of declination, DR latitude, and LHA. Round each argument to the **next lower whole degree**. Enter the Sight Reduction Tables with these whole degree arguments and extract the base azimuth value for these rounded off arguments. Record the base azimuth value in the table.

As the first step in the **triple interpolation** process, increase the value of declination by 1° (to 21°) because the actual declination value was greater than the base declination. Enter the Sight Reduction Tables with the following arguments:

(1) Declination = 21°;
(2) DR Latitude = 33°;
(3) LHA = 316°.

Record the tabulated azimuth for these arguments.

As the second step in the **triple interpolation** process, increase the value of latitude by 1° to 34° because the actual DR latitude was greater than the base latitude. Enter the Sight Reduction Tables with the following arguments:

(1)   Declination =   20°;
(2)   DR Latitude =   34°;
(3)   LHA =   316°.

Record the tabulated azimuth for these arguments.

As the third and final step in the **triple interpolation** process, increase the value of LHA to 317° because the actual LHA value was smaller than the base LHA. Enter the Sight Reduction Tables with the following arguments:

(1)   Declination =   20°;
(2)   DR Latitude =   33°;
(3)   LHA =   316°.

Record the tabulated azimuth for these arguments.

Calculate the Z Difference by subtracting the base azimuth from the tabulated azimuth. Be careful to carry the correct sign.

Z Difference = Tab Z - Base Z

Next, determine the increment for each argument by taking the difference between the actual values of each argument and the base argument. Calculate the correction for each of the three argument interpolations by **multiplying the increment by the Z difference and dividing the resulting product by 60.**

The sign of each correction is the same as the sign of the corresponding Z difference used to calculate it. In the above example, the total correction sums to +0.6'. Apply this value to the base azimuth of 97.1° to obtain the true azimuth 97.7°. Compare this to the compass reading of 096.5° pgc. The compass error is 1.2°E, which can be rounded to 1° for steering and logging purposes.

20-3

End of Chapter USCG Problems
Deviation by Azimuth (Any Body)

Remember: The USCG may ask you to determine Gyro Compass Error, Compass error, Magnetic Compass Deviation or gyro error which is then used to compare Gyro Heading with Magnetic Compass heading to determine Magnetic Compass Deviation using any body, Sun, Moon, Stars or Planets. In the practice problems below we use sun, Stars and planets.

1. 01451. On 11 December 1981, your 1816 zone time DR position is LAT 26° 30.0' N, LONG 140° 35.0' E. At that time, you observe **Venus** bearing 230° pgc. The chronometer reads 09h 14m 52s, and the chronometer error is 01m 02s slow. The variation is 3.5° E. **What is the gyro error?**

A. 2.2° E
B. 3.3° E
C. 3.2° W
D. 4.2° W

2. 01452. On 6 November 1981, your 0752 zone time DR position is LAT 25° 11.0' N, LONG 76° 07.0' W. At that time, you observe the **Sun** bearing 119° psc. The chronometer reads 00h 53m 07s, and the chronometer error is 01m 19s fast. The variation is 3° W. **What is the deviation of the standard compass?**

A. 2.2° W
B. 3.8° W
C. 2.8° E
D. 3.2° E

3. 01453. On 15 October 1981, your 0325 zone time DR position is LAT 26° 51.0' N, LONG 138° 17.0' W. At that time, you observe **Canopus** bearing 167° pgc. The chronometer reads 00h 25m 36s, and the chronometer error is 00m 20s slow. The variation is 2° E. **What is the gyro error?**

A. 1.2° W
B. 3.2° W
C. 3.2° E
D. 4.1° W

4. 01454. On 4 October 1981, your 0734 zone time DR position is LAT 24° 11.0' N, LONG 162° 34.0' E. At that time, you observe the **Sun** bearing 105.5° psc. The chronometer reads 08h 36m 11s, and the chronometer error is 01m 46s fast. The variation is 7° W. **What is the deviation of the standard compass?**

A. 1.2° W
B. 1.9° E
C. 5.3° W
D. 5.8° E

5. 01455. On 4 October 1981, your 1907 zone time DR position is LAT 25° 15.0'S, LONG 105° 44.0' E. At that time, you observe **Deneb** bearing 011.5° psc. The chronometer reads 00h 07m 42s, and the chronometer error is 00m 36s fast. The variation is 7.5° W. **What is the deviation of the standard compass?**

A. 3.2° E
B. 4.3° W
C. 2.1° E
D. 2.1° W

Answers

1. 01451 B
2. 01452 D
3. 01453 A
4. 01454 D
5. 01455 A

USCG Problems Worked-out

Celestial Problems Sight Reduction Azimuth			
Problem # 1 (USCG) (1451)		VENUS	Chapter 20

Date:	11 Dec	Time			LAT: LONG	26° 30.0' N 140° 35.0' E
	ZT	1816	CT	09 14 52	S-	
	ZD	- 9	CE	+ 1 02	C-	
	GMT	0916	CCT	09 15 54		
			GMT	09 15 54	DR	
					Time	
					LAT	
					LONG	

Almanac

		DEC	S 21° 47.4'		
GHA	270° 35.6'	d	- .6 - .2'	T	233.3
M/S	+ 3° 58.5'				
GHA	274° 34.1'	DEC	S 21° 47.2'	E	- 3.3 E
LONG	+ 140° 35.0'			G	230.0
± v (+.8)	+ .2'				
LHA	415° 09.3'				
	55° 09.3'				

LHA	55° 09.3'	DEC	S 21° 47.2'	LAT	26° 30.0' N
Publication 229					
Z (55)	126.1	Z (21)	126.1	Z (26)	126.1
Z (56)	125.4	Z (22)	126.9	Z (27)	126.3
d	- .7	d	+ .8	d	+ .2
Inc Dec (X)	09.3	Inc Dec (X)	47.2	Inc Dec (X)	30.0
Inv	60	Inv	60	Inv	60
correction	- .1	correction	+ .6	correction	+ .1

Base Z	126.1	Z to ZN	360 − 126.7 = 233.3		
tcorr	+ .6	ZN = 360 -Z			
Z	126.7				

Note: CONTRARY
ANSWER B

Celestial Problems
Sight Reduction Azimuth

Problem # 2 (USCG)	(1452)	SUN	Chapter 20

Date:	6 Nov	Time			LAT:	25° 11.0' N
					LONG	076° 07.0' W
	ZT	0752	CT	00:53:07	S-	
	ZD	+ 5	CE	- 1:19	C-	
	GMT	1252	CCT	00:51:48		
			GMT	12:51:48	DR	
					Time	
					LAT	
					LONG	

Almanac

GHA	4° 05.0'	DEC	S 16° 02.3'		T	119.2
M/S	+ 12° 57.0'	d	+.7 +.6'		V	+ 3 W
GHA	17° 02.0'	DEC	S 16° 02.9'		M	121.2
LONG ±	- 76° 07.0'				D	- 3.2 E
LHA	300° 55.0'				C	119.0

LHA	300° 55.0'	DEC	S 16° 02.9'	LAT	25° 11.0' N

Publication 229

Z (300)	118.5	Z (16)	118.5	Z (25)	118.5
Z (301)	119.1	Z (17)	119.4	Z (26)	118.8
d	+ .6	d	+ .9	d	+ .3
Inc Dec (X)	55.0	Inc Dec (X)	2.9	Inc Dec (X)	11.0
Inv	60	Inv	60	Inv	60
correction	+ .6	correction	0	correction	+ .1

Base Z	118.5	Z to ZN		
tcorr	+ .7	ZN = Z = Z	119.2	
Z	119.2			

Note: CONTRARY
ANSWER   D

20-7

Celestial Problems
Sight Reduction Azimuth

Problem # 3 (USCG)	(1453)	**CANOPUS**	Chapter 20

Date:	**15 OCT**	Time			LAT:	26° 51.0' N
					LONG	138° 17.0' W
	ZT	0325	CT	00:25:36	S-	
	ZD	+9	CE	+ 00:20	C-	
	GMT	1225	CCT	00:25:56		
			GMT	12:25:56		

Almanac

GHA Y	203° 55.8'	**DEC**	S 52° 40.9'			
M/S	+ 6° 30.1'	**d**		**T**	165.7	
GHA Y	210° 25.9'	**DEC**	S 52° 40.9'	**E**	+ 1.3 W	
SHA *	+ 264° 06.7'			**G**	167.0	
GHA *	474° 32.6'					
LONG	- 138° 17.0'					
LHA *	336° 15.6'					

LHA	336° 15.6'	**DEC**	S 52° 40.9'	**LAT**	26° 51.0' **N**

Publication 229

Z (336)	165.3	**Z (52)**	165.3	**Z (26)**	165.3
Z (337)	165.9	**Z (53)**	165.7	**Z (27)**	165.3
d	+ .6	**d**	+ .4	**d**	0
Inc Dec (X)	15.6	**Inc Dec (X)**	40.9	**Inc Dec (X)**	51.0
Inv	60	**Inv**	60	**Inv**	60
correction	+ .2	**correction**	+ .3	**correction**	0

Base Z	165.3	**Z to ZN**		
tcorr	+ .5	**ZN = Z**	165.7	
Z	165.7			

Note: CONTRARY
ANSWER A

Celestial Problems
Sight Reduction Azimuth

Problem # (USCG) 4	(1454)	SUN	Chapter 20

Date:	4 Oct		Time				LAT:	24° 11.0' N
							LONG	162° 34.0' E
	ZT	0734	CT	08:36:11			S-	
	ZD	- 11	CE	- 1:46			C-	
	GMT	2034	CCT	08:34:25				
2043 3 Oct			GMT	20:34:25				

Almanac

GHA	122° 46.1'	DEC	S	4° 09.8'		T	104.3
M/S	+ 8° 36.3'	d	+.1	+ .1'		V	+ 7.0 W
GHA	131° 22.4'	DEC	S	4° 09.9'		M	111.3
LONG	+ 162° 34.0'					D	- 5.8 E
LHA	293° 56.4'					C	105.5

LHA	293° 56.4'	DEC	S 4° 09.9'	LAT	24° 11.0' N
		Publication 229			
Z (293)	103.6	Z (4)	103.6	Z (24)	103.6
Z 294()	104.1	Z (5)	104.5	Z (25)	103.9
d	+ .5	d	+ .9	d	+ .3
Inc Dec (X)	56.4	Inc Dec (X)	9.9	Inc Dec (X)	11.0
Inv	60	Inv	60	Inv	60
correction	+ .5	correction	+ .1	correction	+ .1

Base Z	103.6	Z to ZN		104.3
tcorr	+ .7	ZN = Z		
Z	104.3			

Note: CONTRARY
ANSWER D

Celestial Problems
Sight Reduction Azimuth

Problem # (USCG) 5	(1455)	DENEB	Chapter 20

Date:	4 OCT	Time			LAT:	25° 15.0 S
					LONG	105° 44.0 E
	ZT	1907	CT	00:07:42	S-	
	ZD	-7	CE	- 00:36	C-	
	GMT	1207	CCT	00:07:06		
			GMT	12:07:06		

Almanac

GHA Υ	193° 05.3'	DEC	N 45° 13.2'			
M/S	+ 1° 46.8'	d		T	007.2	
GHA Υ	194° 52.1'	DEC	N 45° 13.2'	V	+ 7.5 W	
SHA *	+ 49° 47.8'			M	014.7	
GHA *	244° 39.9'			D	- 3.2 E	
LONG	+ 105° 44.0'			C	011.5	
LHA *	350° 23.9'					

LHA	350° 23.9'	DEC	N 45° 13.2'	LAT	25° 15.0' S
Publication 229					
Z (350)	172.5	Z (45)	172.5	Z (25)	172.5
Z (351)	173.3	Z (46)	172.7	Z (26)	172.6
d	+ .8	d	+ .2	d	+ .1
Inc Dec (X)	23.9	Inc Dec (X)	13.2	Inc Dec (X)	15.0
Inv	60	Inv	60	Inv	60
correction	+ .3	correction	0	correction	0

Base Z	172.5	Z to ZN		
tcorr	+ .3	ZN = 180 -Z	180 – 172.8 = 007.2	
Z	172.8			

Note: CONTRARY
ANSWER A

Additional USCG problems worked-out for this chapter can be found in **Celestial Navigation Calculations (Upon Oceans Endorsement) Worked-Out for Master 500 GT through 2nd Mate Unlimited, Volume 3, part 1, Chapter 3, Magnetic and Gyro Compass Error Calculations.**

Compass Error by Azimuth of Polaris
Chapter 21

The Polaris tables in the Nautical Almanac list the azimuth of Polaris for latitudes between the equator and 65°N. Pages 16-3 and 21-2 show these tables. Compare a compass bearing of Polaris to the tabular value of Polaris to determine compass error. The entering arguments for the table are LHA of Aries and observer latitude.

Example:

01491. On 5 February 1981, your 2320 ZT position is LAT 52° 28' N, LONG 23° 48' W. You observe Polaris bearing 000.2° pgc. At the time of the observation the helmsman noted that he was heading 224° pgc and 244° psc. The variation is 20° W. What is the deviation for that heading?

Solution:

Enter the azimuth section of the Polaris table with the calculated **LHA of Aries**. In this case, go to the column for LHA Aries between **130°** and **139°**. Follow that column down and extract the value for the given latitude. Since the increment between tabulated values is so small, visual interpolation is sufficient. In this case, the azimuth for Polaris for the given LHA of Aries and the given latitude is **358.7°**. In this question first find the Gyro error by Polaris **1.5 W** and the uses the results to compare the Gyro to our magnetic compass.

Celestial Problems							
Compass Deviation By Polaris							
Problem # 3 (USCG) (01491)			Chapter				
Date: **5 Feb.**	Time	23:20 ZT	**LAT:**	52° 28' N			
ZT	23:20	**CT**	**LONG**	23° 48' W			
ZD	+2	**CE**		S-			
GMT	25:20	**CCT**		C-			
6 Feb	01:20	**GMT**					

Almanac		Compass Correction		Deviation			
GHA	151° 04.9'						
M/S	+ 5° 00.8'	T	358.7	T	222.5	T	222.5
GHA	156° 05.7'	E	**1.5 W**	E	**1.5 W**	V	+ 20°.0 W
±SHA/v		G	000.2°	G	224.0°	M	242.5
Sum	156° 05.7'	**Polaris bearing from Almanac**				D	+ 1.5 W
Long	- 23° 48.0'					C	244.0
LHA	132° 17.7'		358.7				

Notes:

Alexander F. Hickethier MBA 1988-2019

POLARIS (POLE STAR) TABLES, 1981
FOR DETERMINING LATITUDE FROM SEXTANT ALTITUDE AND FOR AZIMUTH

L.H.A. ARIES	120°–129°	130°–139°	140°–149	150°–159°	160°–169°	170°–179°	180°–189°	190°–199°	200°–209°	210°–219°	220°–229°	230°–239°
	a_0	a_0	a_0	a_0	a_0	a_0	a_0	a_0	a_0	a_0	a_0	a_0
	° ′	° ′	° ′	° ′	° ′	° ′	° ′	° ′	° ′	° ′	° ′	° ′
0	0 56·4	1 05·0	1 13·3	1 21·2	1 28·5	1 34·8	1 40·0	1 44·1	1 46·7	1 47·9	1 47·7	1 46·0
1	57·2	05·8	14·1	22·0	29·1	35·4	40·5	44·4	46·9	48·0	47·6	45·7
2	58·1	06·7	15·0	22·7	29·8	35·9	41·0	44·7	47·1	48·0	47·4	45·4
3	59·0	07·5	15·8	23·5	30·5	36·5	41·4	45·0	47·2	48·0	47·3	45·2
4	0 59·8	08·3	16·6	24·2	31·1	37·0	41·8	45·3	47·4	48·0	47·2	44·9
5	1 00·7	1 09·2	1 17·4	1 25·0	1 31·8	1 37·6	1 42·2	1 45·6	1 47·5	1 48·0	1 47·0	1 44·6
6	01·5	10·0	18·1	25·7	32·4	38·1	42·6	45·8	47·6	47·9	46·8	44·3
7	02·4	10·8	18·9	26·4	33·0	38·6	43·0	46·1	47·7	47·9	46·6	43·9
8	03·2	11·7	19·7	27·1	33·6	39·1	43·4	46·3	47·8	47·8	46·4	43·6
9	04·1	12·5	20·5	27·8	34·2	39·6	43·7	46·5	47·9	47·8	46·2	43·2
10	1 05·0	1 13·3	1 21·2	1 28·5	1 34·8	1 40·0	1 44·1	1 46·7	1 47·9	1 47·7	1 46·0	1 42·8

Lat.	a_1	a_1	a_1	a_1	a_1	a_1	a_1	a_1	a_1	a_1	a_1	a_1
°	′	′	′	′	′	′	′	′	′	′	′	′
0	0·2	0·2	0·2	0·3	0·4	0·4	0·5	0·6	0·6	0·6	0·6	0·5
10	·2	·3	·3	·3	·4	·5	·5	·6	·6	·6	·6	·6
20	·3	·3	·3	·4	·4	·5	·5	·6	·6	·6	·6	·6
30	·4	·4	·4	·4	·5	·5	·6	·6	·6	·6	·6	·6
40	0·5	0·5	0·5	0·5	0·5	0·6	0·6	0·6	0·6	0·6	0·6	0·6
45	·5	·5	·5	·6	·6	·6	·6	·6	·6	·6	·6	·6
50	·6	·6	·6	·6	·6	·6	·6	·6	·6	·6	·6	·6
55	·7	·7	·7	·7	·6	·6	·6	·6	·6	·6	·6	·6
60	·8	·8	·8	·7	·7	·7	·6	·6	·6	·6	·6	·6
62	0·8	0·8	0·8	0 8	0·7	0·7	0·7	0·6	0·6	0·6	0·6	0·6
64	0·9	0·9	·9	·8	·8	·7	·7	·6	·6	·6	·6	·6
66	1·0	1·0	0·9	·9	·8	·7	·7	·6	·6	·6	·6	·7
68	1·1	1·0	1·0	0·9	0·9	0·8	0·7	0·6	0·6	0·6	0·6	0·7

Month	a_2	a_2	a_2	a_2	a_2	a_2	a_2	a_2	a_2	a_2	a_2	a_2
	′	′	′	′	′	′	′	′	′	′	′	′
Jan.	0·6	0·6	0·6	0·6	0·5	0·5	0·5	0·5	0·5	0·5	0·5	0·5
Feb.	·8	·7	·7	·7	·7	·6	·6	·5	·5	·5	·5	·5
Mar.	·9	0·9	0·9	0·8	·8	·8	·7	·7	·6	·6	·5	·5
Apr.	0·9	1·0	1·0	1·0	0·9	0·9	0·9	0·8	0·8	0·7	0·7	0·6
May	·9	1·0	1·0	1·0	1·0	1·0	1·0	1·0	0·9	0·9	·8	·7
June	·8	0·9	0·9	1·0	1·0	1·0	1·0	1·0	1·0	1·0	0·9	0·9
July	0·7	0·7	0·8	0·9	0·9	0·9	1·0	1·0	1·0	1·0	1·0	1·0
Aug.	·5	·6	·6	·7	·7	·8	0·9	0·9	0·9	1·0	1·0	1·0
Sept.	·4	·4	·5	·5	·6	·6	·7	·7	·8	0·8	0·9	0·9
Oct.	0·3	0·3	0·3	0·3	0·4	0·4	0·5	0·6	0·6	0·7	0·7	0·8
Nov.	·2	·2	·2	·2	·3	·3	·3	·4	·4	·5	·6	·6
Dec.	0·3	0·3	0·2	0·2	0·2	0·2	0·2	0·2	0·3	0·3	0·4	0·4

Lat.	AZIMUTH											
°	°	°	°	°	°	°	°	°	°	°	°	°
0	359·2	359·2	359·2	359·3	359·4	359·5	359·6	359·7	359·9	0·0	0·2	0·3
20	359·1	359·1	359·2	359·3	359·4	359·5	359·6	359·7	359·9	0·0	0·2	0·3
40	358·9	359·0	359·0	359·1	359·2	359·3	359·5	359·7	359·8	0·0	0·2	0·4
50	358·7	358·8	358·8	358·9	359·1	359·2	359·4	359·6	359·8	0·0	0·3	0·5
55	358·6	358·6	358·7	358·8	358·9	359·1	359·3	359·6	359·8	0·0	0·3	0·5
60	358·4	358·4	358·5	358·6	358·8	359·0	359·2	359·5	359·8	0·0	0·3	0·6
65	358·1	358·1	358·2	358·4	358·6	358·8	359·1	359·4	359·7	0·1	0·4	0·7

ILLUSTRATION

On 1981 April 21 at G.M.T. 23h 18m 56s in longitude W. 37° 14′ the apparent altitude (corrected for refraction), Ho, of

From the daily pages:	° ′		Ho	49 31·6
G.H.A. Aries (23h)	194 55·4		a_0 (argument 162° 26′)	1 30·1
Increment (18m 56s)	4 44·8		a_1 (lat. 50° approx.)	0·6
Longitude (west)	−37 14		a_2 (April)	0·9

21-2

End of Chapter USCG Problems

1. 01489. On 23 July 1981, your 2100 ZT position is LAT 36° 43.0' N, LONG 16° 09.8' W, when you observed an azimuth of POLARIS to determine the compass error. POLARIS bears 359.0 per gyrocompass. At the time of the observation, the helmsman noted that he was heading 319.0° per gyrocompass and 331.0° per standard compass. Variation is 12.0° W. Which of the following statements is true?

A. The gyro error is 0.7° E.
B. The gyro error is 1.7° W.
C. The deviation is 1.7° E.
D. The compass error is 13.7° W

2. 01490. On 11 January 1981, your 0450 ZT position is LAT 38° 42' N, LONG 14° 16' W. You observe Polaris bearing 358.5° pgc. At the time of the observation the helmsman noted that he was heading 160° pgc and 173° psc. The variation is 9° W. What is the deviation for that heading?

A. 1° E
B. 1° W
C. 3° W
D. 13° W

3. 01491. On 5 February 1981, your 2320 ZT position is LAT 52° 28' N, LONG 23° 48' W. You observe Polaris bearing 000.2° pgc. At the time of the observation the helmsman noted that he was heading 224° pgc and 244° psc. The variation is 20° W. What is the deviation for that heading?

A. 0°
B. 1.5° W
C. 3.0° W
D. 4.5° W

Alexander F. Hickethier MBA 1988-2019

4. 01492. On 22 February 1981, your 2045 ZT position is LAT 33° 19' N, LONG 52° 06' W. You observe Polaris bearing 358.1° pgc. At the time of the observation the helmsman noted that he was heading 048° pgc and 065° psc. The variation is 19° W. What is the deviation for that heading?

A. 1° E
B. 3° E
C. 1° W
D. 3° W

5. 01493. On 11 July 1981, your 0240 ZT position is LAT 14° 52' N, LONG 34° 23' W. You observe Polaris bearing 359.8° pgc. At the time of the observation the helmsman noted that he was heading 279° pgc and 299° psc. The variation is 19° W. What is the deviation for that heading?

A. 0°
B. 1° E
C. 1° W
D. 3° W

Answers

1. 01489 C
2. 01490 C
3. 01491 B
4. 01492 B
5. 01493 A

Alexander F. Hickethier MBA 1988-2019

USCG Problems worked-out

Celestial Problems							
Compass Deviation By Polaris							
Problem # 1 (USCG) (01489)				Chapter 21			

Date:	23 July	Time		21:00 ZT	LAT:	36° 43.0' N	
		CT			LONG	016° 09.8' W	
ZT	21:00	CE			S-		
ZD	+1	CCT			C-		
GMT	22:00	GMT					

Almanac		Compass Correction		Deviation			
GHA	271° 32.8'						
M/S		T	000.7	T	320.7	T	320.7
GHA	271° 32.8'	E	1.7 E	E	1.7 E	V	+12.0 W
±SHA/v		G	359.0	G	319.0	M	332.7
Sum	271° 32.8'	Polaris bearing from Almanac				D	- 1.7 E
Long	- 16° 09.8'					C	331.0
LHA	255° 23.0'	000.7					

Celestial Problems							
Compass Deviation By Polaris							
Problem # 2 (USCG) (01490)				Chapter 21			

Date:	11 Jan.	Time		04:50 ZT	LAT:	38° 42' N	
		CT			LONG	014° 16' W	
ZT	04:50	CE			S-		
ZD	+1	CCT			C-		
GMT	05:50	GMT					

Almanac		Compass Correction		Deviation			
GHA	185° 37.1'						
M/S	+12° 32.1'	T	359.5	T	161.0	T	161.0
GHA	198° 09.2'	E	1.0 E	E	1.0 E	V	+ 9.0 W
±SHA/v		G	358.5	G	160	M	170.0
Sum	198° 09.2'	Polaris bearing from Almanac				D	+ 3.0 W
Long	- 14° 16.0'					C	173.0
LHA	183° 53.2'	359.5					

Alexander F. Hickethier MBA 1988-2019

Celestial Problems
Compass Deviation By Polaris

Problem # 3 (USCG) (01491)					Chapter 21			

Date:	5 Feb.		Time	23:20 ZT	**LAT:**		52° 28' N	
	ZT	23:20	CT		**LONG**		023° 48' W	
	ZD	+2	CE			S-		
	GMT	25:20	CCT			C-		
	6 Feb	01:20	GMT					

Almanac			Compass Correction		Deviation			
GHA	151° 04.9'		T	358.7	T	222.5	T	222.5
M/S	+5° 00.8'		E	1.5 W	E	1.5 W	V	+ 20.0 W
GHA	156° 05.7'		G	000.2°	G	224.0	M	242.5
±SHA/v			Polaris bearing from Almanac				D	+ 1.5 W
Sum	156° 05.7'						C	244.0
Long	- 23° 48.0'		358.7					
LHA	132° 17.7'							

Celestial Problems
Compass Deviation By Polaris

Problem # 4 (USCG) (01492)					Chapter 21			

Date:	22 Feb		Time	20:45 ZT	**LAT:**		33-19' N	
			CT		**LONG**		052° 06' W	
	ZT	20:45	CE			S-		
	ZD	+3	CCT			C-		
	GMT	23:45	GMT					

Almanac			Compass Correction		Deviation			
GHA	122° 42.9'		T	359.0	T	049.0	T	049.0
M/S	+ 11° 16.8'		E	1.0 E	E	1.0 E	V	+ 19.0 W
GHA	133° 59.7'		G	358.0	G	048	M	068.0
±SHA/v			Polaris bearing from Almanac				D	- 3.0 E
Sum	133° 59.7'						C	065.0
Long	- 52° 06.0'		359					
LHA	81° 53.7'							

Celestial Problems						
Compass Deviation By Polaris						
Problem # 5 (USCG) (01493)			Chapter 21			

Date:	**11 July**	Time		02:40 ZT	LAT:	14° 52' N
			CT		LONG	034° 23' W
	ZT	02:40	CE		S-	
	ZD	+2	CCT		C-	
	GMT	04:40	GMT			

Almanac		Compass Correction			Deviation			
GHA	348° 58.8'							
M/S	+ 10° 01.6'	T	000.8	T	280.0	T	280.0	
GHA	359° 00.4'	E	1.0 E	E	1.0 E	V	19.0 W	
±SHA/v		G	359.8°	G	279°	M	299.0	
Sum	359° 00.4'	Polaris bearing from Almanac				D	0.0 E	
Long	- 34° 23.0'					C	299.0	
LHA	325° 37.4'	000.8						

Additional USCG problems worked-out for this chapter can be found in **Celestial Navigation Calculations (Upon Oceans Endorsement) Worked-Out for Master 500 GT through 2nd Mate Unlimited, Volume 3, part 1, Chapter 3, Magnetic and Gyro Compass Error Calculations.**

Alexander F. Hickethier MBA 1988-2019

SIGHTS TAKEN NEAR GEOGRAPHIC POSITION
Chapter 22

Normally, we take our celestial observation of selected objects at observed altitudes between 30 and 60 degrees. This allows us to plot the circles of equal altitude as a straight line through the use of Publications such as Pub 229 and 249. Occasionally, we will find it necessary to observe the sun at or near it's apparent geographic position. In this unique situation we are required to calculate the True Geographic Position and plot the LOP as a circle of equal altitude, not as a straight line.

The solution to follow will be used when a running fix has two or more observed altitudes of the sun that are greater than 88 degrees.

In our example we will use USCG question and the worksheet on page 22-2.

285 On 18 May 1981, your 1030 ZT DR position is LAT 18° 30' N, LONG 62° 31' W. You are on course 286° T, speed 24 knots. You take the following observations of the Sun:

ZT	GHA	DECLINATION	Ho
1204	61° 54.6'	N 19° 37.6'	88° 39.7'
1210	63° 24.6'	N 19° 37.7'	88° 59.2'

What was the 1200 position?

A.	LAT 18° 33.6' N	LONG 62° 54.3' W
B.	LAT 18° 35.2' N	LONG 62° 49.7' W
C.	LAT18° 38.7'N	LONG 62° 59.2' W
D.	LAT 18° 41.1' N	LONG 62° 53.9' W

We enter the given data, date, Dr, course and speed, ZT of the sights, GHA, Declination and Ho in spaces 1,2,3,4,6,7 and 8 respectively on page 22-2.

Calculating distance run
First we calculate the distance traveled for each sight as shown on the worksheet **space 5**. The results being 1.6 NM for the 1204 sight and 4.0 for the 1210 sight which will be used to retard our LOP's to the time of the required fix 1200.

Calculating Geographic Position
Next, if necessary we convert the GHA to the longitude of the sun's apparent Geographic Position. When we are in **East Longitude the GHA is subtracted from** 360 degrees and when in **West Longitude GHA is longitude.**

Calculating intercept
Finally, we must convert Ho to a circle of equal altitude. This is accomplished by subtracting Ho from 90 degrees and changing the results to minutes of Arc (Nautical Miles), 80.3 NM and 60.8 NM respectively.

22-1

Work form for USCG GP problem 5		
Date: **Time:**	**(1)** 18 May 1981 1030	**(2)** Lat 18° 30' N Long 062° 31' W C-286 S-24
Calculating Distance Run		
Sight	**1**	**2**
(3) ZT	1204	1210
(4) Fix Time	1200	1200
d	4	10
Speed (x)	24	24
inv	60	60
(5) Distance	1.6 NM	4.0 NM
Calculate Geographic Position		
(6) GHA	61° 54.6	63° 24.6
Conversion		
(7) Longitude	61° 54.6	63° 24.6
(8) Dec = Lat	N 19° 37.6	N 19-37.7
Calculation of intercept		
90°	89° 60.0'	89° 60.0'
- HO	88° 39.7'	88° 59.2'
d	1° 20.3'	1° 00.8'
(x) 60	80.3 NM	60.8 NM

With this information we can now plot our running fix.

The plotting of this fix is done differently than any other celestial fix we have learned to date. Following the three steps below and shown below.

1. Plot the Sun's Geographic position using the Declination as Latitude and GHA (corrected if necessary) as the Longitude.

2. Then using the distance calculated in **Step 5** of our worksheet we will retard the Geographic positions along the reciprocal of our course to 1200 the time of the required fix.

3. Finally, we plot the Arc of equal altitude from the retarded position.

4. Our position is the latitude and longitude of the point at which the two arc's cross. In our example this point is at 18° 41.0' N, 62° 53.9' W or USCG Answer D.

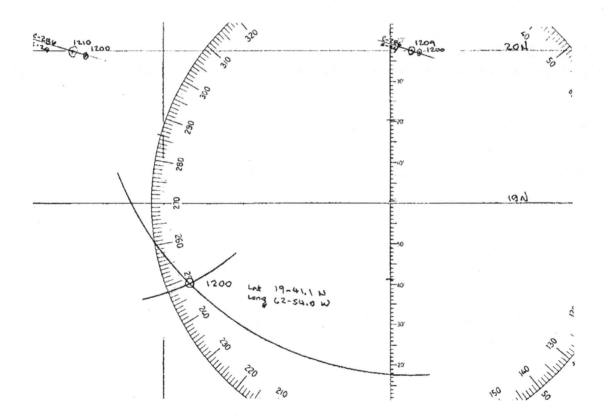

The practice questions on the following pages are actual USCG questions and will require the use of the Universal Plotting Sheet explained in Chapter 11

1.
22. *(5.1.4.1-4)* On 15 November your 1030 ZT, DR position is LAT 17° 25' S, LONG 42° 12' W. You are on course 059° T, speed 22 knots. Determine your 1200 position using the following observations of the Sun.

Zone Time	GHA	Declination	Ho
1128	40° 50.4'	S 18° 33.6'	88° 18.4'
1133	42° 05.4'	S 18° 33.6'	88°37.7'

(A) LAT 17° 00.0' S   LONG 41° 45.8' W
(B) LAT 17° 02.1' S   LONG 41° 48.4' W
(C) LAT 17° 06.8' S   LONG 41° 44.3' W
(D) LAT 17° 08.9' S   LONG 41° 40.4' W

2.
234. *(5.1.4.1-7)* On 30 July your 1030 ZT, DR position is LAT 19° 02' N, LONG 138° 12' W. You are on course 309° T, speed 24 knots. Determine your 1200 position using the following observations of the Sun.

Zone Time	GHA	Declination	Ho
1220	138° 25.0'	N 18° 22.3'	88° 43.3'
1226	139° 55.0'	N 18° 22.2'	88° 24.0'

(A) LAT 19° 28.0' N   LONG 138° 35.2' W
(B) LAT 19° 29.7' N   LONG 138° 42.0' W
(C) LAT 19° 32.6' N   LONG 138° 49.4' W
(D) LAT 19° 34.5' N   LONG 138° 40.9 'W

3.
240. *(5.1.4.1-3)* On 13 November your 1030 ZT, DR position is LAT 19° 03' S, LONG 6° 34' E. You are on course 164° T, speed 12 knots. Determine your 1200 position using the following observations of the Sun.

Zone Time	GHA	Declination	Ho
1112	351° 55.4'	S 18° 00.4'	88° 08.0'
1121	354° 10.4'	S 18° 00.5'	88° 33.9'

(A) LAT 19° 22.3' S   LONG 6° 37.8' E
(B) LAT 19° 20.1' S   LONG 6° 41.4' E
(C) LAT 19° 17.6' S   LONG 6° 39.2' E
(D) LAT 19° 15.8' S   LONG 6° 36.8' E

4.

295. *(5.1.4.1-2)* On 26 July your 1030 ZT, DR position is LAT 18° 25' N, LONG 51° 15' W. You are on course 231° T, speed 15 knots. Determine your 1200 position using the following observations of the Sun.

Zone Time	GHA	Declination	Ho
1228	50° 23.5'	N 19° 21.9'	88° 14.3'
1236	52° 23.5'	N 19° 21.8'	88° 29.0'

(A) LAT 18° 00.9'N   LONG 51° 31.9' W
(B) LAT 18° 03.5'N   LONG 51° 36.2' W
(C) LAT 18° 07.2'N   LONG 51° 30.4' W
(D) LAT 18° 10.6'N   LONG 51 °25.1' W

5.

298. *(5.1.4.1-6)* On 18 May your 1030 ZT, DR position is LAT 20° 41' N, LONG 63° 32' W. You are on course 106° T, speed 24 knots. Determine your 1200 position using the following observations of the Sun.

Zone Time	GHA	Declination	Ho
1204	61° 54.6'	N 19° 37.6'	88° 39.7'
1210	63° 24.6'	N 19° 37.7'	88° 59.2'

(A) LAT 20° 32.6' N   LONG 62° 57.5' W
(B) LAT 20° 30.1' N   LONG 63° 01.9' W
(C) LAT 20° 27.6' N   LONG 62° 52.4' W
(D) LAT 20° 25.2' N   LONG 62° 56.9' W

Answers:

#	USCG #		Answer
1.	**22.**	*(5.1.4.1-4)*	C
2.	**234.**	*(5.1.4.1-7)*	B
3.	**240.**	*(5.1.4.1-3)*	A
4.	**295.**	*(5.1.4.1-2)*	C
5.	**298.**	*(5.1.4.1-6)*	A

Work form for USCG GP problem 1		
	(1)	**(2)**
Date:	15 November	Lat 17° 25' S
Time:	1030 ZT	Long 042° 12' W
		C-059 T
		S-22 Kts
Calculating Distance Run		
Sight	1	2
(3) ZT	1128	1133
(4) Fix Time	1200	1200
d	32	27
Speed (x)	22	22
inv	60	60
(5) Distance	11.7	9.9
Calculate Geographic Position		
(6) GHA	40° 50.4'	42° 05.4'
Conversion		
(7) Longitude	40° 50.4'	42° 05.4'
(8) Dec = Lat	S 18° 33.6'	S 18° 33.6
Calculation intercept		
90°	89° 60.0'	89° 60.0'
- HO	88° 18.4'	88° 37.7'
d	1° 41.6'	1° 22.3'
(x) 60	101.6	82.3

Work form for USCG GP problem 2		
	(1)	**(2)**
Date:	30 July	Lat 19° 02' N
Time:	1030	Long 138° 12' W
		C-309 T
		S-24 Kts
Calculating Distance Run		
Sight	1	2
(3) ZT	1220	1226
(4) Fix Time	1200	1200
d	20	26
Speed (x)	24	24
inv	60	60
(5) Distance	8	10.4
Calculate Geographic Position		
(6) GHA	138° 25.0'	138° 55.0'
Conversion		
(7) Longitude	138° 25.0'	138° 55.0'
(8) Dec = Lat	N 18° 22.3'	N 18° 22.2'
Calculation intercept		
90°	89° 60.0'	89° 60.0'
- HO	88° 43.3'	88° 24.0'
d	1° 16.7'	1° 36.0'
(x) 60	76.7	96.0

Work form for USCG GP problem 3		
	(1)	**(2)**
Date:	13 November	Lat 19° 03' S
Time:	1030	Long 006° 34' E
		C-164 T
		S-12
Calculating Distance Run		
Sight	1	2
(3) ZT	1112	1121
(4) Fix Time	1200	1200
d	48	39
Speed (x)	12	12
inv	60	60
(5) Distance	9.6	7.8
Calculate Geographic Position		
(6) GHA	351° 55.4'	354° 10.4'
Conversion	360° 00.0'	360° 00.0'
(7) Longitude	008°04.6'	005°49.6'
(8) Dec = Lat	S 18° 00.4	S 18° 00.5
Calculation intercept		
90°	89° 60.0'	89° 60.0'
- HO	88° 08.0'	88° 33.9'
d	1° 52'	1°26.1'
(x) 60	112	86.1

Work form for USCG GP problem 4		
	(1)	**(2)**
Date:	26 July	Lat 18° 25' N
Time:	1030	Long 051° 15' W
		C-231 T
		S-15 Kts
Calculating Distance Run		
Sight	1	2
(3) ZT	1228	1236
(4) Fix Time	1200	1200
d	28	36
Speed (x)	15	15
inv	60	60
(5) Distance	7.0	9.0
Calculate Geographic Position		
(6) GHA	50° 23.5'	52° 23.5'
Conversion		
(7) Longitude	50° 23.5'	52° 23.5'
(8) Dec = Lat	N 19° 21.9'	N 19° 21.8'
Calculation intercept		
90°	89° 60.0'	89° 60.0'
- HO	88° 14.3'	88° 29.0'
d	1° 45.7'	1° 31.0'
(x) 60	105.7	91.0

22-6

Work form for USCG GP problem 5		
	(1)	**(2)**
Date: **Time:**	18 May 1981 1030	Lat 20° 41' S Long 063° 32' W C-106 S-24
Calculating Distance Run		
Sight	**1**	**2**
(3) ZT	1204	1210
(4) **Fix Time**	1200	1200
d	4	10
Speed (x)	24	24
inv	60	60
(5) **Distance**	1.6 NM	4.0 NM
Calculate Geographic Position		
(6) **GHA**	61° 54.6	63° 24.6
Conversion		
(7) Longitude	61° 54.6	63° 24.6
(8) Dec = Lat	N 19° 37.6	N 19-37.7
Calculation intercept		
90°	89° 60.0'	89° 60'
- HO	88° 39.7'	88° 59.2'
d	1° 20.3'	1° 00.8'
(x) 60	80.3 NM	60.8 NM

EX – MERIDIAN
Chapter 23

It is the best to determine latitude when a body is at <u>meridian passage</u>, but weather or even our planning may prevent us from being on the bridge at the appropriate time. Thus, if Mother Nature or Murphy's Law is at work we may have to settle for an observation near but not exactly at meridian transit. If our observation is <u>after meridian transit</u> it is called an **upper transit** and if observed <u>prior to meridian transit</u> it is called a **lower transit**.

As in the other chapters, **I will provide the solution to an actual USCG problem step by step, but we will only complete the steps that we have not learned in the earlier chapters.**

Example Ex-Meridian Problem

On **22 July 1981,** in **DR** position Lat **31-40N,** Long **119° 40' W,** you take an ex-meridian observation of the Sun's lower limb. Your vessel is on course **045°** T and a speed of **14** knots. The Chronometer time of the sight is **08h 14m 27s,** and the chronometer error is **01m 27s fast.** The sextant altitude (hs) is **78° 29.1'.** The index error is **2.5' off the arc,** and your height of eye is **39 feet.** What is the latitude at **1200 ZT?**

First, we determine **GMT, Dec, LHA "t"** and **Ho** as shown on our work form found on page 23-4. Reproductions of the appropriate parts of Tables 29 and 30 (Tables 24 and 25 in the new single volume) are shown on pages 23-2 and 23-3.

TABLE 29 (Bowditch volume 2) or **TABLE 24** (Bowditch NEW single volume)

We enter Table 29 (Bowditch) with our latitude 31 and declination 20 finding the **"a"** value of **8.3,** this is our base. Next we enter the table for the next higher latitude (32) and declination (21). We use the same interpolation method as before and shown on the work form page 23-3. The value obtained **(7.9)** is used to enter Table 30. By formulae 1.9635' x (cos 31° 40' x cos 20° 10.4') / sin (31° 40' ~ 20° 10.4') = 7.87268996.

Table 29 (24). Altitude Factors Explained - In one minute of time from meridian transit the altitude of a celestial body changes by the amount shown in this table if the altitude is between 6° and 86°, the latitude is not more than 60°, and the declination is not more than 63°. The values taken from this table are used to enter **Table 30 (25)** for solving the ex-meridian problems.

For upper transit, use the left-hand pages if the declination and latitude are of the same name (both north or both south) and the right-hand pages if of contrary name. For lower transit, use the values below the heavy lines on the last three contrary-name pages. When a factor is taken from this part of the table, the correction from **table 30 (25)** is subtracted from the observed altitude to obtain the corresponding meridian altitude. All other corrections are added.

The table was computed using the formula:

         NOTE (~)   **=**   **- L and d same name,**   **+ L and d contrary name.**

       a = 1.9635" cos L cos d csc (L ~ d)   or   a = 1.9635" cos L cos d / sin (L ~ d) in which **a** is the change of altitude in one minute from meridian transit (the tabulated value), **L** is the latitude of the observer, and **d** is the declination of the celestial body. This formula can be used to compute values outside the limits of the table, but is not accurate if the altitude is greater than 86°.

176

	TABLE 29 — Altitude Factor													
	a, the change of altitude in one minute from meridian transit; used for entering table 30													
Lati-tude	Declination same name as latitude, upper transit: add correction to observed altitude													Lati-tude
	12°	13°	14°	15°	16°	17°	18°	19°	20°	21°	22°	23°	24°	
25	7.7	8.3	9.0	9.9	10.9	12.2	13.9	16.1	19.2	23.8				25
26	7.1	7.6	8.2	8.9	9.8	10.8	12.1	13.7	15.9	18.9	23.5			26
27	6.6	7.0	7.5	8.1	8.8	9.6	10.6	11.9	13.5	15.6	18.6	23.1		27
28	6.2	6.5	7.0	7.4	8.0	8.7	9.5	10.5	11.7	13.3	15.4	18.3	22.7	28
29	5.7	6.1	6.4	6.9	7.3	7.9	8.6	9.4	10.3	11.5	13.1	15.1	18.0	29
30	5.4	5.7	6.0	6.4	6.8	7.2	7.8	8.4	9.2	10.1	11.3	12.8	14.9	30
31	5.1	5.3	5.6	5.9	6.3	6.7	7.1	7.7	8.3	9.0	10.0	11.1	12.6	31
32	4.8	5.0	5.2	5.5	5.8	6.2	6.5	7.0	7.5	8.1	8.9	9.8	10.9	32
33	4.5	4.7	4.9	5.1	5.4	5.7	6.1	6.4	6.9	7.4	8.0	8.7	9.6	33
34	4.3	4.4	4.6	4.8	5.1	5.3	5.6	5.9	6.3	6.8	7.3	7.8	8.6	34
Lati-tude	12°	13°	14°	15°	16°	17°	18°	19°	20°	21°	22°	23°	24°	Lati-tude
	Declination same name as latitude, upper transit: add correction to observed altitude													

TABLE 30 (Bowditch volume 2) or **TABLE 25** (Bowditch NEW single volume)

You have the option of entering Table 30 or using the following formula **a (t)² \ 60** to calculate the correction to **Ho** required to obtain Latitude at ex-meridian. By entering Table 30 with the value obtained from table 29 (7.9) and our LHA (t) of 1° 59.4' we obtain the correction of **8.3**. This correction is applied to observed altitude Ho according to the Table 29 rules found at the top and bottom of each page, in our case it is added to Ho.

Table 30 (24). Change of Altitude in Given Time from Meridian Transit Explained - Enter this table with the altitude factor from **table 24 (29)** and the meridian angle, in either arc or time units, and take out the difference between the altitude at the given time and the altitude at meridian transit. Enter the table separately with whole numbers and tenths of **a**, interpolating for **t** if necessary, and add the two values to obtain the total difference. This total can be applied as a correction to observed altitude to obtain the corresponding meridian altitude, adding for upper transit and subtracting for lower transit.

The table was computed using the formulas:

$$C = at^2/60$$

in which **C** is the tabulated difference to be used as a correction to observed altitude in minutes of arc; **a** is the altitude factor from **table 24 (29)** in seconds of arc; and **t** is the **meridian angle in minutes of time.**

This formula should not be used for determining values beyond the limits of the table unless reduced accuracy is acceptable.

TABLE 30

Change of Altitude in Given Time from Meridian Transit

a (table 29)	1°15'	1°20'	1°25'	1°30'	1°35'	1°40'	1°45'	1°50'	1°55'	2°00'	2°05'	2°10'	2°15'	2°20'	a (table 29)
	5m00s	5m20s	5m40s	6m00s	6m20s	6m40s	7m00s	7m20s	7m40s	8m00s	8m20s	8m40s	9m00s	9m20s	
7.0	2.9	3.3	3.7	4.2	4.7	5.2	5.7	6.3	6.9	7.5	8.1	8.8	9.4	10.2	7.0
8.0	3.3	3.8	4.3	4.8	5.3	5.9	6.5	7.2	7.8	8.5	9.3	10.0	10.8	11.6	8.0
9.0	3.8	4.3	4.8	5.4	6.0	6.7	7.4	8.1	8.8	9.6	10.4	11.3	12.2	13.1	9.0
10.0	4.2	4.7	5.4	6.0	6.7	7.4	8.2	9.0	9.8	10.7	11.6	12.5	13.5	14.5	10.0
11.0	4.6	5.2	5.9	6.6	7.4	8.1	9.0	9.9	10.8	11.7	12.7	13.8	14.8	16.0	11.0
12.0	5.0	5.7	6.4	7.2	8.0	8.9	9.8	10.8	11.8	12.8	13.9	15.0	16.2	17.4	12.0
13.0	5.4	6.2	7.0	7.8	8.7	9.6	10.6	11.7	12.7	13.9	15.0	16.3	17.6	18.9	13.0
14.0	5.8	6.6	7.5	8.4	9.4	10.4	11.4	12.5	13.7	14.9	16.2	17.5	18.9	20.3	14.0
15.0	6.2	7.1	8.0	9.0	10.0	11.1	12.2	13.4	14.7	16.0	17.4	18.8	20.2	21.8	15.0
16.0	6.7	7.6	8.6	9.6	10.7	11.9	13.1	14.3	15.7	17.1	18.5	20.0	21.6	23.2	16.0
17.0	7.1	8.1	9.1	10.2	11.4	12.6	13.9	15.2	16.7	18.1	19.7	21.3	23.0	24.7	17.0
18.0	7.5	8.5	9.6	10.8	12.0	13.3	14.7	16.1	17.6	19.2	20.8	22.5	24.3	26.1	18.0
19.0	7.9	9.0	10.2	11.4	12.7	14.1	15.5	17.0	18.6	20.3	22.0	23.8			19.0
20.0	8.3	9.5	10.7	12.0	13.4	14.8	16.3	17.9	19.6	21.3	23.1				20.0
21.0	8.8	10.0	11.2	12.6	14.0	15.6	17.2	18.8	20.6						21.0
22.0	9.2	10.4	11.8	13.2	14.7	16.3	18.0	19.7	21.6						22.0
23.0	9.6	10.9	12.3	13.8	15.4	17.0	18.8	20.6							23.0
24.0	10.0	11.4	12.8	14.4	16.0	17.8	19.6	21.5							24.0
25.0	10.4	11.9	13.4	15.0	16.7	18.5	20.4								25.0
26.0	10.8	12.3	13.9	15.6	17.4	19.3									26.0
27.0	11.2	12.8	14.4	16.2	18.0	20.0									27.0

In the example used in this chapter page 23-4, I have completed the example problem using the tables from the American Practical Navigator and by formulae, but do to the fact that the USCG examinations are time based I recommend using the calculator in the examinations. The formulas are found in the American Practical Navigator's "Explanation of Tables"

All practice problem on pages 23-7 through 23-11 are worked-out using only the calculator.

Celestial Problems
Sight Reduction Ex-Meridian

Problem # (USCG)			SUN			
Date: 22 July		Time			**LAT:**	31° 40.0' N
					LONG	119° 40.0' W
	ZT	1213	**CT**	08:14:27		S-045
	ZD	+ 8	**CE**	+ 1:27		C-14
	GMT	2013	**CCT**	08 13:00		
			GMT	20:13:00	**DR**	
					Time	
					LAT	
					LONG	

Almanac

GHA	118° 24.4'	**DEC**	N 20° 10.4'		**Hs**	78° 29.1'
M/S	3° 15.0'	**d**	- .5 - .1'		**IE**	+ 2.5'
GHA	121° 39.4'	**DEC**	N 20° 10.3'		**Dip**	- 6.1'
LONG	-119° 40.0'				**Sum**	- 3.6'
± v (+.8)					**Ha**	78° 25.5'
LHA "t"	1° 59.4'				**Alt**	+ 15.7
					Ho	78° 41.2'
"t"	7.96				**Cor**	+ 8.3'
					Ho	78° 49.5'

LAT	31° 40.0' N	**DEC**		N 20° 10.3'		LAN	
		Table 29 corrections					
1 (31)	8.3	**Dec** (20)	8.3		90°	89° 60.0'	
2 (32)	7.5	**Dec** (21)	9.0		**Ho**	78° 49.5'	
d	- .8	**d**	+ .7		**Zd**	11° 10.5'	
Inc Lat (X)	40.0	**Inc Dec (X)**	10.3		**Dec (±)**	20° 10.3'	
Inv	60	**Inv**	60		**LAN 1213**	31° 20.8'	
correction	- .5	**correction**	+ .1		**DLat**	- 2.1	
Base 8.3 - .4 = 7.9		**Table 30 argument**			**Lat 1200**	**31° 18.7'**	
By formulae a = 1.9635" x (cos 31° 40' x cos 20° 10.4')							
/ sin (31° 40' - 20° 10.4') =**7.87268996 = a**							
		Table 30					
a	7.9	**t**	1° 59'	**By calculator Corr = at²/60 = 7.9 x 7.96²/60 = 8.3**			
a (7)	6.9	(1° 55')	6.9				
a +1 (8)	7.8	(2° 00')	7.5				
d	+0.9	d	+0.6		**Base**	6.9	
inv(X)	0.9	inv (x)	59		**tcorr**	+1.4	
inc (1)	1.0	inc (60)	60			8.3	
corr	+0 8	corr	+0.6				

USCG Practice Problems

1.

2. *(5.1.2.1D-12)* On 5 May in DR position LAT 38°34.5'N, LONG 124°20.7'W, you take an ex-meridian observation of the Sun's lower limb. The chronometer time of the sight is 07h 59m 10s, and the chronometer error is 01m 10s slow. The sextant altitude (hs) is 67°27.0'. The index error is 1.4' on the arc, and your height of eye is 30 feet. What is the latitude at meridian transit?

(A) LAT 38°26.4'N
(B) LAT 38°30.2'N
(C) LAT 38°36.0'N
(D) LAT 38°41.2'N

2.

30. *(5.1.2.1D-8)* On 10 March in DR position LAT 21°42.0'S, LONG 57°28.0'E, you take an ex-meridian observation of the Sun's lower limb. The chronometer time of the sight is 08h 28m 17s, and the chronometer error is 00m 00s. The sextant altitude (hs) is 72°08.0'. The index error is 3.4' on the arc, and your height of eye is 52.7 feet. What is the latitude at meridian transit?

(A) LAT 21°32.5'S
(B) LAT 21°40.6'S
(C) LAT 21°45.5'S
(D) LAT 21°50.2'S

3.

68. *(5.1.2.1D-5)* On 27 March in DR position LAT 32°31.0'N, LONG 76°25.0'W, you take an ex-meridian observation of the Sun's lower limb. The chronometer time of the sight is 05h 23m 32s, and the chronometer error is 01m 30s fast. The sextant altitude (hs) is 59°59.0'. The index error is 1.8' off the arc, and your height of eye is 52 feet. What is the latitude at meridian transit?

(A) LAT 32°21.6'N
(B) LAT 32°29.5'N
(C) LAT 32°37.6'N
(D) LAT 32°46.2'N

4.

143. *(5.1.2.1D-9)* On 15 October an ex-meridian altitude of the Sun's lower limb at upper transit was observed at 1146 ZT. Your DR position is LAT 22°42.0'N, LONG 139°52.0'E, and your sextant altitude (hs) is 58°30.4'. The index error is 3.4' on the arc, and your height of eye is 56.7 feet. The chronometer time of the observation is 02h 45m 06s, and the chronometer error is 01m 06s slow. Find the latitude at meridian transit from the ex-meridian observation.

(A) LAT 22°29.1'N
(B) LAT 22°35.2'N
(C) LAT 22°58.1'N
(D) LAT 23°20.6'N

5.

232. *(5.1.2.1D-1)* On 15 December in DR position LAT 23°24.0'N, LONG 55°36.0'W, you take an ex-meridian observation of the Sun's lower limb. The chronometer time of the sight is 03h 45m 19s, and the chronometer error is 00m 00s. The sextant altitude (hs) is 43°02.3'. The index error is 2.6' on the arc, and your height of eye is 65.0 feet. What is the latitude at meridian transit?

(A) LAT 23°33.5'N
(B) LAT 23°35.8'N
(C) LAT 23°38.1'N
(D) LAT 23°40.6'N

Answers for Ex-Meridian

#	USCG #	Answer
1.	**2.** *(5.1.2.1D-12)*	C
2.	**30.** *(5.1.2.1D-8)*	C
3.	**68.** *(5.1.2.1D-5)*	B
4.	**143.** *(5.1.2.1D-9)*	B
5.	**232.** *(5.1.2.1D-1)*	A

USCG Practice Problems Worked-Out

		Celestial Problems					
		Sight Reduction Ex-Meridian					

Problem # 1   (USCG) 2. (5.1.2.1D-12)   SUN

Date:	5 May		Time		**LAT:**		38° 34.5 N
					LONG		124° 20.7 W
	ZT	1213	**CT**	07:59:10		S-	
	ZD	+ 8	**CE**	+ 1:10		C-	
	GMT	2013	**CCT**	08 00:20			
			GMT	20:00:20	**DR**		
					Time		
					LAT		
					LONG		

		Almanac					
GHA	120° 50.7'	**DEC**	N 16° 24.0'	**Hs**	67° 27.0'		
M/S	0° 05.0'	**d**	+ .7 - .0'	**IE**	- 1.4		
GHA	120° 55.7'	**DEC**	N 16° 24.0'	**Dip (30)**	- 5.3		
LONG	-124° 20.7'			**Sum**	- 6.7		
± v (+.8)				**Ha**	67° 20.3'		
LHA	356° 35.0'			**Alt**	+ 15.6'		
-360	003° 25.0'			**Ho**	67° 35.9'		
"t"	13.67			**Cor**	+ 12.0'		
				Ho	67° 47.9'		

Table 29 correction by calculator			LAN
By formulae:		90°	89° 60.0'
		Ho	67° 47.9'
a = 1.9635 x (cos L x cos d / sin (L~d)		Zd	22° 12.1'
		Dec (±)	+16° 24.0'
a = 1.9635" x (cos 38° 34.5' x cos 16° 24.0') / sin (38° 34.5 - 16° 24.0') =**3.844935913 = a**		**LAN**	**38° 36.1'**
		DLat	
		Lat 1200	

Table 30 correction by calculator
By formulae:
Corr = at²/60
Corr= 3.8449 x 13.67²/60 = 11.97

Celestial Problems
Sight Reduction Ex-Meridian

Problem # 2   (USCG) 30. *(5.1.2.1D-8)*   **SUN**

Date:	10 March	Time			**LAT:**	21° 42.0' S
					LONG	057° 28.0' E
	ZT	1228	**CT**	08:28:17	S-	
	ZD	- 4	**CE**	+ 0:00	C-	
	GMT	0828	**CCT**	08 28:17		
			GMT	08 28:17	**DR**	
					Time	
					LAT	
					LONG	

Almanac

GHA	297° 24.6'	**DEC**	S 04° 05.6'	**Hs**	72° 08.0'
M/S	7° 04.3'	**d**	- 1.0 - .5'	**IE**	- 3.4'
GHA	304° 28.9'	**DEC**	S 04° 05.1'	**Dip(52.7)**	- 7.0'
LONG	+ 057° 28.0'			**Sum**	- 10.4'
± v (+.8)				**Ha**	71° 57.6'
LHA	361° 56.9'			**Alt**	+ 15.9'
-360	1° 56.9'			**Ho**	72° 13.5'
"t"	7.7933			**Cor**	+ 6.1'
				Ho	72° 19.6'

Table 29 correction by calculator	LAN	
By formulae:	90°	89° 60.0'
	Ho	72° 19.6'
a = 1.9635 x (cos L x cos d / sin (L~d)	**Zd**	17° 40.4'
	Dec (±)	04° 05.1'
a = 1.9635" x (cos 21° 42.0'x cos 04° 05.1') / sin (21° 42.0' - 04° 05.1') =**6.013219333**	**LAN**	**21° 45.5'**
	DLat	
	Lat 1200	

Table 30 correction by calculator
By formulae:
Corr = at²/60
Corr = 6.0132x 7.7933²/60 = 8.4

Celestial Problems
Sight Reduction Ex-Meridian

Problem # 3   (USCG) 68. *(5.1.2.1D-5)*   **SUN**

Date:	27 March		Time			LAT:	32° 31.0' N
						LONG	076° 25.0' W
	ZT	1222	**CT**	05:23:32		**S-**	
	ZD	+ 5	**CE**	- 1:30		**C-**	
	GMT	1722	**CCT**	05 22:02			
			GMT	17:22:02		**DR**	
						Time	
						LAT	
						LONG	

Almanac

GHA	073° 40.2'	**DEC**	N 02° 45.2'		**Hs**	59° 59.0'	
M/S	5° 30.5'	**d**	+ 1.0 + .4'		**IE**	+ 1.8'	
GHA	079° 10.7'	**DEC**	N 02° 45.6'		**Dip(52)**	- 7.0'	
LONG	- 076° 25.0'				**Sum**	- 5.2'	
± v (+.8)					**Ha**	59° 53.8'	
LHA	2° 45.7'				**Alt**	+ 15.7'	
					Ho	60° 09.5'	
"t"	11.04667				**Cor**	+ 6.8'	
					Ho	60° 16.3'	

Table 29 correction by calculator		LAN	
By formulae:		90°	89° 60.0'
		Ho	60° 16.3'
a = 1.9635 x (cos L x cos d / sin (L~d)		**Zd**	29° 43.7'
		Dec (±)	02° 45.6'
a = 1.9635" x (cos 32° 31.0'x cos 02° 45.6') / sin (32° 31.0'- 02° 45.6') =3.332083		**LAN**	**32° 29.3'**
		DLat	
		Lat 1200	

Table 30 correction by calculator

By formulae:

Corr = $at^2/60$

Corr = $3.332083 \times 11.04667^2/60 = 6.8$

Celestial Problems
Sight Reduction Ex-Meridian

Problem # 4   (USCG) *(5.1.2.1D-9)*   SUN Upper Transit

Date: 15 October		Time			**LAT:**	22° 42.0' N
					LONG	139° 52.0' E
ZT	1146	**CT**	02:45:06		S-	
ZD	- 9	**CE**	+ 1:06		C-	
GMT	0246	**CCT**	02:46:12			
		GMT	02:46:12	**DR**		
				Time		
				LAT		
				LONG		

Almanac

GHA	213° 31.8'	**DEC**	S 08° 25.9'		**Hs**	58° 30.4'
M/S	11° 33.0'	**d**	+ .9 + .7'		**IE**	- 3.4'
GHA	225° 04.8'	**DEC**	S 08° 26.6'		**Dip (56.7)**	- 7.3'
LONG	+ 139° 52.0'				**Sum**	- 10.7'
± v (+.8)					**Ha**	58° 19.7'
LHA	364° 56.8'				**Alt**	+ 15.6'
- 360	004° 56.8'				**Ho**	58° 35.3'
"t"	19.767				**Cor**	+ 23.0'
					Ho	58° 58.3'

Table 29 correction by calculator	LAN	
By formulae:	90°	89° 60.0'
	Ho	58° 58.3'
a = 1.9635 x (cos L x cos d / sin (L~d)	**Zd**	31° 01.7'
	Dec (±)	- 08° 26.6'
a = = 1.9635" x (cos 22° 42.0' x cos 08° 26.6') / sin (22° 42.0' + 08° 26.6') = 3.464496008	**LAN**	**22° 35.1'**
	DLat	
	Lat 1200	

Table 30 correction by calculator

By formulae:

Corr = at^2/60

Corr = = 3.464496008 x 19.967^2/60 = 23.020

Celestial Problems
Sight Reduction Ex-Meridian

Problem # 5 (USCG) 232. *(5.1.2.1D-1)*   SUN

Date:	15 December		Time			LAT:	23° 24.0' N
						LONG	055° 36.0' W
ZT	1145	**CT**	03:45:19			S-	
ZD	+ 4	**CE**	+ 0:00			C-	
GMT	1545	**CCT**	03:45:19				
		GMT	15:45:19		**DR**		
					Time		
					LAT		
					LONG		

Almanac

GHA	046° 11.4'	**DEC**	S 23° 17.0'	**Hs**	43° 02.3'
M/S	11° 19.8'	**d**	+ .1 - .1'	**IE**	- 2.6'
GHA	057° 31.2'	**DEC**	S 23° 17.1'	**Dip(65)**	- 7.8'
LONG	- 055° 36.0'			**Sum**	- 10.4'
± v (+.8)				**Ha**	42° 51.9'
LHA "t"	1° 55.2'			**Alt**	+ 15.2'
				Ho	43° 07.1'
"t"	7.667			**Cor**	+ 2.2'
				Ho	43° 09.3'

Table 29 correction by calculator		LAN	
By formulae:		90°	89° 60.0'
		Ho	43° 09.3'
$a = 1.9635 \times (\cos L \times \cos d / \sin (L\sim d)$		**Zd**	46° 50.7'
		Dec (±)	- 23° 17.1'
$a = = 1.9635'' \times \cos 23° 24.0' \times \cos 23° 17.1' / \sin (23° 24.0' + 23° 17.1' = 2.274948$		**LAN**	23° 33.6'
		DLat	
		Lat 1200	

Table 30 correction by calculator

By formulae:

Corr = $at^2/60$

Corr = 2.274948 x 7.667^2 / 60 = 2.228

UNKNOWN STAR

Chapter 24

The identification of an unknown star that is not one of 57 listed "Navigation Stars" is seldom required, but when necessary it may be our only means of obtaining a reliable celestial fix. This unknown star might well provide the line of position needed to complete a fix during poor weather conditions, when we are lucky to get a fix. Of course this only happens at that one time when all other forms of navigation have failed. As a professional navigator you know the "tricks of the trade" and will be able to save the day.

As with every other new calculation, we have presented each step using a USCG question as an example. In this case we will use USCG question # 1. (5.1.1.3-12). The calculation will require the use of the reproductions of the 1981 Almanac and Pub 229 on pages 3 and 4 and the work form on page 5. I will not work through steps learned in previous chapters of Celestial Navigation for Masters Upon Oceans (GHA Chapter 8, LHA 9, Ho Chapter 7, and GMT Chapter 6).

On 12 June, your 1845 DR position is LAT 21° 47' N, LONG 46° 52' W when you observe a faint unidentifiable star through a break in the clouds. The star bears 313° T at a sextant altitude (hs) of 14° 56.3'. The index error is 0.5' on the arc, and the height of eye is 45 feet. The chronometer reads 09h 43m 27s, and the chronometer error is lm 46s slow. What star did you observe?

A. Alnitak
B. Mirzam
C. Menkalinan
D. Theta Aurigae

ANSWER: C

We determine GMT, GHA and Ho as shown on our work form.

UNKNOWN STAR WORK FORM

Example		12 June			(1) LAT 21° 47' N, LONG 46° 52' W	
ZT 18:45		CT	09:43:27			
ZD + 3:00		CE	+ 1:46			
GMT 2145		CCT	09:45:13			
		GMT	21-45-13			

GHA ♈h	216° 05.6'		Hs	14° 56.3'	(2) Brg (Zn) 313°	
m/s	11° 20.1'		Ic	- 0.5'		
GHA ♈	227° 25.7'		Dip (45)	- 6.5'		
Long	- 46° 52.0'		Ha	14° 49.3'		
LHA ♈	180° 33.7'		Alt	- 3.6'		
			(3) Ho	14° 45.7'		

From PROBLEM	Enter PUB 229			From PUB 229		
(1) LAT	22 N	= LAT		(4) Hc N 45	= DEC	
(2) ZN	313	= LHA	L	(5) Z 090.6	= t	
(3) Ho	15	= Dec				

Rule (5) If the azimuth angle respondent is extracted from above the C-S Line, the supplement of the tabular value is the meridian angle, t, of the body.

Rules for (6)
If body is east of observer's meridian, subtract t from 360 (LHA = 360 – t)
If body is west observer's meridian, LHA = t

(6) t 090.6W = LHA *

Rule for (7)
SHA = LHA * - LHA ♈

SHA = 091– 181° = 271

(7) 271 = SHA *

Extracts from the 1981 Nautical Almanac

118   JUNE 12, 13, 14 (FRI., SAT., SUN.)

G.M.T.	ARIES G.H.A.	VENUS −3.3 G.H.A.	Dec.	MARS +1.7 G.H.A.	Dec.	JUPITER −1.7 G.H.A.	Dec.	SATURN +1.1 G.H.A.	Dec.	STARS Name	S.H.A.	Dec.
12 00	260 13.9	161 11.8 N24 16.5		197 22.8 N21 11.1		78 57.6 N 0 56.7		76 27.7 N 1 03.9		Acamar	315 37.2	S40 22.7
01	275 16.4	176 10.9 16.4		212 23.4 11.5		93 59.9 56.6		91 30.2 03.8		Achernar	335 45.2	S57 19.7
02	290 18.8	191 10.0 16.3		227 24.0 11.8		109 02.3 56.6		106 32.6 03.8		Acrux	173 36.5	S63 00.0
03	305 21.3	206 09.1 ·· 16.2		242 24.6 ·· 12.2		124 04.7 ·· 56.5		121 35.1 ·· 03.8		Adhara	255 32.1	S28 56.9
04	320 23.8	221 08.2 16.1		257 25.2 12.5		139 07.0 56.5		136 37.5 03.8		Aldebaran	291 17.8	N16 28.2
05	335 26.2	236 07.3 16.0		272 25.8 12.9		154 09.4 56.4		151 39.9 03.8				
06	350 28.7	251 06.5 N24 15.8		287 26.4 N21 13.2		169 11.8 N 0 56.3		166 42.4 N 1 03.7		Alioth	166 41.9	N56 04.0
07	5 31.1	266 05.6 15.7		302 27.0 13.6		184 14.1 56.3		181 44.8 03.7		Alkaid	153 17.8	N49 24.7
08	20 33.6	281 04.7 15.6		317 27.6 13.9		199 16.5 56.2		196 47.3 03.7		Al Na'ir	28 14.2	S47 02.9
F 09	35 36.1	296 03.8 ·· 15.5		332 28.2 ·· 14.3		214 18.8 ·· 56.2		211 49.7 ·· 03.7		Alnilam	276 11.5	S 1 12.9
R 10	50 38.5	311 02.9 15.3		347 28.8 14.6		229 21.2 56.1		226 52.1 03.7		Alphard	218 20.3	S 8 34.7
I 11	65 41.0	326 02.0 15.2		2 29.4 15.0		244 23.6 56.1		241 54.6 03.6				
D 12	80 43.5	341 01.2 N24 15.1		17 30.0 N21 15.3		259 25.9 N 0 56.0		256 57.0 N 1 03.6		Alphecca	126 31.4	N26 46.8
A 13	95 45.9	356 00.3 15.0		32 30.6 15.6		274 28.3 56.0		271 59.5 03.6		Alpheratz	358 08.9	N28 59.0
Y 14	110 48.4	10 59.4 14.8		47 31.2 16.0		289 30.7 55.9		287 01.9 03.6		Altair	62 31.8	N 8 49.1
15	125 50.9	25 58.5 ·· 14.7		62 31.8 ·· 16.3		304 33.0 ·· 55.8		302 04.3 ·· 03.5		Ankaa	353 39.9	S42 24.3
16	140 53.3	40 57.6 14.6		77 32.4 16.7		319 35.4 55.8		317 06.8 03.5		Antares	112 55.9	S26 23.4
17	155 55.8	55 56.7 14.4		92 33.0 17.0		334 37.7 55.7		332 09.2 03.5				
18	170 58.3	70 55.9 N24 14.3		107 33.6 N21 17.4		349 40.1 N 0 55.7		347 11.6 N 1 03.5		Arcturus	146 17.8	N19 16.9
19	186 00.7	85 55.0 14.2		122 34.2 17.7		4 42.5 55.6		2 14.1 03.5		Atria	108 19.1	S68 59.7
20	201 03.2	100 54.1 14.0		137 34.8 18.0		19 44.8 55.6		17 16.5 03.4		Avior	234 28.5	S59 27.2
21	216 05.6	115 53.2 ·· 13.9		152 35.4 ·· 18.4		34 47.2 ·· 55.5		32 19.0 ·· 03.4		Bellatrix	278 58.6	N 6 19.9
22	231 08.1	130 52.3 13.8		167 36.0 18.7		49 49.5 55.5		47 21.4 03.4		Betelgeuse	271 28.1	N 7 24.2
23	246 10.6	145 51.4 13.6		182 36.6 19.1		64 51.9 55.4		62 23.8 03.4				

[21] [216 05.6] ⇐

44ᵐ   INCREMENTS AND CORRECTIONS   45ᵐ

44ᵐ	SUN PLANETS	ARIES	MOON	v or Corrⁿ d		v or Corrⁿ d		v or Corrⁿ d		45ᵐ	SUN PLANETS	ARIES	MOON	v or Corrⁿ d		v or Corrⁿ d		v or Corrⁿ d	
00	11 00·0	11 01·8	10 29·9	0·0	0·0	6·0	4·5	12·0	8·9	00	11 15·0	11 16·8	10 44·3	0·0	0·0	6·0	4·6	12·0	9·1
01	11 00·3	11 02·1	10 30·2	0·1	0·1	6·1	4·5	12·1	9·0	01	11 15·3	11 17·1	10 44·5	0·1	0·1	6·1	4·6	12·1	9·2
02	11 00·5	11 02·3	10 30·4	0·2	0·1	6·2	4·6	12·2	9·0	02	11 15·5	11 17·3	10 44·7	0·2	0·2	6·2	4·7	12·2	9·3
03	11 00·8	11 02·6	10 30·6	0·3	0·2	6·3	4·7	12·3	9·1	03	11 15·8	11 17·6	10 45·0	0·3	0·2	6·3	4·8	12·3	9·3
04	11 01·0	11 02·8	10 30·9	0·4	0·3	6·4	4·7	12·4	9·2	04	11 16·0	11 17·9	10 45·2	0·4	0·3	6·4	4·9	12·4	9·4
05	11 01·3	11 03·1	10 31·1	0·5	0·4	6·5	4·8	12·5	9·3	05	11 16·3	11 18·1	10 45·4	0·5	0·4	6·5	4·9	12·5	9·5
06	11 01·5	11 03·3	10 31·4	0·6	0·4	6·6	4·9	12·6	9·3	06	11 16·5	11 18·4	10 45·7	0·6	0·5	6·6	5·0	12·6	9·6
07	11 01·8	11 03·6	10 31·6	0·7	0·5	6·7	5·0	12·7	9·4	07	11 16·8	11 18·6	10 45·9	0·7	0·5	6·7	5·1	12·7	9·6
08	11 02·0	11 03·8	10 31·8	0·8	0·6	6·8	5·0	12·8	9·5	08	11 17·0	11 18·9	10 46·2	0·8	0·6	6·8	5·2	12·8	9·7
09	11 02·3	11 04·1	10 32·1	0·9	0·7	6·9	5·1	12·9	9·6	09	11 17·3	11 19·1	10 46·4	0·9	0·7	6·9	5·2	12·9	9·8
10	11 02·5	11 04·3	10 32·3	1·0	0·7	7·0	5·2	13·0	9·6	10	11 17·5	11 19·4	10 46·6	1·0	0·8	7·0	5·3	13·0	9·9
11	11 02·8	11 04·6	10 32·6	1·1	0·8	7·1	5·3	13·1	9·7	11	11 17·8	11 19·6	10 46·9	1·1	0·8	7·1	5·4	13·1	9·9
12	11 03·0	11 04·8	10 32·8	1·2	0·9	7·2	5·3	13·2	9·8	12	11 18·0	11 19·9	10 47·1	1·2	0·9	7·2	5·5	13·2	10·0
13	11 03·3	11 05·1	10 33·0	1·3	1·0	7·3	5·4	13·3	9·9	13	11 18·3	11 20·1	10 47·4	1·3	1·0	7·3	5·5	13·3	10·1
14	11 03·5	11 05·3	10 33·3	1·4	1·0	7·4	5·5	13·4	9·9	14	11 18·5	11 20·4	10 47·6	1·4	1·1	7·4	5·6	13·4	10·2
15	11 03·8	11 05·6	10 33·5	1·5	1·1	7·5	5·6	13·5	10·0	15	11 18·8	11 20·6	10 47·8	1·5	1·1	7·5	5·7	13·5	10·3
16	11 04·0	11 05·8	10 33·8	1·6	1·2	7·6	5·6	13·6	10·1	16	11 19·0	11 20·9	10 48·1	1·6	1·2	7·6	5·8	13·6	10·3
17	11 04·3	11 06·1	10 34·0	1·7	1·3	7·7	5·7	13·7	10·2	17	11 19·3	11 21·1	10 48·3	1·7	1·3	7·7	5·8	13·7	10·4
18	11 04·5	11 06·3	10 34·2	1·8	1·3	7·8	5·8	13·8	10·2	18	11 19·5	11 21·4	10 48·5	1·8	1·4	7·8	5·9	13·8	10·5
19	11 04·8	11 06·6	10 34·5	1·9	1·4	7·9	5·9	13·9	10·3	19	11 19·8	11 21·6	10 48·8	1·9	1·4	7·9	6·0	13·9	10·5

⇒ [11 20·1]

Extract from the Sight Reduction Tables

Pub 229, Vol 2

47°, 313° L.H.A. **LATITUDE SAME NAME AS DECLINATION** N. Lat. { L.H.A. greater than 180° .....Zn=Z / L.H.A. less than 180°.............Zn=360°−Z

Dec.	15° Hc	d	Z	16° Hc	d	Z	17° Hc	d	Z	18° Hc	d	Z	19° Hc	d	Z	20° Hc	d	Z	21° Hc	d	Z	22° Hc	d	Z	Dec.
°	° ′	′	°	° ′	′	°	° ′	′	°	° ′	′	°	° ′	′	°	° ′	′	°	° ′	′	°	° ′	′	°	°
0	41 12.3	+20.3	103.6	40 57.8	+21.5	104.4	40 42.5	+22.7	105.3	40 26.3	+23.9	106.1	40 09.2	+25.2	106.9	39 51.4	+26.4	107.7	39 32.8	+27.5	108.5	39 13.4	+28.7	109.3	0
1	41 32.6	+19.4	102.3	41 19.3	+20.7	103.2	41 05.2	+22.0	104.0	40 50.2	+23.3	104.9	40 34.4	+24.5	105.7	40 17.8	+25.6	106.5	40 00.3	+26.9	107.3	39 42.1	+28.0	108.1	1
2	41 52.0	+18.5	101.0	41 40.0	+19.9	101.9	41 27.2	+21.1	102.8	41 13.5	+22.4	103.6	40 58.9	+23.7	104.5	40 43.4	+25.0	105.3	40 27.2	+26.1	106.2	40 10.1	+27.3	107.0	2
3	42 10.5	+17.7	99.8	41 59.9	+19.0	100.7	41 48.3	+20.4	101.5	41 35.9	+21.6	102.4	41 22.6	+22.9	103.3	41 08.4	+24.1	104.1	40 53.3	+25.4	105.0	40 37.4	+26.6	105.8	3
4	42 28.2	+16.8	98.5	42 18.9	+18.2	99.4	42 08.7	+19.5	100.3	41 57.5	+20.8	101.2	41 45.5	+22.1	102.0	41 32.5	+23.4	102.9	41 18.7	+24.6	103.8	41 04.0	+25.8	104.6	4
5	42 45.0	+16.0	97.2	42 37.1	+17.3	98.1	42 28.2	+18.6	99.0	42 18.3	+20.0	99.9	42 07.6	+21.2	100.8	41 55.9	+22.5	101.7	41 43.3	+23.8	102.5	41 29.8	+25.1	103.4	5
6	43 01.0	+15.0	95.9	42 54.4	+16.4	96.8	42 46.8	+17.8	97.7	42 38.3	+19.1	98.6	42 28.8	+20.5	99.5	42 18.4	+21.8	100.4	42 07.1	+23.1	101.3	41 54.9	+24.3	102.2	6
7	43 16.0	+14.1	94.5	43 10.8	+15.4	95.5	43 04.6	+16.8	96.4	42 57.4	+18.2	97.3	42 49.3	+19.5	98.2	42 40.2	+20.9	99.2	42 30.2	+22.2	100.1	42 19.2	+23.5	101.0	7
8	43 30.1	+13.1	93.2	43 26.2	+14.6	94.1	43 21.4	+16.0	95.1	43 15.6	+17.3	96.0	43 08.8	+18.7	97.0	43 01.1	+20.0	97.9	42 52.4	+21.4	98.8	42 42.7	+22.7	99.7	8
9	43 43.2	+12.2	91.8	43 40.8	+13.6	92.8	43 37.4	+15.0	93.7	43 32.9	+16.4	94.7	43 27.5	+17.8	95.6	43 21.1	+19.2	96.6	43 13.8	+20.5	97.5	43 05.4	+21.9	98.4	9
10	43 55.4	+11.2	90.5	43 54.4	+12.6	91.4	43 52.4	+14.0	92.4	43 49.3	+15.5	93.4	43 45.3	+16.9	94.3	43 40.3	+18.2	95.3	43 34.3	+19.6	96.2	43 27.3	+21.0	97.2	10
11	44 06.6	+10.3	89.1	44 07.0	+11.7	90.1	44 06.4	+13.1	91.1	44 04.8	+14.5	92.0	44 02.2	+15.9	93.0	43 58.5	+17.4	94.0	43 53.9	+18.7	94.9	43 48.3	+20.1	95.9	11
12	44 16.9	+9.2	87.7	44 18.7	+10.7	88.7	44 19.5	+12.2	89.7	44 19.3	+13.6	90.7	44 18.1	+15.0	91.6	44 15.9	+16.4	92.6	44 12.6	+17.8	93.6	44 08.4	+19.1	94.6	12
13	44 26.1	+8.2	86.4	44 29.4	+9.7	87.3	44 31.7	+11.1	88.3	44 32.9	+12.6	89.3	44 33.1	+14.0	90.3	44 32.3	+15.4	91.3	44 30.4	+16.9	92.3	44 27.5	+18.3	93.2	13
14	44 34.3	+7.2	85.0	44 39.1	+8.6	86.0	44 42.8	+10.1	86.9	44 45.5	+11.5	87.9	44 47.1	+13.0	88.9	44 47.7	+14.5	89.9	44 47.3	+15.9	90.9	44 45.8	+17.3	91.9	14
15	44 41.5	+6.2	83.6	44 47.7	+7.7	84.6	44 52.9	+9.1	85.6	44 57.0	+10.6	86.6	45 00.1	+12.0	87.5	45 02.2	+13.4	88.5	45 03.2	+14.9	89.5	45 03.1	+16.4	90.6	15

45 03.1 +16.4 90.6

Extract from the 1981 Nautical Almanac

STARS, JULY—DECEMBER 273

Mag.	Name and Number		S.H.A. JULY	AUG.	SEPT.	OCT.	NOV.	DEC.	Dec. JULY	AUG.	SEPT.	OCT.	NOV.	DEC.
		°	′	′	′	′	′	′	° ′	′	′	′	′	′
1·6	Castor	246	39·4	39·2	39·0	38·8	38·5	38·2	N. 31 55·8	55·8	55·7	55·7	55·7	55·6
3·3	σ Puppis	247	50·9	50·8	50·6	50·3	50·1	49·9	S. 43 15·8	15·7	15·6	15·5	15·6	15·8
3·1	β Canis Minoris	248	28·3	28·2	28·0	27·8	27·6	27·4	N. 8 19·7	19·7	19·7	19·7	19·6	19·6
2·4	η Canis Majoris	249	10·1	10·0	09·8	09·6	09·3	09·1	S. 29 16·0	15·9	15·8	15·8	15·8	16·0
2·7	π Puppis	250	53·2	53·1	52·9	52·7	52·4	52·2	S. 37 03·8	03·7	03·6	03·6	03·7	03·8
2·0	Wezen	253	05·9	05·8	05·6	05·4	05·2	05·0	S. 26 21·8	21·7	21·6	21·6	21·7	21·8
3·1	o Canis Majoris	254	26·7	26·6	26·4	26·2	26·0	25·8	S. 23 48·3	48·2	48·1	48·2	48·2	48·3
1·6	Adhara 19	255	32·0	31·9	31·7	31·5	31·3	31·1	S. 28 56·8	56·6	56·6	56·6	56·6	56·8
2·8	τ Puppis	257	38·4	38·3	38·0	37·8	37·5	37·3	S. 50 35·5	35·4	35·3	35·3	35·4	35·5
−1·6	Sirius 18	258	55·5	55·4	55·2	55·0	54·8	54·6	S. 16 41·4	41·3	41·3	41·3	41·4	41·5
1·9	Alhena	260	50·9	50·8	50·5	50·3	50·1	49·9	N. 16 24·9	24·9	25·0	24·9	24·9	24·9
−0·9	Canopus 17	264	07·5	07·3	07·0	06·7	06·4	06·3	S. 52 41·1	40·9	40·8	40·9	41·0	41·1
2·0	Mirzam	264	32·2	32·1	31·9	31·7	31·5	31·3	S. 17 56·8	56·7	56·6	56·6	56·7	56·8
2·7	θ Aurigæ	270	23·8	23·5	23·3	23·0	22·7	22·6	N. 37 12·6	12·6	12·6	12·6	12·6	12·7
2·1	Menkalinan	270	28·2	27·9	27·6	27·3	27·0	26·8	N. 44 56·7	56·6	56·6	56·6	56·7	56·7
Var.‡	Betelgeuse 16	271	28·0	27·8	27·6	27·4	27·2	27·0	N. 7 24·2	24·3	24·3	24·3	24·3	24·2
2·2	κ Orionis	273	17·3	17·1	16·9	16·7	16·5	16·4	S. 9 40·5	40·5	40·4	40·4	40·5	40·6
1·9	Alnitak	275	03·1	02·9	02·7	02·5	02·3	02·2	S. 1 57·1	57·1	57·0	57·0	57·1	57·1
2·8	Phact	275	15·8	15·6	15·4	15·2	15·0	14·9	S. 34 05·0	04·8	04·8	04·8	04·9	05·1
3·0	ζ Tauri	275	52·5	52·3	52·0	51·8	51·6	51·4	N. 21 07·8	07·9	07·9	07·9	07 9	07·9

GREEK ALPHABET

A	α	ALPHA
B	β	BETA
Γ	γ	GAMMA
Δ	δ	DELTA
E	ε	EPSLION
Z	ζ	ZETA
H	η	ETA
Θ	θ	THETA
I	ι	IOTA
K	κ	KAPPA
Λ	λ	LAMBDA
M	μ	MU
N	ν	NU
Ξ	ξ	XI
O	ο	OMICRON
Π	π	PI
P	ρ	RHO
Σ	σ, ς	SIGMA
T	τ	TAU
Y	υ	UPSILON
Φ	φ	PHI
X	χ	CHI
Ψ	ψ	PSI
Ω	ω	OMEGA

1.

35. *(5.1.1.3-6)* On 13 September your 1830 ZT DR position was LAT 23°03'S, LONG 105°16'E when you observed a faint unidentifiable star through a hole in the clouds. The star bore 351.5°T at a sextant altitude (hs) of 62°05.6'. The chronometer read 11h 24m 39s and is 5m 08s slow. The index error is 1.0' off the arc, and the height of eye is 52 feet. What star did you observe?

(A) Kappa Scorpii
(B) Alpha Herculis
(C) Alpha Arae
(D) Beta Ophiuchi

2.

42. *(5.1.1.3-1)* On 12 June your 1845 DR position is LAT 21°47'N, LONG 46°52'W when you observe a faint unidentifiable star through a break in the clouds. The star bears 019.0°T at a sextant altitude (hs) of 53°56.2'. The index error is 0.5' on the arc, and the height of eye is 45 feet. The chronometer reads 09h 43m 27s, and the chronometer error is 1m 46s slow. What star did you observe?

(A) Phecda
(B) Mizar
(C) Mimosa
(D) Gamma Ursae Minoris

3.

87. *(5.1.1.3-4)* On 2 October your 1845 DR position is LAT 28°09.2'S, LONG 167°48.1'E. You observe a faint star through a hole in the clouds at a sextant altitude (hs) of 63°29.1' bearing 237.5°T. The index error is 1.3' off the arc, and the height of eye is 42 feet. The chronometer reads 07h 46m 19s and is 0m 51s fast. What star did you observe?

(A) Beta Draconis
(B) Kappa Scorpii
(C) Alpha Arae
(D) Beta Ophiuchi

4.

139. *(5.1.1.3-5)* On 13 September your 1830 ZT DR position was LAT 23°03'S, LONG 105°16'E when you observe a faint unidentifiable star through a hole in the clouds. The star bore 132.3°T at a sextant altitude (hs) of 29°34.6'. The chronometer read 11h 24m 39s and is 5m 08s slow. The index error is 1.0' off the arc, and the height of eye is 52 feet. What star did you observe?

(A) Alpha Indi
(B) Beta Gruis
(C) Scheat
(D) Sigma Capricorni

5.

208. *(5.1.1.3-2)* On 12 June your 1845 DR position is LAT 21°47'N, LONG 46°52'W when you observe a faint unidentifiable star through a break in the clouds. The star bears 162°T at a sextant altitude (hs) of 28°36.5'. The index error is 0.5'on the arc, and the height of eye is 45 feet. The chronometer reads 09h 43m 27s, and the chronometer error is 1m 46s slow. What star did you observe?

(A) Mimosa
(B) Gamma Virginis
(C) Spica
(D) Iota Centauri

ANSWERS:

#		USCG #	ANSWER
1.	**35.**	*(5.1.1.3-6)*	D
2.	**42.**	*(5.1.1.3-1)*	B
3.	**87.**	*(5.1.1.3-4)*	B
4.	**139.**	*(5.1.1.3-5)*	B
5.	**8.**	*(5.1.1.3-2)*	D

Problem 1	13 September		**(1)** LAT 23° 03' S, LONG 105° 16' E

ZT	18:30		CT	11:24:39
ZD	- 7:00		CE	+ 5:08
GMT	11:30		CCT	11:29:47
			GMT	11:29:47

GHA ϒ h	157° 20.9'		Hs	62° 05.6'	**(2)** Brg (Zn) 351.5°
m/s	7° 28.0'		Ic	+ 1.0'	
GHA ϒ	164° 48.9'		Dip (52)	- 7.0'	
Long	+ 105° 16.0'		Ha	61° 59.6'	
LHA ϒ	270° 04.9'		Alt	- 0.5'	
			(3) Ho	61° 59.1'	

From	Enter			From	
PROBLEM	**PUB 229**			**PUB 229**	
(1) LAT	23 S	= LAT		(4) Hc N 05	= DEC
(2) ZN	352– 180 = 172	= LHA	R	(5) Z 176	= t
(3) Ho	62	= Dec		(004)	

Rule (5) If the azimuth angle respondent is extracted from above the C-S Line, the supplement of the tabular value is the meridian angle, t, of the body.

Rules for (6)
If body is east of observer's meridian, subtract t from 360 (LHA = 360 – t)
If body is west observer's meridian, LHA = t

(6) t 004W =   LHA *

Rule for (7)
SHA * = LHA * - LHA ϒ

SHA * = 004 – 270° = 094

(7) 094 = SHA *

The answer is on page **Beta Ophiuchi** is found on pg 268-9 of the 1981 Almanac. N 05, SHA 094

Problem 2	12 June			(1) LAT 21° 47' N, LONG 46° 52' W
ZT 18:45		CT	09:43:27	
ZD + 3:00		CE	+ 1:46	
GMT 2145		CCT	09:45:13	
		GMT	21-45-13	

GHA ♈ h	216° 05.6'		Hs	53° 56.3'	(2) Brg (Zn) 019°
m/s	11° 20.1'		Ic	- 0.5'	
GHA ♈	227° 25.7'		Dip (45)	- 6.5'	
Long	- 46° 52.0'		Ha	53° 49.3'	
LHA ♈	180° 33.7'		Alt	- 0.7'	
			(3) Ho	53° 48.6'	

From	Enter				From		
PROBLEM	**PUB 229**				**PUB 229**		
(1) LAT	22 N	= LAT			(4) Hc N 55	= DEC	
(2) ZN	019	= LHA	L		(5) Z 19	= t	
(3) Ho	54	= Dec					

Rule (5) If the azimuth angle respondent is extracted from above the C-S Line, the supplement of the tabular value is the meridian angle, t, of the body.

* Rules for (6)
If body is east of observer's meridian, subtract t from 360 (LHA = 360 – t)
If body is west observer's meridian, LHA = t

(6) t   360 – 19 E = 341 LHA *

**Rule for (7)
SHA = LHA * - LHA ♈

SHA = 341 – 181° = 159

(7) 159 = SHA *

The answer is on page **Mizar** is found on pg 271 of the 1981 Almanac. N 55, SHA 159

Problem 3		2 October		**(1)** LAT 28° 09.2' S, LONG 167° 48.1' E
ZT	18:45	CT	07:46:19	
ZD	- 11:00	CE	- 0:51	
GMT	07:45	CCT	07:45:28	
		GMT	07-45-28	

GHA ♈ h	115° 54.7'		Hs	63° 29.1'	**(2)** Brg (Zn) 237.5°
m/s	11° 23.9'		Ic	+ 1.3'	
GHA ♈	127° 28.6'		Dip (42)	- 6.3'	
Long	+ 167° 48.1'		Ha	63° 24.1'	
LHA ♈	295° 16.7'		Alt	- 0.5'	
		(3)	Ho	63° 23.6'	

From **PROBLEM**	Enter **PUB 229**			From **PUB 229**		
(1) LAT	28 S	= LAT		(4) Hc	S 39	= DEC
(2) ZN	238– 180 = 058	= LHA	L	(5) Z	30	= t
(3) Ho	63	= Dec				

Rule (5) If the azimuth angle respondent is extracted from above the C-S Line, the supplement of the tabular value is the meridian angle, t, of the body.

Rules for (6)
If body is east of observer's meridian, subtract t from 360 (LHA = 360 – t)
If body is west observer's meridian, LHA = t

(6) t   030 W = LHA *

Rule for (7)
SHA = LHA * - LHA ♈

SHA = 030 – 295° = 095

(7) 095   = SHA *

The answer is on page **Kappa Scorpii** is found on pg 268-9 of the 1981 Almanac. S 39, SHA 095

Problem 4	13 September	(1) LAT 23° 03' S, LONG 105° 16' E

ZT	18:30	CT	11:24:39
ZD	- 7:00	CE	+ 5:08
GMT	11:30	CCT	11:29:47
		GMT	11:29:47

GHA ♈ h	157° 20.9'	Hs	29° 34.6'	(2) Brg (Zn) 132.3°
m/s	7° 28.0'	Ic	+ 1.0'	
GHA ♈	164° 48.9'	Dip (52)	- 7.0'	
Long	+ 105° 16.0'	Ha	29° 28.6'	
LHA ♈	270° 04.9'	Alt	- 1.7'	
		(3) Ho	29° 26.9'	

From **PROBLEM**	Enter **PUB 229**			From **PUB 229**	
(1) LAT	23 S	= LAT		(4) Hc S 47	= DEC
(2) ZN	180 – 132 = 48	= LHA	L	(5) Z 070	= t
(3) Ho	29	= Dec			

Rule (5) If the azimuth angle respondent is extracted from above the C-S Line, the supplement of the tabular value is the meridian angle, t, of the body.

Rules for (6)
If body is east of observer's meridian, subtract t from 360 (LHA = 360 – t)
If body is west observer's meridian, LHA = t

(6) t   360 - 070 E = 290 LHA *

Rule for (7)
SHA = LHA * - LHA ♈

SHA = 290 – 270° = 020

(7)   020 = SHA *

The answer is on page **Beta Gruis** is found on pg 268 of the 1981 Almanac. S 47, SHA 020

Problem 5		12 June		**(1)** LAT 21° 47' N, LONG 46° 52' W
ZT 18:45		CT	09:43:27	
ZD + 3:00		CE	+ 1:46	
GMT 2145		CCT	09:45:13	
		GMT	21-45-13	

GHA ♈ h	216° 05.6'	Hs	28° 36.5'	**(2)** Brg (Zn) 162°
m/s	11° 20.1'	Ic	- 0.5'	
GHA ♈	227° 25.7'	Dip (45)	- 6.5'	
Long	- 46° 52.0'	Ha	28° 23.5'	
LHA ♈	180° 33.7'	Alt	- 1.8'	
		(3) Ho	28° 21.7'	

From	Enter			From		
PROBLEM	**PUB 229**			**PUB 229**		
(1) LAT	22 N	= LAT		**(4)** Hc S 37	= DEC	
(2) ZN	162	= LHA	R	**(5)** Z 160.0	= t	
(3) Ho	28	= Dec		(020)		

Rule (5) If the azimuth angle respondent is extracted from above the C-S Line, the supplement of the tabular value is the meridian angle, t, of the body.

Rules for (6)
If body is east of observer's meridian, subtract t from 360 (LHA = 360 – t)
If body is west observer's meridian, LHA = t

(6) t   360 – 020 E = 340 LHA *

Rule for (7)
SHA = LHA * - LHA ♈

SHA = 340 – 180° =

(7)   160 = SHA *

The answer is on page **Iota Centuri** is found on pg 270-1 of the 1981 Almanac. S 37, SHA 160

Annex 1
Practice Examination Questions

Celestial Practice Examination #1

1. 0301

You depart LAT 28° 55.0' N, LONG 89° 10.0' W, enroute to LAT 24° 25.0' N, LONG 83° 00.0' W. Determine the true course and distance by mid-latitude sailing?

a) 418 miles, 122° T
b) 427 miles, 129° T
c) 436 miles, 133° T
d) 442 miles, 122° T

2. 0410

A vessel steams 666 miles on course 135° T from LAT   40° 24.0' N, LONG 74° 30.0' W. What is the latitude and longitude of the point of arrival by Mercator sailing?

a) LAT 32° 30.0' N,   LONG 64° 41.0' W
b) LAT 32° 33.0' N,   LONG 64° 46.0' W
c) LAT 32° 36.0' N,   LONG 64° 49.0' W
d) LAT 32° 39.0' N,   LONG 64° 53.0' W

3. 0452

Determine the great circle distance and initial course from LAT 35° 17.6' N, LONG 144° 23.0' E to LAT 47° 36.0' N, LONG 124°22.0' W.

a) 3946 miles, 312° T
b) 3931 miles, 048° T
c) 3881 miles, 042° T
d) 3718 miles, 318° T

4. 0528

You depart LAT 38° 12' S, LONG 12° 06' W and steam 1543 miles on course 270°. What is the Longitude of arrival?

a) 44° 49' W
b) 45° 12' W
c) 45° 37' W
d) 45° 42' W

A-3

5. 0616

At 0800 zone time, on 15 April, your vessel is heading west in position LAT 15° 10.0' N, LONG 165° 15.0' W at a speed of 22 knots. The distance to your destination at LAT 15° 10.0' N, LONG 135° 15.0' E is 3, 600 miles. What is your ETA?

a) 1439, 21 April
b) 0539, 22 April
c) 2339, 22 April
d) 0539, 23 April

6. 0726

On 16 December 1981, your 1810 zone time DR position is LONG 129° 46.5' W. At that time you observe Polaris with a sextant altitude (hs) of 23° 56.8'. The chronometer time of the sight is 03h 12m 31s, and the chronometer error is 02m 16s fast. The index error is 2.5' off the arc, and the height of eye is 52.6 feet. What is your latitude by Polaris?

a) 23° 07.8' N
b) 23° 12.3' N
c) 24° 11.9' N
d) 24° 18.6' N

7. 0844

On 12 September 1981, your 0600 zone time (ZT) fix gives you a position of LAT 22° 51.9' N, LONG 133° 40.1' W. Your vessel is on course 062° T, and your speed is 12.3 knots. Local apparent noon (LAN) occurs at 1142 ZT, at which time a meridian altitude of the Sun's upper limb is observed. The observed altitude (Ho) for this sight is 70° 33.2'. What is the calculated latitude at LAN?

a) 23° 23.0' N
b) 23° 24.8' N
c) 23° 26.5' N
d) 23° 27.9' N

8. 0976

On 7 November 1981, your 0830 zone time position was LAT 27° 36.0' N, LONG 162° 19.0' W. Your vessel was steaming on course 289° T at a speed of 19.0 knots. An observation of the Sun's lower limb was made at 0945 ZT. The chronometer read 08h 43m 11s and was slow 01m 51s. The observed altitude (Ho) was 38° 21.1'. Local Apparent Noon (LAN) occurred at 1138 zone time. The observed altitude (Ho) was 45° 35.0'. What was the longitude of your 1200 zone time running fix?

a) 163° 38.8' W
b) 163° 34.0' W
c) 163° 30.2' W
d) 163° 26.0' W

9. 979

At 0900 zone time, on 23 September 1981, your DR position is LAT 28° 48.0' N, LONG 153° 11.5' W. You are steering course 257° T at a speed of 18.0 knots. You observed 3 morning sun lines. Determine the latitude and longitude of your 1020 running fix?

ZONE TIME	GHA	OBSERVED ALTITUDE	DECLINATION
0915	110° 44.9'	40° 01.9'	S 0° 15.8'
0950	119° 27.4'	46° 22.9'	S 0° 16.3'
1020	127° 00.9'	51° 21.7'	S 0° 16.8'

A. 28° 43.3' N,   153° 32.1' W
B. 28° 46.4' N,   153° 34.6' W
C. 28° 49.1' N,   153° 37.0' W
D. 28° 52.8' N,   153° 30.6' W

10. 1175

On 12 February 1981, your 0900 zone time DR position is LAT 16° 43.0' N, LONG 51° 42.0' W. Your vessel is on course 093° T at a speed of 18.5 knots. What is the zone time of local apparent noon (LAN)?

a) 1237
b) 1233
c) 1230
d) 1226

11. 1253

On 8 August 1981, your 0400 ZT DR position is LAT 23° 16.0' S, LONG 105° 33.0' W. You are on course 295° T at a speed of 25 knots. What will be the zone time of sunrise at your vessel?

a) 623
b) 629
c) 636
d) 654

12. 1852

On 26 November 1981, at 0535 ZT, while taking sights for a morning fix, you observe an unidentified planet bearing 074° T at an observed altitude (Ho) of 38° 29.8'. Your DR position is LAT 27°18.9' S, LONG 30°18.4' E. The chronometer time of the sight is 03h 33m 16s, and the chronometer is 01m 48s slow. What planet did you observe?

a) Saturn
b) Jupiter
c) Mars
d) Venus

13. 2005

On 17 July 1981, your 1951 zone time DR position is LAT 24° 26.0' N, LONG 51° 16.0' W. Considering their magnitude, azimuth, and altitude, which group includes the three bodies best suited for a fix at star time?

a) Hadar, Deneb, Alphard
b) Regulus, Venus, Antares
c) Mars, Vega, Dubhe
d) Kochab, Jupiter, Rasalhague

14. 2282

You observe the lower limb of the Sun at a sextant altitude (hs) of 42° 44.0' on 22 June 1981. The index error is 0.8' off the arc. The height of eye is 70 feet (21.3 meters). What is the observed altitude (Ho)?

a) 42° 19.8'
b) 42° 21.7'
c) 42° 51.7'
d) 42° 54.2'

Answers to Celestial Practice Examination #1

1.   0301   B
2.   0410   B
3.   0452   B
4.   0528   A
5.   0616   C
6.   0726   A
7.   0844   B
8.   0976   A
9.   0979   C
10.   1175   A
11.   1253   C
12.   1852   A
13.   2005   D
14.   2282   C

Celestial Practice Examination #2

1. 0303
A vessel steams 576 miles on course 260° T from LAT 40° 36' N, LONG 50° 24' W. What are the latitude and longitude of the point of arrival by mid-latitude sailing?

a) LAT 39° 12' N,   LONG 62° 28' W
b) LAT 39° 06' N,   LONG 62° 34' W
c) LAT 39° 02' N,   LONG 62° 37' W
d) LAT 38° 56' N,   LONG 62° 38' W

2. 0411
A vessel steams 3312 miles on course 282° T from LAT 34° 24' S, LONG 18° 18' E. What is the latitude and longitude of the point of arrival by Mercator sailing?

a) LAT 22° 39' S,   LONG 43° 17' W
b) LAT 22° 42' S,   LONG 43° 14' W
c) LAT 22° 47' S,   LONG 43° 10' W
d) LAT 22° 55' S,   LONG 43° 05' W

3. 0454
Determine the great circle distance and initial course from LAT 26° 00.0' S, LONG 56° 00.0' W to LAT 34° 00.0' S, LONG 18° 15.0' E.

a) 3705 miles, 153° T
b) 3841 miles, 068° T
c) 3849 miles, 248° T
d) 3805 miles, 117° T

4. 0534
You depart LAT 52° 01' N, LONG 176° 09' E, for LAT 52° 01' N, LONG 178° 46' W. What are the course and distance by parallel sailing?

a) 090° T, 95 miles
b) 090° T, 188 miles
c) 270° T, 95 miles
d) 270° T, 188 miles

5. 0622

You are on a voyage from Limoy, Costa Rica, to Los Angeles, CA. The distance from departure to arrival is 3150 miles. The speed of advance is 14.0 knots. You estimate 24.0 hours for bunkering at Colon, and 12.0 hours for the Panama Canal transit. If you take departure at 1836 hours (ZD +6), 28 January, what is your ETA (ZD +8) at Los Angeles?

a) 1736, 9 February
b) 1736, 8 February
c) 1336, 8 February
d) 0536, 8 February

6. 0728

On 2 January 1981, your 1759 zone time DR position is LONG 45° 17.6' W. At that time you observe Polaris with a sextant altitude (hs) of 24° 16.5'. The chronometer time of the sight is 08h 57m 10s, and the chronometer error is 02m 16s slow. The index error is 3.5' on the arc, and the height of eye is 42.5 feet. What is your latitude by Polaris?

a) 22° 50.2' N
b) 23° 18.8' N
c) 23° 30.2' N
d) 24° 07.3' N

7. 0846

On 22 February 1981, your 0612 zone time fix gives you a position of LAT 27° 16.2' S, LONG 37° 41.6' W. Your vessel is on course 298° T, and your speed is 14.2 knots. Local apparent noon (LAN) occurs at 1147 zone time, at which time a meridian altitude of the Sun's lower limb is observed. The observed altitude (Ho) for this sight is 73° 33.3'. What is the calculated latitude at LAN?

a) 26° 31.4' S
b) 26° 29.5' S
c) 26° 27.1' S
d) 26° 24.8' S

8. 0978

On 11 November 1981, your 0730 zone time position was LAT 19° 58.0' N, LONG 143° 54.0' W. Your vessel was steaming on course 084° T at a speed of 15.0 knots. An observation of the Sun's lower limb was made at 0931 ZT. The chronometer read 07h 29m 22s and was slow 02m 22s. The observed altitude (Ho) was 44° 17.6'. LAN occurred at 1125 zone time (ZD +10). The observed altitude (Ho) was 52° 17.4'. What was the longitude of your 1200 zone time running fix?

a) 142° 34.7' W
b) 142° 37.1' W
c) 142° 40.2' W
d) 142° 44.2' W

9. 992

At 0100 zone time, on 23 September 1981, your DR position is LAT 24° 25.0' N, LONG 83° 00.0' W. You are steering course 315° T. The speed over the ground is 10.0 knots. You observed 3 morning sun lines. Determine the latitude and longitude of your 1100 running fix?

ZONE TIME	GHA	OBSERVED ALTITUDE(Ho)	DECLINATION
0700	17° 20.1'	21° 09.0'	S 00° 09.7'
0900	47° 03.0'	46° 05.0'	S 00° 11.6'
1100	77° 06.4'	63° 16.1'	S 00° 13.5'

A. LAT 25° 35.3' N,   LONG 84° 17.0' W
B. LAT 25° 42.6' N,   LONG 84° 18.7' W
C. LAT 25° 30.4' N,   LONG 84° 28.6' W
D. LAT 25° 28.3' N,   LONG 84° 34.3' W

10. 1178

On 27 August 1981, your 0900 zone time DR position is LAT 24° 25.0' N, LONG 94° 20.0' W. Your vessel is on course 071° T at a speed of 20.0 knots. What is the zone time of local apparent noon (LAN)?

a) 1214
b) 1208
c) 1206
d) 1158

11. 1256

On 17 May 1981, your 0300 ZT DR position is LAT 27° 21.0' N, LONG 146° 14.0' E. You are on course 107° T at a speed of 18knots. What will be the zone time of sunrise at your vessel?

a) 457
b) 511
c) 519
d) 522

12. 1855

On 22 July 1981, your 0442 ZT DR position is LAT 26° 35.6' N, LONG 22° 16.7' W. You observe an unidentified star bearing 112° T, at an observed altitude (Ho) of 44° 16.0'. The chronometer reads 05h 39m 03s and is 03m 14s slow. What star did you observe?

a) Hamal
b) Rigel
c) Menkar
d) Acamar

13. 2009

On 16 July 1981, your 1920 ZT DR position is LAT 25° 36.0' N, LONG 172° 18.9' W. Considering their magnitude, azimuth, and altitude, which group includes the three bodies best suited for a fix at star time?

a) Rasalhague, Spica, Arcturus
b) Venus, Antares, Vega
c) Vega, Mars, Antares
d) Saturn, Acrux, Spica

14. 2276

You observe the lower limb of the Sun at a sextant altitude (hs) of 46° 20.3' on 1 April 1981. The index error is 4.5' off the arc. The height of eye is 57 feet (17.4 meters). What is the observed altitude (Ho)?

a) 46° 24.2'
b) 46° 27.9'
c) 46° 30.1'
d) 46° 32.6'

Answers to Celestial Practice Examination #2

1. 0303 D
2. 0411 D
3. 0454 D
4. 0534 B
5. 0622 C
6. 0728 B
7. 0846 A
8. 0978 C
9. 0992 A
10. 1086 A
11. 1178 A
12. 1256 D
13. 1855 C
14. 2009 B
15. 2276 D

Celestial Practice Examination #3

1. 0307

A vessel at LAT 28° 00'N, LONG 116° 00' W is to proceed to LAT 34° 00' N, LONG 123° 40' W. What is the course and distance by mid-latitude sailing?

a) 323° T, 428 miles
b) 324° T, 453 miles
c) 312° T, 533 miles
d) 302° T, 539 miles

2. 0412

A vessel steams 1650 miles on course 077° T from LAT 12° 47' N, LONG 45° 10' E. What is the latitude and longitude of the point of arrival by Mercator sailing?

a) LAT 18° 54' N,   LONG 72° 58' E
b) LAT 18° 58' N,   LONG 72° 52' E
c) LAT 19° 02' N,   LONG 72° 44' E
d) LAT 19° 06' N,   LONG 72° 36' E

3. 0455

Determine the great circle distance and initial course from LAT 24° 52.0' N, LONG 78° 27.0' W to LAT 47° 19.0' N, LONG 06° 42.0' W.

a) 3593 miles, 048.1° T
b) 3457 miles, 053.3° T
c) 3389 miles, 042.4° T
d) 3367 miles, 045.0° T

4. 0536

Determine the distance from LAT 63° 54.0' N, LONG 04° 52.0' E to LAT 63° 54.0' N, LONG 18° 24.0' W by parallel sailing.

a) 608.6 miles
b) 610.9 miles
c) 612.3 miles
d) 614.2 miles

5. 0627

You are on a voyage form Halifax, Nova Scotia, to Galveston, TX. The distance is 2138 miles, and the speed of advance is 12.5 knots. You estimate 18.0 hours for bunkering enroute at Port Everglades, FL. If you sail at 0648 hours (ZD +4), 12 June, what is your ETA (ZD +5) at Galveston?

a) 0250, 20 June
b) 0350, 20 June
c) 0550, 20 June
d) 1350, 20 June

6. 0731

On 2 January 1981, your 1759 zone time DR position is LONG 45° 17.6' W. At that time you observe Polaris with a sextant altitude (hs) of 24° 16.5'. The chronometer time of the sight is 08h 57m 10s, and the chronometer error is 02m 16s slow. The index error is 3.5' on the arc, and the height of eye is 42.5 feet. What is your latitude by Polaris?

a) 22° 50.2' N
b) 23° 18.8' N
c) 23° 30.8' N
d) 23° 48.8' N

7. 0812

On 28 July 1981, your 0800 zone time (ZT) fix gives you a position of LAT 25° 16.0' N, LONG 71° 19.0' W. Your vessel is on course 026° T, and your speed is 17.5 knots. Local apparent noon (LAN) occurs at 1150 ZT, at which time a meridian altitude of the Sun's lower limb is observed. The observed altitude (Ho) for this sight is 82° 28.7'. What is the latitude at 1200 ZT?

a) 26° 25.0' N
b) 26° 27.6' N
c) 26° 29.8' N
d) 26° 32.0' N

Alexander F. Hickethier MBA © 2010-2019

8. 0980

On 29 April 1981, your 0530 zone time position was LAT 23° 04.0' S, LONG 162° 12.0' E. Your vessel was steaming on course 120° T at a speed of 9.0 knots. An observation of the Sun's upper limb was made at 0830 ZT. The chronometer read 09h 27m 32s and was slow 02m 24s. The observed altitude (Ho) was 24° 58.0'. LAN occurred at 1205 zone time. The observed altitude (Ho) was 52° 04.0'. What was the longitude of your 1200 zone time running fix?

a) LONG 163° 02.1' E
b) LONG 163° 06.0' E
c) LONG 163° 09.5' E
d) LONG 163° 11.3' E

9. 993

Your 0745 ZT, 15 July 1981, position is LAT 29° 04.0' N, LONG 71° 17.5' W. You are on course 165° T, and your speed is 8.0 knots. You observed 3 morning sun lines. Determine the latitude and longitude of your 1130 running fix?

ZONE TIME	GHA	OBSERVED ALTITUDE	DECLINATION
0830	21° 01.8'	44° 16.4'	N 21° 29.2'
0930	36° 01.7'	57° 25.5'	N 21° 28.8'
1130	66° 01.6'	81° 30.2'	N 21° 28.0'

A. LAT 28° 35.0' N,   LONG 71° 08.5' W
B. LAT 28° 39.8' N,   LONG 71° 04.0' W
C. LAT 28° 40.5' N,   LONG 71° 13.0' W
D. LAT 28° 43.3' N,   LONG 71° 02.5' W

10. 1180

On 3 May 1981, your 1009 zone time DR position is LAT 30° 1.0' N, LONG 123° 15.0' W. Your vessel is on course 330° T at a speed of 8.6 knots. What is the zone time of local apparent noon (LAN)?

a) 1206
b) 1208
c) 1211
d) 1214

11. 1259

On 10 April 1981, your 1630 ZT DR position is LAT 21° 03.0' N, LONG 63° 11.0' W. You are on course 324° T at a speed of 22 knots. What will be the zone time of sunset at your vessel?

a) 1805
b) 1814
c) 1818
d) 1833

12. 1859

On 22 March 1981, your 0519 ZT DR position is LAT 27° 20.6' N, LONG 69° 25.6' W. You observe an unidentified star bearing 094° T, at an observed altitude (Ho) of 30° 15.0'. The chronometer reads 10h 16m 47s and is 02m 15s slow. What star did you observe?

a) Acamar
b) Enif
c) Menkar
d) Rigel

13. 2012

On 24 March 1981, your vessel is enroute from Cadiz to Norfolk. Evening twilight will occur at 1830 zone time, and your vessel's DR position will be LAT 35° 06' N, LONG 60° 48'W. Considering their azimuth, altitude, and magnitude, which group of stars is best suited for plotting a star fix at star time?

a) Adhara, Rigel, Suhail
b) Regulus, Denebola, Alkaid
c) Adhara, Procyon, Alphard
d) Sirius, Dubhe, Mirfak

14. 2290

You observe the lower limb of the Sun at a sextant altitude (hs) of 75° 12.3' on 6 August 1981. The index error is 1.5' off the arc. The height of eye is 32 feet (9.8 meters). What is the observed altitude (Ho)?

a) 75° 18.6'
b) 75° 24.0'
c) 75° 30.7'
d) 75° 34.6'

Answers to Celestial Practice Examination #3

1. 0307   C
2. 0412   B
3. 0455   A
4. 0536   D
5. 0627   A
6. 0731   B
7. 0812   B
8. 0980   B
9. 0993   A
10. 1180   C
11. 1259   D
12. 1859   B
13. 2012   D
14. 2290   B

54216742R00163